THE PENGUIN SWAMI CHINMAYANANDA READER

The Penguin
Swami Chinmayananda Reader

Edited by

ANITA RAINA THAPAN

PENGUIN
VIKING

VIKING
Published by the Penguin Group
Penguin Books India Pvt. Ltd, 11 Community Centre, Panchsheel Park, New Delhi
110 017, India
Penguin Group (USA) Inc., 375 Hudson Street, New York, New York 10014, USA
Penguin Group (Canada), 10 Alcorn Avenue, Toronto, Ontario, Canada M4V 3B2
(a division of Pearson Penguin Canada Inc.)
Penguin Books Ltd, 80 Strand, London WC2R 0RL, England
Penguin Ireland, 25 St Stephen's Green, Dublin 2, Ireland (a division of Penguin
Books Ltd)
Penguin Group (Australia), 250 Camberwell Road, Camberwell, Victoria 3124,
Australia (a division of Pearson Australia Group Pty Ltd)
Penguin Group (NZ), cnr Airborne and Rosedale Roads, Albany, Auckland 1310,
New Zealand (a division of Pearson New Zealand Ltd)
Penguin Group (South Africa) (Pty) Ltd, 24 Sturdee Avenue, Rosebank, Johannesburg
2196, South Africa

Penguin Books Ltd, Registered Offices: 80 Strand, London WC2R 0RL, England

First published in Viking by Penguin Books India 2004

This anthology copyright © Central Chinmaya Mission Trust, Mumbai 2004
Introduction copyright © Anita Raina Thapan 2004

All rights reserved

10 9 8 7 6 5 4 3 2 1

Typeset in Sabon by Mantra Virtual Services, New Delhi
Printed at International Print-O-Pac, Noida

To

Swamini Gurupriyananda, karma yogi and bhakta,

through whom I met the Master

CONTENTS

~

FOREWORD

Pujya Gurudev Swami Chinmayananda devoted his life to teaching the highest form of knowledge—Self-knowledge. The goal of this knowledge is freedom in the true sense of the term, that is liberation from all negativity and from slavery to the senses and the mind. By this freedom alone can an individual live in a steady state of mental equipoise and have access to boundless reserves of energy and creativity. A peaceful mind entertains noble thoughts, which, in turn, inspire noble actions. Such an enlightened individual becomes a catalyst of change in the wider society. In a nutshell, Swamiji sought world perfection through individual perfection.

I am very happy that Penguin India has decided to bring out *The Penguin Swami Chinmayananda Reader*. The selection of articles in this volume will be of interest to a wide public: the curious lay person, those interested in philosophy, religion and spirituality, the sceptic, the seeker as also the devotee who may be happy to have this collection of writings and talks in book form.

The life, personality and contribution of Swami Chinmayananda have been very ably brought out by Anita Raina Thapan in the Introduction. They bear eloquent testimony to the potential latent in each one of us. The key to the transformation of an ordinary person into an extraordinary one is available to all who seek it. The articles in this reader will, I hope, offer some insights into how it may be found.

Swami Tejomayananda
Chinmaya Mission Head, Worldwide

Swami Chinmayananda (1916–93)

Of the many great spiritual Masters of India in the twentieth century, Swami Chinmayananda has the distinction of having made the textual study of the Bhagavad Gita and the Upanishads accessible to every Indian. Through a structured and systematic approach to these texts he revived an understanding of the ancient philosophy of Vedanta. This philosophy, he believed, contained the basic and eternal truths underlying all religions and was, therefore, the heritage of all Indians. His mission, beginning in 1951, was 'to convert Hindus to Hinduism' and thereby usher in a cultural, spiritual and social renaissance in a country newly awakened to nationhood. He was convinced that neither political regimes nor economic or social measures would bring about a transformation of society. Such a state could be achieved only by individuals who were spiritually awakened. And this awakening would be realized through a revival of the timeless spiritual values embodied in the Hindu scriptures.

Defying the tradition of students seeking a guru, he sought out his students through a novel method of instruction. Believing that an intense and concentrated exposure to the scriptures was an essential first step to awaken the interest of the Western-educated elite in the Hindu religion, he introduced a series of discourses which he named the jnana yajna. The term, borrowed from the Bhagavad Gita (XVIII:70), signifies, in his words, 'the kindling of the fire of knowledge in the seeker's heart and into this is offered, as oblation, his or her false values and negative tendencies'.

A typical jnana yajna lasted for seven days and focussed on two specific texts: one of the shorter Upanishads or a section of a larger Upanishad covered in one-hour lectures in the early morning and one chapter of the Gita over one and a half hours every evening. The first jnana yajna was held in Pune in 1951 and lasted a hundred days. Gradually, however, as the number of devotees increased, centres multiplied and the demands on the guru grew in proportion, the number of days for the yajna were reduced and eventually fixed at a standard one-week. This continues to be the tradition of the Chinmaya Mission even today.

The jnana yajna represented a total experience. At the intellectual level, the Upanishads and the Gita were approached with the scientific spirit of enquiry and logic. At each step Swami Chinmayananda cautioned the questioning mind to accept neither the words of the scriptures nor the interpretation of the sages with blind faith. The ideas were to be tested by individual contemplation, integration and experience. Alongside the intellectual understanding of the Upanishads and the Gita, spiritual disciplines such as chanting the Lord's name, devotional music and meditation were also introduced. In this manner, an atmosphere charged with a spiritual aura was created. The emphasis on bhakti (devotion) was indispensable, for without it intellectual knowledge remained dry and a potential source of arrogance—the great stumbling block on the spiritual journey. The jnana yajna also offered the opportunity for karma or selfless service. The volunteers who organized the discourses were encouraged to do meticulous planning, with careful thought to all aspects of the management of these large-scale gatherings.

With such a concentrated and simultaneous exposure to jnana (knowledge), bhakti and karma, Swami Chinmayananda provided an environment that inspired countless individuals to commence spiritual practice. The yajnas were marked by orderliness and silence in contrast to the noise and disorder in many temples.

Chinmayananda's punctuality became legendary. On several occasions, heads of state, Ministers or other VIPs who were invited for the inauguration of the talks arrived a few minutes late only to find the lecture in full swing.

Swami Chinmayananda also introduced an innovative teaching aid which came to be known as the body-mind-intellect (BMI) chart. To facilitate the comprehension of some complex yet key concepts of Vedanta, he devised this visual aid which was always present at his discourses. It helped him explain how and why individuals remained limited by their conditionings of body, mind and intellect and how the knowledge of the Upanishads and the Gita was the key to transcending this limiting state to experience the divinity within.* This chart proved to be of great benefit to numerous lay persons who had to grapple with several new terms and concepts constantly alluded to by Chinmayananda during the yajna.

Over a span of forty-two years Swami Chinmayananda spent virtually every day teaching the Upanishads and the Bhagavad Gita to an ever-swelling audience across India and, eventually, around the

---

* The three conditionings of the Self (atman) are: body, mind and intellect (hence, BMI). Individuals identifying with the body, mind and intellect experience, respectively, the world of objects, emotions and thoughts (OET). This identification is responsible for intellectual restlessness, emotional cravings and physical appetites. The quality of the BMI equipment is determined by the innate tendencies or vasanas of each individual. These are impressions gathered by a personality as a result of its own thoughts and actions over several lifetimes. The vasana-patterns in each individual are what cause the differences between individuals. Vasanas prevent individuals from realizing the Higher Self, the divine Principle, which lies beyond the BMI but which animates the body, mind and intellect and causes them to function. The key to Self-realization is the knowledge in the Upanishads and the Bhagavad Gita. It alone empowers the individual to dissolve the vasanas, transcend the BMI and realize the divinity within himself or herself.

world. English remained his language of instruction throughout his life. It had been his first language in school and college and he was, therefore, acutely conscious of the shortcomings of the knowledge and attitude of the Western-educated elite. Besides, English was the common language of the educated class throughout the country. And, finally, Malayalam, his native language, was restricted to only one state, Kerala. Nevertheless, through English he succeeded in awakening an interest in and appreciation of the richness of the Sanskrit language, thereby giving an impetus to the study of the language at the conclusion of each yajna.

His idea of the revival of Indian culture and society was holistic. He encouraged industrialists, scientists and leaders in the field of technology to have a thorough knowledge of the Indian ethos so that they would find Indian solutions to Indian problems. Moreover, spiritual awareness would shape their ideals and determine the manner in which they would choose to use their knowledge and technology. With his modern outlook he believed that no nation can live in pride if it is steeped in poverty. Material success was indeed necessary and the Hindu scriptures never opposed prosperity. Managers were urged to inculcate in workers a philosophy of work. In his words: 'Without this philosophy, the best in each of us can never be churned out and poured into our productive work. The earlier we give them this, the sooner we shall find the nation ready to bring into different fields of work the subtler powers of integrity, loyalty and efficiency.'

To those who were in positions of power, he urged humility and dedicated service. Once at a dinner hosted in honour of a Chinmaya Mission Board Member who was elected Sheriff of Bombay, he was asked to say a few words. With his characteristic humour and frankness he began by saying: 'Actually there's nothing to commend when a person does his duty in his country. Such a thing is only noticed in a country like ours because it is so rare!'

To his critics who felt that he was giving too much importance to religion which could be detrimental in the long run, he would say: 'A community or nation is constituted of its members and its strength and happiness depend not only upon the material wealth and environmental circumstances, but pre-eminently upon the texture and composition of the individuals concerned . . . The secular plans and scientific achievements of the present age are certainly magnificent and acceptable but, when applied in practical life, they seem to entomb our peace and happiness. The redemption lies in the happy marriage between the secular and the sacred, between science and religion.' In fact, as he put it: 'Religion is like a friendly policeman who guides man through this traffic of life to reach the goal of a perfectly happy and successful living.'

In his effort to foster respect for all religions, he associated many of his activities and events with leaders of these different faiths believing in the necessity for them to publicly demonstrate their respect for each other. He believed that the only path towards a truly secular India was for each Indian to be steadfast to his or her own religion and at the same time to be loving and respectful to fellow Indians, whatever their background. To him, this was the highest form of patriotism. He neither encouraged nor appreciated conversion. To those non-Hindus who became his disciples, he insisted that they stick to their own religion, for Vedanta, he said, is a universal philosophy that can enhance any religious system. It aims at making a Hindu a better Hindu, a Christian a better Christian and so on.

Early Life and Development

Born on 8 May 1916, into a family of well-to-do landowners in Ernakulam, Kerala, Balakrishnan Menon, as he was known, grew up in a traditional matriarchal joint family. Named by the well-known yogi and saint, Chattambhi Swamigal (1853–1924), Balan grew up in an atmosphere where religious rituals and the visits of holy men were a part of family life. The loss of his mother in early childhood and the extra indulgence on the part of the aunts and grandmothers were held by his father as reasons for his excessive playfulness and non-conformity of conduct during his growing years.

After graduating from an English-medium school and college in Kerala, he joined Lucknow University for an MA in English literature. An over-confident teenager, he was partial to good clothes, vocally sceptical about the existence of God and his passion for tennis and debate far exceeded his interest in academics. The general consensus among family and friends was that the lad had a brilliant mind but lacked application.

While enrolled in Lucknow University, Menon was one of the thousands of students who joined Quit India Movement. Arrested and imprisoned, he spent several months languishing in jail. It was while recovering from illness, after his release from prison, that he first took to reading books on Western and Eastern philosophy. At the same time he also came to read about Swami Sivananda, founder of the Divine Life Society in Rishikesh, and about other spiritual figures residing in the Himalayas. Possibly the desire to write was born at this point, for when he returned to the University, in addition to English literature, he took several courses in journalism. Thereafter, armed with an MA degree, he embarked on a career as a journalist in Bombay with the *Free Press Journal*. Soon after, in 1945, he moved to Delhi as a sub-editor with the *National Herald*. His articles focussed mainly on the lives of the poor and less fortunate. One of his columns called 'The View from the Footpath' by Mr Tramp was regularly published in the *Commonweal*.

It was in 1947, while working in Delhi, that Menon first visited Rishikesh and met Swami Sivananda whose work and writings had so deeply impressed him. The idea of doing research on the lives of sadhus and swamis of the Himalayan region began to take shape. He sought to understand what they really represented in Indian society and what it was that inspired men to renounce family, career and comfort to live the austere life of renunciation. What was behind this tradition that had continued unbroken through the centuries despite the upheavals in society and the vicissitudes of history? Was it pure escapism or was there something deeper to it?

This enquiry necessitated repeated trips to the region and the ashram of Swami Sivananda became a base. Soon the trips became more frequent and the stays longer. At the same time Menon continued to read about the lives and works of Vivekananda, Dayanand Sarasvati, Ram Tirtha, Aurobindo and Ramana Maharishi all of whom fascinated him.

The article on the sadhus of the Himalayas never got written. Instead, on 25 February 1949, two years after his first visit to Rishikesh, Menon was initiated into the *sannyasa ashram* by Swami Sivananda and named Swami Chinmayananda Saraswati. Because of his great appetite for learning, Sivananda directed him to study Vedanta from Swami Tapovan. This great Vedantin was renowned for his scholarship, austere lifestyle, and extraordinary spiritual experiences. Chinmayananda spent the next two and a half years moving with Swami Tapovan between Rishikesh, Uttarkashi and Gangotri according to the vagaries of the climate, living a life of extreme austerity and trying to grapple with the greatest spiritual treasures of the Vedanta philosophy.

In 1952 Chinmayananda set out as a wandering mendicant visiting various temples and places of pilgrimage to gain a first-hand knowledge of the state of religion and the religious establishments in the country. The experience only reinforced his determination to bring the knowledge of the Vedanta philosophy to his countrymen. Swami Tapovan was sceptical of such a venture believing that religion was only for the sincere seeker. However, seeing the enthusiasm of his disciple, he finally blessed him and sent him on his mission. Chinmayananda never looked back after having delivered his first talk in Pune in 1951. However, until 1956, when Swami Tapovan left his mortal body, he faithfully returned for some months every year to serve his guru.

Chinmayananda's meteoric rise as a spiritual teacher must be understood against the social and political background of the country. The young swami emerged on the scene when the success of the freedom struggle had brought home to the people the fact that the power of the spirit is far superior to the most insolent might. Indians were ready for a spiritual awakening. Chinmayananda firmly believed that India had a major role to play on the world stage. As he put it: 'India has always been the guru of the world. This generation has been called upon to lead and guide the world. The time has come, not for killing, not for destroying, not for warfare, but for learning and understanding how to face the problems of the outer world. It is absolutely necessary to study the scriptures and learn to practise the teachings in our everyday lives.' He had the spiritual authority of traditional India, but the ideas and approach of a modern, educated intellectual. He easily became a role model.

Several devotees have said how they were struck by the physical appearance of the young Swami in the 1950s. Tall and lean with striking features, a fiery glow in his eyes and a powerful ring in his voice, his presence was almost mesmerizing. Others felt the compelling power of his words, urging them to transform, to realize their Higher Self. His Christian followers in India and abroad found he looked like Jesus Christ. He inspired awe, reverence and devotion. But, above all, it was his boundless compassion, understanding and sense of humour that endeared him to his followers.

Swami Chinmayananda spent very little time in any one place, so there was never a core group that was continually with him. He repeatedly emphasized that the spiritual path is a lonely one but that the guru is always there as a guide, to point out the pitfalls along the way. However, he was always available to his followers through letters and over the telephone. Young children and adults of all ages received a prompt personal response to their queries and complaints. His memory was prodigious and he could place people, events and names with amazing speed and accuracy. Full of love and concern when the need arose, he would not mince his words with devotees who complained and indulged in self-pity. One of his remarks to someone who continually complained of feeling lonely was: 'If you don't like your own company why inflict it on others?'

In August 1993 he was to have been honoured with the Gobal Vision 2000 award. In September that same year he was to represent Hinduism at the Meeting of the Parliament of World Religions, exactly a hundred years after Vivekananda's historical address at the same forum. Yet, this was not to be, for on 3 August 1993, when he was at San Diego, USA, Swami Chinmayananda attained *mahasamadhi*. His mortal remains rest at the Sidhbari Ashram in Kangra, northern Himachal Pradesh, at a spot earlier chosen by him as his final resting place. The majestic Dhauladhar ranges that formed the backdrop of his many talks and that were a perennial source of joy and inspiration for him, stand as silent witness to the power of human potential when it has realized the Higher Self.

The Chinmaya Mission

It was a small team of enthusiasts in Madras who, inspired by the first jnana yajna in the city, formed a Society in 1953 and planned a programme of activity to sustain what they had gained from Swami Chinmayananda's teachings. The Society was named the Chinmaya Mission. Thereafter, Swami Chinmayananda was approached for its recognition and ratification. Gradually branches sprang up in different cities and eventually in several countries, as, in the words of Chinmayananda, 'a sort of divine contagion, almost an epidemic of spiritual enthusiasm!'

By 1964 there were over one hundred centres. From 1965, Swami Chinmayananda began to take his message overseas at the repeated invitation of Indians settled abroad who had had the opportunity of listening to him in India. In 1975, Chinmaya Mission West was established in California. Numerous centres sprang up in the US, Canada, Singapore, and elsewhere in Asia and Europe. Today the Chinmaya Mission is a world body run with the expertise of well-trained monks and professionals in different fields. They seek to realize, through spiritual and secular activities, the wisdom of the teachings imbibed through the Mission.

The foundation of the organization is the Vedanta gurukula where young men and women are trained in the scriptures so that they can further the work of their founder. There are a total of six such institutes in India and all of them are called Sandeepany (named after the great sage of yore, Sandeepany, at whose gurukula numerous students, including Lord Krishna, gained spiritual knowledge). The oldest is the Sandeepany at Mumbai where the medium of instruction is English. Sandeepany Himalayas at Sidhbari (Himachal Pradesh) trains students in Hindi. The other Sandeepanies are located in Andhra Pradesh, Tamil Nadu, Kerala and Karnataka where instruction is given in the regional languages. Today over sixty swamis/swaminis, and about 150 brahmacharis/brahmacharinis sustain the work of the Chinmaya Mission around the world and head the ever-growing number of projects undertaken by the Mission.

There are a number of programmes that have become a part of all the centres. Bal Vihar, or weekly culture classes for children, are held under the guidance of a trained and dedicated teacher. Here children hear stories from the epics and the *itihasa–purana* tradition, and learn the significance of festivals and the rituals associated with them. They are also taught Sanskrit shlokas and bhajans. Children from the Bal Vihar graduate to the Yuva Kendra or youth group. At this stage the basic concepts of Vedanta philosophy are introduced. Yuva Kendra members eventually join study groups where adults meet once a week, in groups of eight to ten, and collectively read and discuss a prescribed syllabus of texts on Vedanta. The swami or brahmachari heading each centre also offers regular classes on different texts of Vedanta for the general public. Visiting swamis hold jnana yajnas several times a year. All this is offered free of cost, so any interested person has an opportunity to have a regular and sustained exposure to this knowledge. There are, in addition, correspondence courses on Vedanta and, of late, such a course over e-mail has been introduced. For senior citizens there are Vanaprastha Sansthans which organize talks and lectures dealing with topics relevant to the elderly. Women have the possibility of joining devi groups and most of these provide an opportunity to learn devotional singing and organize pujas and other social and religious rituals for the community.

The Bal Vihar have played a particularly important role among the Indian diaspora. They have contributed to a resurgence of interest in Indian culture providing children and youth, growing up in a foreign environment, an organized approach to the study of the Hindu religion. In many centres outside India, Sunday Bal Vihar have an attendance of as many as three to five hundred children. Dedicated workers have devised a graded syllabus that corresponds to the school terms and sees the children through their school years.

Besides these core activities, the Chinmaya Mission runs several projects and programmes: schools, colleges, training courses in nursing, free food centres, slum renovation programmes, institutes of management, hospitals, old-age homes, *goshalas*, vocational training institutes, youth centres, social and welfare organizations, rural development programmes, research and publication, construction and management of temples and so on. The publication division has over 600 titles in English and the regional languages. Some of the books have been translated into foreign languages as well.

Many of these projects have been the initiative of inspired individuals from the community and they provide the field for dedicated service to the ever-growing number of those seeking to devote their lives to the ideals propounded by Swami Chinmayananda. The secular programmes serve the same purpose as the jnana yajnas. Besides being activities with a vision of nation-building, they also serve to bring about the understanding that dharma embraces every aspect of life.

In the US, which is home to around 1.2 million Indians, temples have been built by the Mission in Orlando (Florida), Washington DC, Houston and Dallas (Texas), Chicago, Langhorne (Pennsylvania), San Jose and Los Angeles (California), Flint and Ann Arbor (Michigan) and Sugarland (Texas). In Canada there is one temple at Toronto and one has been established in Sri Lanka as well. In India the Mission has constructed twenty temples.

Swami Chinmayananda's vision for education has culminated in the Chinmaya Vision Programme (CVP). A comprehensive value-based educational programme, it is being incorporated in the seventy-seven schools and eight colleges established by the Mission all over the country as well as in scores of other institutions. The Mission also runs the Chinmaya International Residential School at Coimbatore, Tamil Nadu, founded to give the best of academics and Indian culture to the children of non-resident Indians.

The message of the Gita has today reached the grass-root level. Approximately 100–150 yajnas per week are conducted simultaneously in different parts of the country in all the different regional languages. These are organized in small towns and rural areas where they are addressed to simple peasants. Gita quizzes and Gita chanting are part of the programme of the eighty-five schools and colleges run by the Mission around the country. Such programmes are also organized by local Mission centres for the schools in the different cities and at the national level. Talks on the Gita are given by the numerous swamis and swaminis in colleges, clubs, business forums, and labour groups in factories and to householders.

Since 1993 Swami Tejomayananda heads the Mission. While the organization has continued to expand geographically, numerically and institutionally, he has also brought his own flavour to it. A gifted singer, completely trilingual (English, Marathi and Hindi), and the epitome of bhakti, he reaches out to a larger cross-section of society and is able to offer the same incisive talks in a language and tone that even the common man understands. In addition to the Upanishads and the Gita, he has made the *Ramcharitmanas* of Tulsidas and the *Bhagavatam* known to an ever-widening audience just as a generation before, his guru had done with the Upanishads and the Gita. Through the medium of the common man's literature, he highlights Vedantic principles bringing fresh insights into these texts.

If Swami Chinmayananda revelled in classical music and dance as an intrinsic aspect of Indian cultural heritage, Swami Tejomayananda has brought about, in addition, an appreciation of mediaeval bhakti literature and music. Above all, he has brought cohesiveness to the ever-expanding world body and given a global vision to many local groups, facilitating contact and cooperation among Chinmaya Centres and individual members across the country and the globe.

Vedanta and Its Place in the Religious Life of India

The Upanishads (also known as Vedanta, that which comes at the end of the Vedas) constitute the third and last portion of the Vedas. Their subject matter is the highest knowledge of the Self and represents the culmination of the spiritual seeker's quest as stated in the Vedas. Because they are expressed in a highly condensed language that requires interpretation, the original statements of the Upanishads have been interpreted and explained in many different ways, by many different schools of thought, over the centuries. Swami Chinmayananda's teachings are based on the Advaita Vedanta tradition of the eighth-century philosopher-saint, Adi Shankara. This tradition focuses on a philosophical rather than a theological or mystical approach.

The essential purpose of the philosophical approach of Adi Shankara is to stimulate reflection and rational enquiry, as a first step. The Upanishadic truths challenge the intellect, urging it to use all its resources, to stretch itself to the maximum. Once awakened and stimulated, a rational intellect can discover in these texts an intellectual and spiritual content, which a simple reading of the Vedas does not enable one to even suspect. In fact, the Upanishads represent a highly specialized training which the traditional teacher was free to either impart or withhold. The pupil had to be truly an adhikarin (competent student) to receive such esoteric lore, very mature and perfectly fit to bear the revealed wisdom. The list of qualifications that Shankara lays down for a student of philosophy include discrimination between things eternal and non-eternal, renunciation of the enjoyment of the fruits of action, detachment and a longing for liberation. This brings out how, for Shankara, philosophy is not an intellectual pursuit but a dedicated life. The purpose of philosophy is not so much knowledge as wisdom, not so much logical learning as spiritual freedom.

Shankara laid the foundation for much of the later philosophical thought in India. His contribution, in a nutshell, was to systematically interpret the Vedas—and especially the Upanishads—in order to reduce all diversity in the world to one unified whole, the Brahman, which is, devoid of distinction, unlimited, eternal, and which is beyond all qualities. Hence the name a–dvaita (non-duality). The philosophy is summed up in the classical adage, *Brahman satyam jagan mithya*: Brahman alone is real, the world is illusory. Brahman is characterized as Existence (*sat*), Knowledge (*cit*) and Bliss Absolute (*ananda*).

One criticism levelled against the Advaita approach is that it proclaims the world in which we all move and act to be unreal. This unfortunately is a misunderstanding of the philosophy. According to Advaita, as long as Self-realization does not take place, the world of experience is all that constitutes reality in a worldly sense. In other words, Brahman is what appears as the world and, therefore, the appearance is true for all purposes. It is only from the standpoint of the state of Brahman realization, which is a higher state of experience and knowledge, that the world is called unreal. This state of realization is known as moksha and it can be attained while living in the world itself, in which case it is called the jivanmukta stage. In terms of Advaita Vedanta, jivanmukti is understood as a return to a state of freedom which the individual had, in fact, never left. It constitutes the essence of the human condition which is presented or appears as an event in time. The jivanmukta abides serene in uninterrupted consciousness of the essence of imperishable being. In other words, he or she 'lives in the world but is not of it'.

In Shankara's own time, popular Hinduism was on the rise while the Vedic rites had declined in importance and following. The bhakti movement in the south, spearheaded by the Shaivite Nayanars and Vaishnavite Alvars, was popularizing the path of devotion. At the same time Buddhism, although on the decline in the south, still had numerous followers. Jainism was at its zenith. Shankara blazed on the scene as an eager champion of the orthodox faith of the Vedas and as a spiritual reformer. He sought to give a new spiritual direction to his age by formulating a philosophy and religion, which could satisfy the ethical and spiritual needs of the people better than the systems of Buddhism, Jainism, Bhakti and the other existing schools of religio-philosophical thought such as the Mimansa. The Advaita philosophy alone, in his opinion, could do justice to the truth of the conflicting creeds, and so he wrote all his works with the one purpose of helping the individual to a realization of the identity of his soul with the Brahman that serves as means of liberation from samsara.

Shankara destroyed many an old dogma, not by violently attacking it, but by quietly suggesting something more reasonable which was at the same time more spiritual too. He generally attacked the philosophical views of the rival schools and not their religious tenets. He put into general circulation a vast body of important knowledge and formative ideas which, though contained in the Upanishads, had been forgotten by the people. He thus recreated for them the ideas from the distant past. He gave a common basis to the prevalent forms of belief and worship—Vaishnavism, Shaivism, Shaktaism, etc.—and related them all to the central coordinating idea of his philosophy. He emphasized the religion of truth rooted in spiritual inwardness. From his philosophical point of view he declares that, though the Absolute is visualized in many ways, the underlying reality is the same. He showed his sincerity of conviction by composing hymns to the different deities, hymns which have hardly been surpassed for their moving power.

Shankara's great genius enabled him to combine tradition with a new way of radical thinking, thereby laying the foundation for much of the later philosophical thought in India. In fact, the entire ethos and culture of India is permeated with a lot of what Shankara preached and taught. The oft-quoted example of the rope and the snake, is a contribution of Shankara. The implicit acceptance of the divinity of man because of the identity of the jivatma with the paramatma and the understanding of the immortality of atman, were also concepts popularized by him.

Shankara's Advaita Vedanta continued to inspire hundreds of works, commentaries and treaties in the succeeding centuries. Advaita concepts were presented in the Puranas in the form of myths and stories to appeal to the understanding of the majority. Bhakti texts like the *Ramcharitmanas* of Tulsidas, for example, expressed the same ideas in local idioms (in this case Avadhi), carrying the message to grass-root levels. In this manner Upanishadic concepts—such as maya, avidya, jivatma, paramatma, Brahman and so on—became the common heritage of the Indian people and through this means, an interest in metaphysics on the part of the multitude was achieved. The Upanishads and the Gita (which contains the essence of the Upanishads) became over the years both the great literature of the country and at the same time vehicles of the great systems of thought.

In the centuries succeeding Shankara, philosophical interpretations of Advaita continued to grow. Side by side, there were a number of other philosophical traditions which, unlike Advaita, remained important only at a regional level. These include Vedic traditions inspired by those other than Shankara such as the Dvaita (dualist) Vedanta of Sri Madhava at Mysore, and also the philosophies of multiple sects and religious movements that appeared in the course of the centuries: Pancharatra, Shaivasiddhanta, Kashmiri Shaivism, Virashaiva, and so on. As for the philosophies of classical Brahmanism, a few like Mimansa or Vaisesika became virtually unproductive. Others such as Samkhya were assimilated by Advaita. The Yoga of Patanjali also declined as a school of philosophy but continued to subsist as a practice among certain ascetic sects. Nyaya evolved into the Navyanyaya and was transformed into a technical discipline, little concerned with metaphysics and religious problems or concerns. From about the sixteenth century onwards, Advaita tends to increasingly appear as the Indian philosophy par excellence. But it is a relatively syncretic form of Advaita which includes, or at least highlights, a number of yogic meditative practices, Samkhya terminology, and gives a large place to bhakti.

From the second half of the eighteenth century, in the early stages of colonial rule, there appears to have been a relative stagnation of non-dualist thought for about a hundred years. Contact with Christianity and with European philosophy made the intellectual and religious elite, especially in Bengal, re-examine and re-question their tradition. They became acutely conscious of what Hinduism had degenerated into. Institutions such as hereditary caste, untouchability, child marriage, sati and so on were held as major reasons for India's weakness and, therefore, for her submission to colonial powers. Reaction towards colonialism gave an impetus to the development of vernacular literature, social-reform movements, and a number of religious movements. These movements sought different solutions. While some opted for modern secularism based on legislation of the European type as well as on science and technology, others wished a return to the source, that is, to the Vedas. Only Advaita Vedanta was capable of realizing this second great ambition. Other schools of Brahmanical philosophy had become either too specialized, thus inapt for universal application, or had only a regional following. Advaita Vedanta was the ideal formula for a counter-attack of the Hindu intellectuals for it enabled them to demonstrate that the other religions and visions of the world which confronted Hinduism, could be shown as only partial realizations or historical approximations of an eternal truth which ancient India had been able to express in its purest form.

Of all the reformers in the nineteenth century, the one who contributed the most to the spread of Advaita Vedanta was Vivekananda (1863–1902), and his memorable speech at the World Parliament of Religions in Chicago in 1893 marks the beginning of a new era, that of the diffusion of Vedanta across the Western world. He founded the Ramakrishna Mission in 1897 with the objective of promoting the message of Advaita everywhere and to everyone. Vivekananda rethought traditional Advaita in a historical context, that of globalization. He was the first to make an alliance of tradition and modernity, to see the parallels between mysticism and science. He put forward the idea that the real solution to the problems of mankind lie not in the realm of the socio-political or technical order but in the realm of metaphysics and religion.

Twentieth-century India has produced an impressive number of spiritual masters who have developed their own personal interpretations of the Vedantic heritage, trying to reformulate it in the context of modernity. Sri Aurobindo, for example, while using Advaita as the basis for his thought, also adds elements borrowed from the yoga tradition and proposes a spiritual path termed as integral yoga. Swami Sivananda and Maharishi Mahesh Yogi, in addition to Vedanta, liberally integrated elements from yoga, particularly tantric yoga, and were also greatly influenced by Western scientific thought which was part of their education (Swami Sivananda had studied medicine and Maharishi Mahesh Yogi, physics).

There is a second group which represents the 'orthodox' stream and for whom the doctrine of Shankara is to be accepted as it is in its eternal perfection. Ramana Maharishi belongs to this category. After a profound spiritual experience at the age of seventeen in which he had the experience of Brahman, he confirmed to his disciples that the Upanishads and Shankara's understanding of them, which he discovered subsequent to this experience, pinpointed what had been his experience.

Swami Chinmayananda is also situated in this 'orthodox' category. He repeatedly claimed that his purpose was to give back to Hindus, the greatest aspect of their spiritual and intellectual heritage in its pristine purity. The degeneration of Hindu society had been declared by Vivekananda to be the symptom of a disease caused by a lack of knowledge of the scriptures. The cure was an understanding of these ancient texts and this is what Chinmayananda was so successfully able to accomplish. What he did was to restate the old doctrine, something that Shankara had done twelve centuries earlier. And this restatement of the old doctrine, based on Shankara's work, is just as valuable as a spiritual discovery. Adi Shankara was able to revive the old heritage by expressing the ancient ideas of the Vedas in the language of his day, so that they were grasped and understood. Swami Chinmayananda used the main corpus of Shankara's works[*] with their detailed commentary and taught them, in the light of modern ideas and concepts, in the English language. For instance, although he upheld the importance of such concepts as jnana, dana and tapa in modern life, he interpreted the terms differently from Shankara.[†] Similarly, the interpretations of the terms *tyaga* and *sannyasa* are given in the light of modern times.[‡] Chinmayananda repeatedly emphasized that respect for the past has produced a regular continuity in Indian thought, where the ages are bound to each other by natural piety. The way to grow is to take in all the good that has gone before and add to it something more. It is to inherit the faith of the fathers and modify it by the spirit of the time.

While Shankara's spiritual faith needs no shrines and ritual, still, he had the spiritual depth combined with a sense of the historic to recommend them to those who were in want of them. This combination of Upanishadic jnana with Pauranic ritual and bhakti is also clearly visible in the jnana yajnas organized by the Chinmaya Mission and in the programmes of the Mission centres around the world.

---

[*] These include commentaries on the principal Upanishads, the Bhagavad Gita and the Vedanta Sutra. In addition there are the compositions of Shankara such as *Vivekachudamani* and the shorter texts such as *Atma Bodh* and *Tatva Bodh*. Also included are his popular hymns to the different forms of Godhead, such as *Dakshinamurti Stotra*, *Anandalahari* and *Saundaryalahari*, to name a few.

[†] See Swami Chinmayananda, *Holy Gita*, Chap. XVIII.

[‡] Ibid., Chap. V.

Shankara founded four *maths**. However, although these institutions are the direct inheritors of an incomparable master, they have not adapted to changed needs and historical conditions. This role has been taken over by the several institutes of Vedanta, the Sandeepanies, founded by Swami Chinmayananda. They are the prime institutions for in-depth study of Advaita Vedanta in English as well as Hindi and several regional languages and draw the cream of young educated spiritual aspirants who wish to dedicate their lives to missionary activity of this nature.

If the teaching of Vedanta has retained its freshness and relevance throughout the long centuries until today, it is because it really expresses the depth of Indian spirituality: the aspiration to experience non-duality and not just approach it in an intellectual conceptual manner. Swami Chinmayananda has ensured that it will remain the bedrock of modern Hinduism.

The Structure and Purpose of This Book

The articles in this volume are selections from a large collection of talks given on special occasions or published as articles for commemorative volumes or in the monthly publications of the Mission. They do not form part of the core texts published by the Central Chinmaya Mission Trust (CCMT). By core texts, I mean those texts which form the subject of jnana yajnas and which are central to the teachings of the Mission. These include the commentaries on the Bhagavad Gita, the principal Upanishads, several works of Adi Shankara and so on. All these are exhaustive studies meant for those deeply interested in the subject.

---

* Shringeri in the south (Karnataka), Dwarka in the west (Gujarat), Badrinath in the north (Uttaranchal) and Puri in the east (Orissa). Each was headed by one of his four direct disciples.

The selection of articles for this book and their arrangement is necessarily subjective. Yet, no matter what the structure, all the writings and talks of Swami Chinmayananda clearly reflect the content of his message, his style of teaching, and also his multifaceted personality. I have presented the topics in the order that they appear in this book because I believe that they permit a lay person to actually walk in the footsteps of Swami Chinmayananda and follow his own process of evolution from a sceptical young man to a towering spiritual figure. It is to enable the interested person to understand the significance of religion and spiritual practice from the perspective of someone who lived an ordinary life and asked himself similar questions. The quest for the answers set off a process of change that culminated in his transformation into an extraordinary person.

I have chosen to begin with the topic 'The Relevance of Religion' precisely because that was the question that plagued the mind of the teenager who would one day become Swami Chinmayananda. Later he was to declare to the young: 'Test religion before condemning it! Try the spiritual life for two years, then decide for yourself its benefits.'

Among those who condemn religion altogether, few have devoted time to read or reflect upon any of the scriptures. Among those who have read them, many have had access to only scholarly interpretations of these texts. Scholars are rarely able to provide deep spiritual insights and are not able to offer guidance on spiritual practices that are so vital a part of any study of the scriptures. After all, scriptures were not written for the intellect alone. Secondly, a mere reading of these texts does not provide an indispensable aspect of scriptural study—the presence and vibration of a Master who lives by these teachings. Great saints communicate more by vibrations than by words. Many a seeker has found answers to long-standing dilemmas in the silent presence of a great Master. Swami

Chinmayananda consistently repeated that just as people were at different levels of evolution, so also they required different kinds of gurus. He maintained that there simply were not enough gurus!

The second topic of this book presents some core concepts of Vedanta, so that the reader can gain some idea about the principles of Vedanta. Even a basic understanding of this philosophy reveals how religion, in the popular sense, is ultimately something to be transcended. Religious consciousness with its distinctions comes to an end when the goal of the Upanishads is reached. A 'personal god' has meaning only for the practical religious consciousness and not for the highest insight. However, on the journey to Self-realization the practice of religion is indispensable.

Once the relevance of religion is accepted and the fundamentals of Vedanta philosophy become clear, the question that would arise in the mind of a lay person would be what embarking on the spiritual path implies. How is it at all possible in the context of modern secular life?

In the third section it is clear that faith or shraddha is an indispensable quality for the seeker of Truth. The Upanishads attempt to say things that are not fully 'sayable'. Men of vidya, or vision, convey what language and logic are not equipped to say. Hence, those who have had no direct insight into Reality are obliged to trust the Vedic views which record the highest experiences of some of the greatest minds who have wrestled with this problem of apprehending Reality. This is only possible through faith and a mind that is pure. Faith requires humility and the recognition that there is a higher power than the intellect which enables us to *live* Reality rather than to *think* it and to *become* it rather than *know* it.

This leads to the question of the role of the guru, the next topic. Swami Chinmayananda, trained in the traditional guru–shishya parampara, always stressed the importance of a spiritual guide. Yet, as he pointed out, the guru is only a guide and not a crutch. In the contemporary context when people are educated and trained in rational enquiry, when they have access to detailed discourses of the Master in print and audio-visual format, it is the individual intellect, above all, that must be the constant guru.

Association with a guru invariably leads to some spiritual practices being recommended and these form the fifth topic. These practices are always advised by the guru in addition to the reading of the scriptures. For most people they are an aid to what remains otherwise a dry intellectual exercise. They are practices that have aided the great Masters in their own process of Self-realization and, therefore, to follow their path, the seeker must have the faith to try them. Only then is he or she in a position to reject them. Usually, these practices are kept up only because of the difference the individual begins to experience in his or her own life. Many seekers have found that after prolonged practice many spiritual impulses refuse to be set aside at the bidding of logic. It becomes clear that logic by itself leads to scepticism, whereas when partnered by spiritual practice, leads one to experience the deepest insights.

The purpose of spiritual exercises such as japa and meditation is to inculcate in the individual the highest values that make the seeker fit to walk the spiritual path, to avoid the many pitfalls along the way and to stand up after each fall. These values form the topic of the sixth section of this book. They are indeed common to all religions and are not the preserve of any one community, ethnic group or faith. In fact, it is often argued that these values can be lived without any practice of religion, that you can be a good human being without practising religion. That is, indeed, indisputable. However, when the study of the scriptures and spiritual practices go hand in hand and are undertaken on a daily basis with devotion and mindfulness, these values get re-inforced in the mind, eventually becoming second nature. Ultimately they pave the way for the highest spiritual practice—meditation. Successful meditation requires a mind that is pure and peaceful. Only such a mind is easily focussed. At the same time, regular meditation reinforces the higher values.

Finally, the last section of this book throws light on how a student of Vedanta is expected to act in the everyday world and tackle some of the common difficulties that arise in the course of modern living. Swami Chinmayananda sought to emphasize to his devotees that the teachings of the Bhagavad Gita and the Upanishads were meaningful only if they were applied in daily life. That was the test of knowledge being fully assimilated and internalized. It is the intimate relation between the truth of philosophy and the daily life of people that makes religion always alive and real.

Vedanta is a philosophy (a view of life) that approaches religion and spirituality (a way of life) with the scientific spirit of enquiry and experimentation. It therefore has a special relevance and appeal for the intellectual. Its study is, however, encouraged with some form of devotional practice, for otherwise it remains, for most people, a dry intellectual exercise. Vedanta is also a philosophy that highlights the importance of intuition. The latter is not necessarily opposed to reason and understanding. Intuition can throw light on the dark areas where the intellect in not able to penetrate. Only by the comradeship of scientific knowledge and intuitive experience can true insight be attained. If this book stimulates in the mind of the reader a desire to know more about Vedanta and the spiritual quest that it implies, its purpose will have been served.

I

THE RELEVANCE OF RELIGION

We glorify religion, calling it the watchdog of our culture. Yet we conveniently make it a scapegoat on which we heap our mistakes and failings.

—Swami Chinmayananda

~

ONE

ON BELIEF IN GOD*

One day during an afternoon session, Swami Chinmayananda invited questions. 'I do not believe in God,' began Ram, a sophisticated young man from the audience.

Swamiji beamed, 'Excellent'. With a broad welcoming smile, nodding his head slowly, Swamiji continued: 'That is fine. I like you. You are the man I have been wanting to meet. I like your outspokenness. You are intelligent and you think independently. You have the courage to speak your convictions. Now, what kind of God is it that you do not believe in?'

The young man was pleasantly surprised at Swamiji's cordial tone and benign smile and, feeling encouraged, went on: 'The one who sits above the clouds and judges men and dispenses favours and punishments by remote control at his own sweet will. Do you think, Swamiji, that it is all hocus pocus?'

Swamiji laughed. 'Shake hands, young man. I am entirely with you. I also do not believe in that kind of God. But let me ask you something, did you have breakfast this morning?'

'Yes, Swamiji.'

'What did you have for breakfast?'

'The usual things: porridge, toast, scrambled eggs, and coffee.'

---

* From *The Power of Faith*, The Mananam Publication Series, Vol. XIII, No. 1, Chinmaya Mission West Publications Division, Piercy, California, 1991.

'Eggs, that is interesting. Now, where did the eggs come from, Ram?'

Ram with his brow raised, feeling that Swamiji was leading up to something, said: 'I do not know exactly, probably one of those new poultry farms near Pune.'

Swamiji said: 'I do not mean that. How are the eggs made? Do they grow in fields, or are they made in factories?'

'I think you are pulling my leg, but I will answer you just the same. Hens, of course, lay eggs, you know,' Ram said with an air of flippancy.

Nodding his head thoughtfully, Swamiji continued: 'I see, so the eggs come from hens. Now where do the hens come from?'

Ram, an intelligent man, could see the trap he was being led into. He started saying: 'Of course from . . .' Then, wide-eyed, he looked at Swamiji silently.

Swamiji smiled: 'So eggs come from hens, hens from eggs, which again come from other hens, and so on, ad infinitum. Can you say with any certainty which was the first cause? The egg or the hen? How and why?'

The First Cause

Swamiji, now addressing the entire audience, continued: 'You see, God is not just a person or an individual, sitting in a palace above the clouds, dispensing favours. It stands to reason that every effect must have had a cause prior to it. The watch you are wearing did not make itself. Your breakfast did not cook itself. In each case there was a cause. That cause must have emerged from a previous cause. God is now the very first cause. The sole cause. The uncaused cause. There was no cause before Him. He is the oldest, the most ancient. He existed before time. This causation hunting is the favourite pastime of the evolving human intellect—trying to trace everything to its ultimate origin. That which is beyond the point at which the intellect gets stalled is G-O-D. The intellect cannot come to a conclusion as to the ultimate cause. Thus far and not further is the limitation of the capacity of the human intellect.'

Ram was flushed with excitement. He was thrilled. In a faltering voice he asked, 'There does seem to be something in what you say, Swamiji. Am I to understand that, That is God?'

'That which you now speak of as God is the Allah of the Muslims, the Father in Heaven of the Christians, and the Ahura Mazda of the Parsees. These are a few of the different ways in which He or It is referred to, but all refer to the same supreme principle. The Cause behind all causes. The Source of all that was, now is, and ever will be. The Vedas refer to it as Brahman, the Absolute, the Infinite. The Truth is one, the wise speak of it in various ways.'

'But Swamiji, the description does not seem to be complete. Is that all that God is? How can one come to know Him?'

The Life Principle

'Now, you are really getting somewhere. I have not described God. He cannot be described. To define Him is to defile Him. What I pointed out only constitutes one way, one manner, of approaching the Truth. It is just one aspect. Now, your second question asks: How can one come to know Him? Know Him? He cannot be known as you know this table or this chair. He is not an object of the intellect. He is the very Subject.

'Have you heard of the great disciple of the *Kenopanishad* who approached the Master and inquired: "Revered Sir, what is It, directed by which the mind cognizes objects, the eyes see, the ears hear?" The Master cryptically answered: "It is the Eye of the eye, the Ear of the ear, the Mind of the mind." In fact It is the very Subject that enables the eye to see, the ear to hear, and so on. It is not an object

5

of the senses or the mind or the intellect. Hence, to answer your question, I have to tell you that you cannot make God an object of knowledge.

'Let us take an example: You are walking along a dark country road at night, occasionally illuminating your path with the help of a flashlight. You want to know how the flashlight gives off light, so you unscrew it, take the battery out, and try to see it with the light of the flashlight. But you will not be able to see the battery, for the bulb will not emit light unless powered by the battery. Similarly, the eyes, ears, mind, and intellect, all of which get their own power to function from the life principle, cannot understand It as an object. God is thus conceived of as the life principle in everyone.'

The audience was listening spellbound to Swamiji's exposition of a difficult Vedantic truth in such an easy lucid style.

'Then Swamiji, you say that God or Truth is something abstract, that cannot be seen, heard, touched, or even thought of. Am I right?'

'You are very much right. In fact, God is all this and much more. The Bhagavad Gita says: "Weapons cleave It not; fire burns It not; water wets It not; wind dries It not. This Self cannot be cut nor burned nor wetted nor dried." It is not material; It is not matter, understand.'

'Why did you say Self?'

'The supreme life principle is also the Self in you, in me, and in everyone. It is the innermost core of one's personality. The popular misconception is that man is a body with a soul. However, the truth is that man is the soul in a body; he is eternal. The role of the body is likened to a worn-out garment that is discarded by the wearer at his will.'

Another member of the audience who had been listening with awe and reverence took the opportunity to clear his doubt.

'Swamiji, if God is an abstraction and cannot be seen or thought of, is there any significance of idol worship?'

'Of course there is. When your beloved son is in America and you cannot see him whenever you want, you find solace by looking at his photograph. You know that the photo is only a piece of paper with various tones of grey, but it reminds you of your beloved boy and his great love for you. So also the idols in temples are there to remind the devotees of the ideal, the Supreme. Since the human mind cannot conceive of a formless Supreme, God is conceived of in form as represented by an idol. To the earnest devotee, the idol appears as a living embodiment of his Lord, and he goes into ecstasy at its sight. It is, however, necessary to remember that the idol is not God, but represents God.

'Constant practice and frequent association with the good are needed. The temple visits and worship should elevate the mind of the seeker and help to keep his mind on a higher plane. He should also take other steps to continue the purification of the mind at all times of the day, at home, in the office, and at the marketplace.'

TWO

LIFE AND THE ART OF LIVING[*]

The modern materialist who denounces religion and claims to be an atheist probably does not know that the super structure of his scepticism is built upon the sands of eighteenth-century materialism. In the eighteenth century, scientists discovered that matter was composed of mere physical units called 'atoms'. They claimed that a combination of atoms constituted molecules and that molecules packed together formed a substance. To them, therefore, the concept of a God or a Creative Power behind all names and forms seemed absurd and redundant. In that age of materialism, the biologist–prophet, Darwin, was the seer and his theory of evolution gave a fillip to the materialism advocated and demonstrated by physicists in their laboratories.

But this was in the eighteenth century. Today, the very sceptical West has discovered that the atom is further divisible and is, in content, nothing but energy. Though science has progressed to prove that energy is the fundamental factor in matter, a corresponding change in the view of the scriptures has yet to come about. Though people in the West claim to be progressive and scientific-minded, they are, in fact, conservative and intolerant. If they were to readjust their view of life, according to the new discoveries in the laboratories, they would certainly turn more of their attention towards the

---

[*] From Swami Chinmayananda, *A Sweeping Look at Vedanta*, Central Chinmaya Mission Trust, Mumbai (reprint, 1984).

spiritualization of their lives. Indeed, for any society where the scientific spirit predominates, Vedanta is bound to prove to be the most satisfying religion.

According to Darwin's theory, evolution is measured in terms of the development of the physiological equipment and the level of mind and intelligence in the specimen. But for the Eastern philosophers, while they accept different strata of beings, the measuring rod for the level of evolution is not the physical or mental development. It is *the amount of awareness, manifested in a thing or being.*

In stone life there is a mere expression of existence, but no awareness or intelligence as such. A piece of rock does not seem to feel bothered by the kicks of a mule, nor does it exult because a king has chosen to dine over it! It is totally unaware of the external climatic conditions, the place or the treatment it receives. In the vegetable kingdom, however, we find a greater degree of awareness. A plant is aware of the external conditions of humidity or the conditions of the soil. When there is a dearth of moisture, the plants dry up. When water is supplied, they react to the external condition and absorbing the same, seem to smile with liveliness and charm. Plants react to the seasons and their corresponding climatic conditions. During spring they bloom fully and joyously. Thus, the more sympathetically we observe mineral and vegetable life, the more we find to our complete satisfaction that there is a greater degree of awareness in plant life.

When plant life is compared to the animal kingdom, we find the latter manifests a yet greater degree of consciousness. An animal not only reacts to external circumstances but also seems to feel, perhaps only to a limited extent, the conditions of its own mind and intellect. Birds and animals feel an instinctive responsibility towards their young and display towards them a great amount of consideration, sympathy, tolerance and love, at least for a short period. Birds and animals also prepare for themselves proper shelter for the changing climatic conditions. Birds and fishes living in the upper regions of the Ganges start moving down as winter approaches. Birds move into the higher valleys as summer sets in the plains. So too, we are told that in the jungle, wild animals migrate from place to place seeking better caves, safer dens, and healthier environments.

Of all beings, man seems to be most intensely aware of the external world and internal states of the mind. This intensity of consciousness is, again, perceptibly different from man to man. It is not all men that are at all times fully aware or conscious of all the external or internal life, but it is only a rare few that are the most sensitive, not only to their outer life, but also to the patterns of their thoughts, emotions, feelings and ideas.

Thus, to the ancient seers of our scriptures, the theory of evolution is a story of the slow unfoldment of consciousness through more and more complex and highly evolved equipment. It is the great Plan of Nature expressed from stone life to human life, the one continuous golden vein of growth and development running through all manifestations culminating in the complete unfoldment of Consciousness.

The seers were not mere scientists meddling with material equipment on an insignificant table in a corner of a laboratory. They were men of giant wisdom observing life as a whole, in the canvas of their own mind and intellect, to study the great theme of life, in a spirit of pure detachment. Even here, it is not life of a given period of history, but life in its totality gushing out through the channels of ages. Each master conditioned and trained his disciples for such a study of observed life and passed down his conclusions to them. They, in turn, observed all through their lives, their own generations, working through the same truths. It is the sum total of their unanimous conclusions that constitute the declarations of the Vedantic philosophy.

If philosophy is a set of conclusions arrived at after a diligent and scientific analysis of life as a whole, our study of philosophy or inquiry into the nature of the Creative Power in us cannot be complete unless we know the meaning of 'life'. Certainly, none among us is a stranger to life. It is the business of every one of us, through despair and dejection, through laughter and tears, to wend our way. Life seems to be the only factor common to all of us at all times irrespective of our individual conditions or environment. If life be thus the main business of every one of us, we must certainly know what Life means, before we can hope to live consciously.

And yet, how few of us have ever given a thought to this problem of what life really is! I request you all to ask yourselves this question: 'What is life?' Are you silent? Do you know the reason for your silence? The silence is but the 'language of confusion' in which the intellect expresses its own foolhardiness in living so long without knowing what life is! This is not strange either; not even one per cent of the generation living 'life' is truly conscious of what it means, and in this intellectual ignorance, the wise ones of the world come to suffer the agonies of incomplete living.

The great Rishis of old analysed life and as a result of their observation, came to the conclusion that it is the sum total of one's experiences gained by contact with the external world of objects and circumstances. Moment to moment, time is marching towards us carrying on its surface, as it were, different circumstances and varied challenges. Reacting to them, we live through these circumstances earning for ourselves what we call residual impressions or experiences. The sum total of these experiences is life.

From this perspective, the 'unit of life' becomes an 'experience'. When we analyse an experience, we can certainly understand that in order to produce an experience, there must be an experiencer and the experienced with a relationship between the two, called the experiencing. The experiencer of circumstances in our life is certainly not an unintelligent physical body but an intelligent agent, 'mind'. The mind is the 'subject' and the 'object' is the world outside and the circumstances. In its relationship or reaction to the object, the subject gains the phenomenon called 'experience'.

On closer analysis, we also observe that a given set of circumstances does not produce the same kind of experience in all the individuals reacting to it. For example, house no. 5 on the third street is reported to be on fire. To many, the news will only be an incident of a house on fire. But to those living on that street, it is a more poignant incident. However, to the individual to whom the house belongs, it is the greatest tragedy. Thus, the external circumstance remaining the same, different subjects having different relationships with the object, come to gain their varied textures of experiences. Certainly then, a lot of attention is to be given by each individual to developing a correct relationship between himself and the world outside so that a healthy reaction between the two may permit a glorious experience for the individual.

Based upon these conclusions, the great Rishis continued their heroic adventure of ripping open the stuff of life and discovering the secret treasure chambers within. They found that the finite world of objects is in a constant state of flux. To adjust to this kaleidoscopic variety of continuous change in order to gain a joyous experience at all times is both frivolous and fatiguing for the subject. Therefore, they concluded that the only way in which an individual could gain a certain and permanent victory over the external world was by adjusting the mind in such a way as to maintain equilibrium in every given set of circumstances.

This assertion is the unanimous declaration of all the prophets and great seers of the world. In one voice they all declare that such a perfect equilibrium of the mind is possible. The technique by which this equipoise is gained is advised in all religions of the world. Philosophy explains life and provides us with the healthy values of life. Religion shows us how to train ourselves to fulfil the promises of philosophy. When I say spiritualism, I do not mean the outgrowths of redundant show and pomp that have now come to predominate in temples, churches and mosques. I mean the great spiritual exercises in concentration, mental control, and application of mental energy in diligent and continuous meditation.

With this understanding, if we peep into the history textbooks, we shall discover the main reason for the repeated failure of man in bringing about a perfect state of peace and prosperity in society through wars and revolutions. The history of man, in fact, reads as a melancholic story of repeated wars and revolutions. In the name of peace, we have learnt to make weapons of destruction and to kill each other with ruthless, monstrous efficiency! The peace that we know of today is but the exhausting pause between two wars. After every spasm of cruelty and bloodshed, the animal in us, in sheer exhaustion, seeks a shelter wherein to mourn or to roll upon itself until it licks dry its wounds and gets ready to fight again!

History has been a repetition of such callous suicidal mistakes; and yet, each spirited warrior, each revolutionary leader who had set the wheel of destruction in motion was, in fact, intrinsically not cruel or bloodthirsty. Each one of them believed that by bringing about a special pattern in life or a new order, he could establish the maximum happiness for the maximum number of people. And that was at the cost of so many lives!

But we know that all the revolutions and wars we have had so far have ended only in failure. Even today we have not discovered that secret prescription for joy or that ever-elusive system of perfect government whereby each citizen can bloom in the maximum happiness he is capable of. This failure is the result of our ignorance of the real meaning of life.

In the understanding of the revolutionaries, the constitutionalists, the politicians, the economists, joy or sorrow is the result of a

13

reorganization of the pattern of things and circumstances in the outer world. Unfortunately, they do not realize that the external pattern of objects cannot and will not consistently remain in any given scheme formulated through the force of the pen, the tongue or the sword. The pattern eternally changes. Individual minds constantly change. In this welter of change, to hope to maintain equilibrium is a mere dream. Thus, all revolutionary plans for a congenial living pattern are necessarily doomed to failure, so long as they ignore the subject-unit constituted by the mental, the intellectual and spiritual personalities of man.

Is philosophy, then, a despairing dream of life? If it were so, man could have thrown it overboard long ago and relieved himself of its severe implications. On the other hand, true philosophy is the most optimistic call to man to act diligently and wisely, carving out for **him**self from moment to moment a greater state of perfection whereby he can come to live in a fuller world of noble endeavours, pursuing values that endure!

The solution for the world, according to the seers, seems to be a call to accomplish this inner revolution. According to them, the revolutionaries in the outer world cannot accomplish the promises they make from time to time. The true goal of joy can be reached only if the minds and intellects of individuals are controlled and patterned so as to find for themselves their equipoise amidst the changing vicissitudes of life.

If this mental culture is to be cultivated, resulting ultimately in an inner revolution, what are the strategies to be followed, what methods are to be adopted? A detailed description of these techniques constitutes the contents of spiritual literature. There is a perfectly scientific method of purifying our thoughts, and controlling them, thereby gaining mastery over their application. By this art of self-perfection an ordinary man can steadily and easily come to gain a complete victory over his mind. One who is the master of his own mind is indeed the master of the world.

Now that I have explained the benefits of the practical aspect of religion, you might ask: 'How is it that religion today has drifted away from our life to flounder upon the rocks of decadence, become the debris of a past vain glory?'

The present generation's failure to realize the blessings of religious wisdom is not so much because of the ignorance of religious beliefs or spiritual truths among the people. It is due mainly to their growing incapacity to live up to the ideals of religion. There seems to be in every one of us an endless conflict between the head and the heart. Though our discriminating intellects are fully convinced of the blessings of the higher values of life, our hearts lack the courage and the heroism to translate those ideas into our everyday thoughts and actions. We know truth, but we are not truthful. We do appreciate love, but we hardly live in love. The most hardened criminal can give the most beautiful discourses on the divine qualities of his higher nature, and yet in his everyday life he acts as though he is an irredeemable animal.

All spiritual literature glorifies truthfulness as one of the most important cornerstones in the edifice of a perfect life. In many of our Upanishads, truth has been described thus: 'To Truth, the path lies through Truth, and it is laid out all along with Truth!' In Shankara's commentaries, truth has been defined as 'a conformity of thoughts with actions'. In its subjective application, this implies that a heart that throbs truly to the dictates of the intellect is the honest heart. So, to summarize, the more we attune our actions to our intellectual conviction, the more spiritually truthful we become.

In an era of materialism, when men run after simple and fleeting sense-ticklings, the alignment of their heart to the dictates of their intellect can never easily happen. In such an era, therefore, we find that the noble ideals or the noble values insisted upon by religion cannot bless the generation. And this is only because of our failure to live religion and not due to the lack of capacity and efficiency of religion.

A philosophy, however great it may be, cannot of its own accord bless any generation. Though I know that Aspro can cure me of my headache, the knowledge in itself is not a guarantee against headache. When I am suffering, I will have to go out and procure the medicine, administer it to myself and wait patiently until it is completely absorbed in my system. Similarly, a philosophy, be it political, economic or spiritual, cannot by itself bless the generation simply because we have codified it and adorned our libraries with writings on it. A nation is wise or a community happy, only to the degree to which its behaviour and transactions are attuned to its intellectually accepted philosophical truths.

Philosophy lived in our day-to-day life is called religion. Various easy methods are discovered and prescribed by the seers. If they are followed even unconsciously, a generation can be made to live the creative instincts and philosophical values in life. Religion is not only in temples: it is in our heart, to be faithfully followed at all times in our life.

~

THREE

RETURNING THE GIFT[*]

If the world was not there, we could not have survived upon the surface of the globe for even a moment. When I say the world, it includes everything: the sun, the moon, the stars, the plant and animal kingdoms, the earth, and the rivers and the oceans. The entire world is necessary for us to exist. This is why in the scriptural narration of creation all religions declare that the world was created first and then man was introduced, and not the other way round. Christianity relates the story of how Adam was formed in the Garden of Eden. In ancient Hinduism too, the world was created first and the last masterpiece of creation was man. The Lord was so happy in making His masterpiece that He sent him to the world with certain instructions, 'You do not need to approach the Lord to improve the condition of the world, but you are the master of the entire universe.'

These are not just stories: it is true. The world is necessary for our existence. To that extent we are all slaves to the world. If the sun, the moon, and the stars were not there, if the gravitational or phenomenal forces, the air in the atmosphere, or water were not there, we could not have existed. All of nature is necessary for us to survive and enjoy life.

Everything that exists, the entire world, is given to us as a gift

---

[*] From *The Path of Love*, The Mananam Series (Writings from the Spiritual Traditions of the World), Chinmaya Mission West Publications Division, Piercy, California, 1995.

from the creator, the Lord. Are the sun, the moon, the stars, and the oxygen not free? If these are not there, of what use is our technology? Not only the outer world, but the equipment to contact that world—our eyes, ears, nose, tongue, mind and intellect—are also gifts. Yet, in our vanity we think that we have achieved certain things, but we could not have achieved anything had it not been for all these gifts. Therefore, our achievements are also ultimately only gifts. When we start thinking deeply about these ideas, the logic of it becomes self-evident.

When a gift is received, the recipient is a slave and the giver is the master. We, the entire humanity, are slaves, recipients, in the sense that the Lord is the giver, the Master. An employee who receives a monthly salary from her employer is a recipient, and in spite of what the labour law says, is a slave to her employer.

The True Meaning of Spirituality

The great thinkers of the past, the Rishis, were strongly against the idea of slavery. They did not want to be slaves to anyone, not even to God. Their entire system revolted against the idea that they would only be recipients, beggars at His door at every moment. So these great revolutionaries started thinking, is it possible that even though He is the omnipotent, omnipresent, omniscient Lord of the entire universe, I can still become the Master? And their great discovery for humanity was that we can conquer Him, and He can be our implicit slave. The method of achieving this is the meaning of spirituality.

Whatever we have been given is His gift to us. How can we give Him anything when nothing is ours? The great Rishis pondered over this question and found a strategy by which the Lord can be walking behind us, wagging His tail as an implicit slave. How is this possible? It is true that whatever we have is His gift to us, but what we do with what we have is our gift to Him. When we start giving

Him the gift, He becomes the recipient. When He becomes the recipient, He is a slave and we are the master.

Let me give an example. Suppose there is a servant who has been faithfully working for your family for the last twenty years. Today he will be the head of the family; although he is still paid by you and working in the kitchen, yet everybody surrenders to him implicitly. How did this happen? It is because of the way he worked for you with total loyalty and honesty, taking even better care of your health than you would yourself, that you now do whatever he says. Once this is understood, we should learn to apply all our faculties—physical, mental, and intellectual—in His service. All scriptures advise us to have the attitude, 'Thy will be done, not mine, not mine. I am only an instrument, Oh Lord, make use of me.'

In Advaita philosophy, this omnipotent, omnipresent Brahman is the cause of the universe. Cause is never far away from the effect. All effects are nothing but the cause in different forms. All waves are nothing but the ocean in different forms. The entire universe around us has come from Him, the cause. That cause is unachieved, ever pursued, pervading in all beings. Therefore, if all my faculties are made use of or employed for the benefit of others and not for my own selfish desires, am I not offering Him the very faculties that He has given to me?

No doubt, I am a limited creature, and cannot be omnipresent, but He is present everywhere—in every plant, animal, and human being. I can serve Him anywhere as every name and form is nothing but His moving temple—a touch of life. This vitality that vibrates through every living being is the Self, the Lord.

Thus, when I start serving everybody, without consideration of caste, creed, colour, belief or behaviour, whether he is a cruel monster or a divine individual, I am serving none other than the Lord. So when we surrender our stupid egos, our vulgar selfishness, and start using all our faculties for the service of others, we know that He is the one who receives through all these names and forms.

Try this method for six months and then just look back. You will find the Lord standing there, ready to do whatever you want Him to do. He has to, because He has become the recipient. He is an employee, and I am now the employer. I am giving to Him and He has to accept. He has no choice. We cannot deny His gift because it is thrust upon us. Similarly, when we fling our works upon Him, the poor Lord will have to be our slave. The Lord is always a slave to his devotees. When I use the word 'devotee' do not think of one who goes on pilgrimages every year and gives money and gold to the temple. That is not devotion. Devotion means devotion to the Lord at every moment. This kind of devotion is now sadly lost in the world.

Faith and Devotion

With the arrival of the scientific revolution, the West said farewell to devotion and faith. No doubt a lot has been achieved, but the loss of faith and devotion has caused harmful results. We have achieved significant conquests over nature, but the callous aspects of our own nature within have rapidly gained possession over us. In thoughts, ideas, and actions, some people have become worse than animals. This is what is now called technological development!

The virtues of compassion, mercy, tenderness, love and forgiveness, which add to the glory of humanity, have all but disappeared. All over the world, the entire order of things has become disturbed. Years ago it was discovered that tampering with nature leads to disastrous results, and out of this came a new science called ecology. If damage to nature continues in this way, man will disappear from the surface of the globe.

The purely material outlook and values that have replaced devotion and faith in man—that have made him selfish to the extreme, that have propagated the philosophy that only the fittest can survive—have caused a maladjusted economy all over the world, where the rich continue to grow richer and the poor helplessly become poorer. Markets slump while the poor find prices of goods increasing beyond their means.

We are desperately in need of tranquillity and peace to alleviate the hardships of vast populations living in appalling conditions all over the world. But instead we have had undeclared wars in many parts of the world—South Africa, South America, the Middle East, North Africa, Afghanistan, Iraq, Iran, and Kampuchea—which are directly or indirectly supported by certain big powers. Not to mention the ecological imbalances—the depletion of the ozone layer that causes untimely rains, the failure of monsoons, and unseasonal snowfalls—upsetting the natural rhythm of life.

Nature Only Reflects

Nature only reflects humanity, however. An echo is dependent on the sound we make. When we are in a valley and we cry out 'you are a fool,' the valley echoes back 'you are a fool' three times. If we hate the world, we receive hatred back threefold. If, on the other hand, we learn to love the world, we will receive triple that love. We ourselves are the deciding factors. If we act poorly, nature will behave poorly. If we act wisely, nature changes immediately and will be beneficial and benevolent to us. In the third chapter of the Bhagavad Gita, Lord Krishna says that the Creator ordered that when we are cherished by the yajna spirit, by nature, society or the community, we shall cherish them back.* Thus mutually, man cherishing nature

---

* Bhagavad Gita, Chapter III, Shlokas 10-11. The Creator created the world along with the 'spirit of service' and the 'capacity for sacrifice'. This means that no achievement is impossible for man, if he knows how to act in the discipline of cooperation and if he is ready to bring forth into his activities the required amount of non-attachment and spirit of sacrifice.

21

and nature cherishing man, we may reach the highest prosperity, peace, and joy.

Until we change, the world is not going to change. To the modern world of politics or sociology, the world outside, called nature, is something to be manipulated, just as though it is a machine that can be corrected and repaired. But it is not an inanimate thing. The outer world is a living, pulsating organism. The great thinkers of India recognized that it is His form, the infinite Reality. It is not a thing to be manipulated, but something to be cultivated and nourished, respected and revered. If nature is approached with the right attitude we can get things done by invoking His grace and blessings.

We may say, 'But what is the use. I am just a nobody. How can I make a difference?' But any one of us can conquer and direct the universe around us, because we are the centre. The best definition of infinity is, 'The infinite is a circle whose circumference is nowhere and whose centre is everywhere.' Meaning, every one of us is a centre of the entire universe. When we change, the world will change. We may wonder why our country is the way it is, but we ourselves are the cause. Why? Because we have not purified ourselves.

If I am an alcoholic right now, only alcoholics will befriend me, and I say that they are the cause for my drinking. But if I decide to stop drinking only teetotallers will surround me. Now how did I change the world around me? I changed the world by changing myself.

When we feel that nobody loves or respects us what should we do? Begin to respect everyone, love everyone with a full heart, and they will in turn love and respect us. It cannot be any other way. Do not ask anyone's permission first! Splash it around. Love means love without any desire. Love with desire is called lust. Share pure love and anyone coming near us must feel that love. If we go near a fire we must feel hot, not cold. It cannot be otherwise; it is a universal law. Similarly, love generates love.

We have forgotten all these beautiful techniques of mastering the world around us, improving the country, beautifying our society, in short, transforming the world by changing ourselves. Without changing ourselves the world is not going to change. Revolutions or changes in the Constitution will not change or bring peace to the world.

What we have been given is His gift to us, but what we do with what we have is our gift to Him. I give Him a gift by more intelligently putting to use what has been given to me. With my gift I conquer Him and make Him a slave. He will be there, behind me. Why? Because I am serving the entire world. If that attitude is adopted by everyone, improvement of the country will come about and the world will change by itself.

When we are healthy, our reflection in the mirror is healthy. When we are unhealthy, we may want to break all mirrors because we do not like what we see; but the mirror is honest, it reflects exactly what is in front of it. So remember how others may be enjoying or suffering when they have to look at us.

When we develop our own health—physical, mental, and spiritual—our reflection, the world, will change. The outside world is a mirror of ourselves because it is ruled and determined by the condition of our own inner world. Each of us is responsible for the condition of the world today. Therefore, let us try to change the world by changing ourselves.

FOUR

~

RELIGION AND HUMAN VALUES[*]

Had this been a debate, I would not be addressing you today. It is
only a dialogue and as the other participants have placed their ideas,
I too shall place my point of view on the topic 'Religion and Human
Values' before you for consideration.

Up to this moment none of the participants have tried to define
religion. They have just accepted that religion is exactly what we
now see in the churches, the mosques and the temples and the so-
called religious institutions, the missions and the *maths*, the ashrams
and the seminaries. On this basis it has been criticized as being the
cause of communal riots, of untouchability, of the various religious
wars and, also, of the demeaning dependence of man on a God,
which is considered an insult to human dignity and freedom.
Religion has also been held responsible for creating divisions and
disagreements between man and man, between nation and nation
and as such has been considered as the main cause for disunity and
hatred amidst humanity, thus implying that it is anti-humanistic.
Further, a fantastic claim has been made that twentieth-century man
is not afraid of anything; he can create anything and is capable of
taking care of himself without any guidance from any super-human
God. So God and religion have been considered unnecessary in the

---

[*] Swami Chinmayananda's address on 'Religion and Human Values', delivered
in 1978 and reprinted by the Central Chinmaya Mission Trust, Mumbai,
2003.

modern age of spectacular human progress. If at all religion still persists in modern society it is said to be because certain people sustain or maintain religious institutions for their own glorification. This is the basic concept of religion that has been assumed so far in the dialogue here and so you all have naturally concluded 'therefore religion is not necessary'.

If this be the case, there is no difference of opinion, because if this be religion, certainly I too feel such a religion is not necessary. But then is this religion? As a hypothesis let us suppose, as it has been said, that this is religion. Then friends, how is it that this institution has remained with us all these centuries, from the very dawn of recorded history till today? Today also it is very much with us and hence this dialogue. Do you mean to say that all our forefathers were fools who never understood the emptiness of religion and who never could see it as the greatest obstacle to human progress and unity? Does it mean that our generation alone has all of a sudden acquired the wisdom to see the hollowness of it all?

There must have been something valuable in religion, or else humanity would not have suffered it so long and allowed it amidst them as an institution. We must try to know what exactly religion was conceived to be, and how with the passage of time it got enshrouded by other alien factors, so that we, some of us at least, have come to detest it and reject it. It is dangerous and even an insult to human intelligence if we take an aspect of social life and declare that because of some ugliness in its working it must be entirely discarded. Instead, is it not more intelligent to find out what the weaknesses and drawbacks in it are, eliminate these weaknesses and try to preserve those valuable factors that have served humanity so long?

Whenever I pass the various hospitals in our country, I often think that hospitals are multiplying, new medicines are being discovered, the number of medical colleges and the doctors are

25

increasing, and yet we find every hospital overflowing with patients groaning in agony. We find that the more medical research advances and discovers new medicines for existing diseases, the more new kinds of diseases appear, if not physical at least psychological. Thereby are we justified if we insist 'we must close down all hospitals as they are useless'? Would it be right or intelligent? Because human beings still suffer in spite of the increasing number of hospitals and doctors, medicines and treatments, it does not mean that the science of medicine is to be condemned or the hospitals are to be closed!

Even if there is inhuman exploitation in the matter of selling drugs and the fees claimed by doctors, we cannot afford to do away with drugs and doctors, hospitals and dispensaries. An intelligent conclusion should be that there is something fundamentally wrong with either the people who are suffering or with the doctors who are prescribing these medicines or with the chemists who make the medicines. There cannot be any other conclusion.

Similarly, I consider religion as an institution which has developed 'institutionalism'. Whenever anything is institutionalized its good effects get vitiated. 'Gandhism' is a wonderful ideology. The moment it becomes an institutionalized thing, it decays. Man by his contact always, it seems, compromises the higher ideals and defiles anything that is sacred and noble. We have this habit of compromising with the ideal, and the longer an institution has been in existence the more and more the compromises creep in. Thus it becomes more and more confusing and even disastrous to people. Such is the corroding effect of time and the corrupting influence of compromises. But whenever such conditions have come to prevail, intelligent and healthier generations in the past have thrown up the right type of leadership, and these men have repaired the damage and revived the institution through a renaissance. So is the case with the Hindu religion.

We find that in the past many masterminds came into existence at appropriate moments and renewed the original vitality of the Hindu culture and religion. Those mighty men of vision readjusted the then existing religion to suit the necessities and conditions of their contemporary society. They revived it by discarding the evils in it and gave it a new lease of life in the service of society. Thus, when the Vedic religion and culture decayed, the Pauranic religion came up. As the Pauranic culture decayed, the Buddha arose to remind men of the essentials of ethical and moral values in religion. When Buddhism itself decayed into perversions, Adi Shankaracharya appeared to reform the religious institutions and bring Advaita philosophy to the forefront. Ramanuja came after Shankara when religious people had become merely lip-Vedantins. After him came Madhava, Vallabha, Nimbarka, Gnaneshwar, Tulsidas, Kabir, Tukaram and Ramdas. Later on in the nineteenth century, when we as a culture became tamasic in the name of religion, came Sri Ramakrishna and Swami Vivekananda with their message of universal harmony and dynamic service. So we can see that these rejuvenating waves of a refreshing renaissance have been taking place in the religious history of this land. The basic spiritual values remaining the same, each mastermind reinterpreted their application to suit the demand and problems of the society of his age.

But how are those fundamental spiritual values or philosophy to be applied in the world? What are the techniques by which each individual in a society could come to live and practise them? It is these gymnasiums, where the fundamental truths discovered by the Upanishadic seers are practised, that are called religions in our country. There are religions (plural) within our Hinduism! This is usually a source of great confusion to most people. So many religions exist in this country: all of them are called Hinduism in a general sense! It was and is necessary. Each aspect of this federation of religions called Hinduism arose in different historical periods to cater to the special demands of its adherents. It seems that the last renaissance, which occurred in the nineteenth century, has not been enough to rub out the evils accumulated in our society and its institutions during the past few centuries of political slavery and domination by alien races. At this moment, after many years of political independence, we have become more and more conscious of the weaknesses in our society and its institutions including the religions. But alas! The right type of leadership has not yet arisen to weed out the weaknesses.

The method of curing illness is not to kill the patient. The parasites on a tree may weaken the vitality of the tree, and it may not be producing the fruits expected of it. But to cut down the tree is not an intelligent method of growing its fruits. We have to remove the weeds in a garden or the parasites on a tree so that the garden may flourish well with the seedlings we have planted, and the tree may grow healthily to yield the fruits. Similarly, the social institutions called religion all over the world, and not only in our country, have developed or accumulated many ugly practices. But the very fact that religion can still harbour and serve some people shows that there are aspects of human value in it which need to be nourished and developed by discarding its ugly and evil aspects. In the modern age when science is dehumanizing man through its technology, we cannot afford to throw away whatever there is of human value in the time-tested institution called religion.

As I mentioned earlier, a claim was made that modern man knows no fear at all. Alas! If man in this age of ours has no fear, then which age had it? Our forefathers? What did they fear? They feared the storm or the jungle with its beasts, the mighty rivers with their currents, the mountains, the rains, the thunder and lightning and such natural phenomena. Don't we also fear them even now? But apart from these natural phenomena modern man has the additional fear of the products of human science and technology—the A-bombs and H-bombs, the hallucinogenic drugs, the atmospheric pollution, the increasing population, the political revolutions and military coups!

In short, our entire generation is going through a fear psychosis. If science and technology have blessed us with comforts, they have also given us grave political, social and psychological problems which many of us do not realize; and those who do, are unable to find a solution. Modern man living in apartments in skyscrapers with plenty of food, shelter and clothing seems more melancholic, gloomy and worry-ridden than ever before. Even his laughter is forced and artificial. The entire generation is fear-stricken, frustrated and disillusioned about the revolutions in science and technology. Yet you say that there is no fear, that man needs no guidance and that he can look after himself!

If religion started with fear, then it can be said with equal justice that science and democracy also have their origin in fear: fear of the phenomenal forces in one case and fear of tyranny and oppression in the other. Fear as a springboard to greater adventure is nothing wrong. Just as we are still afraid of many things in the world, our forefathers also might have been afraid because man is indeed a very tiny fellow compared with the trees and the mountains, the rivers and the jungles. Hence he must have started the inquiry, from where did all this come? Who is responsible for this creation? What is my relation with this world and who created it? Such could have been the basic enquiries which led to the religious quest and attitude. Ultimately, some intelligent ones came to the conclusion that there must be some mighty Truth or Reality or God behind this whole drama of the cosmos, from whom this has emanated and who sustains this. What is wrong with this inquiry and conclusion? Even if they did not inquire about the universe as a whole, they must have surely asked questions about themselves. Why am I here? Who made me? Why do I behave in this way? Why can I not behave in another way? How can I become more efficient, more happy, more cheerful, etc.? The discoveries made as the result of such questionings and investigation are called spiritual truths and values in the ancient

Upanishadic tradition. As modern political leaders try to evaluate the world and reorganize society upon the basis of political values and economic facts, these ancient Rishis, who discovered truths about human life and existence, tried to reorganize their society on the basis of their discovery. They were interested in rehabilitating the emotional and intellectual life of individual men rather than changing the political and economic set-up of society. Whenever a pure science or abstract philosophy is to be made useful to society, we need practical techniques.

Science applied becomes technology. Pure philosophy applied to social conditions becomes religion. This applied aspect of philosophy slowly evolved, giving rise to religious practices or rituals: worship, tapas, meditation, etc. Religion thus became the training ground for living spiritual and philosophic truths in a social context. I am now talking of the ideal. This is not the case today.

In certain periods of human history, in certain places, wars have taken place in the name of religion. Admitted. Thereby if we are to jump to the conclusion that religion is useless and should be discarded, then before that or simultaneously we have to reject all politics because more wars have taken place in the name of political disagreements and ambitions. In the name of economics how many wars have taken place or how much human slavery has been perpetrated by colonization and indentured labour! Wars will go on in one form or another because of man's selfishness. How to eliminate this is the problem. How to make him rise above his lower selfish demands? Can politics and economics help us? Has science helped us? In the past, religion alone has been influential in making man less selfish and more loving both through persuasion and example. A Buddha or a Christ or a Ramakrishna has inspired thousands to love their fellow men as equals, and serve them wholeheartedly at the cost of great sacrifices to themselves. So religions and religious masters have both through precept and example tried to make men give up their selfishness and egocentric viewpoint of the world. Religious practices have been prescribed to achieve this selflessness. These practical details have been changing and have to change with the changes taking place in society. Individuals who live in such changing patterns, have to be re-instructed as to how to apply the basic spiritual truths in the new conditions. So religion as 'practical philosophy' has to be remodelled and readjusted from time to time. But religion would be needed in one form or another to make man truly human. There are countries in the world where religion has been removed and rituals banned. Yet, even in such places new substitutes have come in the form of army parades, cultural and political festivals, May days and Revolution days. The political leader has taken the place of God, and his writings have become the Bibles and the Korans or scriptures by which people try to fashion their lives. The fear of God is now the fear of 'Big Brother'; his displeasure, the sinful act; his words, the Gospels. If you remove rituals and worship in one form they appear in another form — that is all the difference. Men need places and occasions to gather together and be inspired by higher ideals so as to expand their minds beyond the confines of day-to-day life and its petty problems.

We have been told by the other participants that religion is not necessary to give this inspiration and expansion to human beings, but that human values are sufficient. Everyone knows what human values are and so no special banners and institutions are necessary under which men should be made conscious of such values. Admitted, Sir, that all of us know what human values are. To look after my wife and children is a human value. But how I look after them will be my value. Is it not? I pick your pocket. It is my human value! Similarly, you too have your concept of human value. If everyone follows his own special brand of human value, even the murderer would justify his killing because the victim, say, insulted him and his family. Thus if each individual is allowed to practise his own human value there will be chaos in society. There must be a standard. Just as if every shopkeeper says that 'this is my metre and it is only eight inches or ten inches or six inches,' no transaction is possible. To avoid this we have a standard metre kept in Paris to which all other metres must measure up. So when we say human values, what is the standard, Sir? The Muslim considers another man being converted to his opinion a good thing, I consider to be a Hindu is great. You may say kindness, tolerance, mercy, service, etc., are all known to us. But then, my notion of mercy, when applied, will be different from yours. Stalin's method of serving his country was quite different from Gandhiji's concept of serving his country. Both of them are human beings behaving according to their notion of human values. To liquidate one-third of the population is to people like Hitler serving and saving their country! It was said that religion is not necessary to bring about cohesiveness in society but that nationalism was sufficient. Yes, we have seen in our lifetime what calamitous things can happen if we have a nationalism like that of Hitler.

Humanistic ideas are to an extent acceptable. Comparatively, it is right that instead of living a self-centred life of bachelorhood if I feel for a wife and children, my family—it is indeed an expansion. If I consider that I must sacrifice my home and comforts for the sake of the society and the community in which I live—it is still greater expansion. From the community if I am ready to sacrifice the community's happiness for the sake of the country or the state, it is still more wonderful. The wider my vision and the more comprehensive my viewpoint and identification, the nobler I become in my human values. I should become a nationalist, that was one of the substitutes suggested for religion. Certainly acceptable. But will I not become a brute when I face a Chinese or a Pakistani or a Russian because they are different nationals? When you want to have love for the whole universe of living creatures such parochial identifications will not do. We must have a more expansive vision;

we must have the feeling known as *vasudhaiva kutumbakam*—the whole earth is one family.

But how can I get this idea of universal oneness and brotherhood unless I identify myself with a greater ideal? Identifying with my home or community or nation I am ready to fight and destroy other homes, communities, parties or nations. Suppose on the other hand I identify myself with something more vast, the Infinite Reality of which the whole universe is a manifestation. I can in my expanded vision afford to embrace in love all living creatures, nay the whole cosmos itself. This was the ideal of our forefathers—the Rishis. But even though we may aspire, you and I cannot immediately reach this pinnacle. We must proceed step by step. Even he who is now the greatest and fastest sprinter in the world, must also have started walking in his childhood and repeatedly kept falling at each faltering step he took. Similarly every one of us may not be able at once to achieve this infinite expansion of universal oneness. But all of us are trying. Religion's original task was to help us in achieving this elevated vision gradually. To lift the limited and selfish human being from his passions, greeds and hatreds to a loftier vision of the world is the essential ideal of religion. Whenever religion has been true to this mission it has been a blessing to humanity. But on the contrary, whenever it has shrunk to 'my prophet', 'my holy book', 'my rituals', 'my ways of doing things', and all such narrow fanaticism, it has become divisive and exclusive. This has happened because of institutionalization.

Now let us look at this aspect. Why is religion institutionalized? Because you and I, its followers, need it. The Rishis or the prophets never wanted it. It is the psychological weakness of ordinary human beings. When an institution becomes too large and unwieldy it has to be subdivided into smaller ones. Which is the political party in this country which does not have splinter groups? We have CPI, CPI(M), CPI(M-L) and we don't know how many more there will be in future. Why is this necessary? It is because in the vast concourse of mankind each individual does not feel a sense of belonging. Ignore religion and politics; go to a big city, you will find hundreds of clubs, big and small. Someone, after being in a club for decades, suddenly resigns from it. Why did he do it? He will say it has become too crowded, too large, he felt lost therein. Now he and some friends have started a new exclusive club. Here he feels a sense of belonging, more at home. Throughout the day I am lost in the marketplace. I go to the club to feel I belong somewhere. When it is not possible, I change or resign. Denominational differences must necessarily arise when intellectuals join together. It is only the masses that can to an extent form a large organization and yet feel quite at home because they rarely think independently. The thinking few always form themselves into small groups. Thus a splintering process usually sets in when institutions become too large. In religion we have the counterpart of this general malady of institutions: the various sects and denominations. There is nothing essentially wrong about this. The difficulty arises when they start feeling that they are separate competitive forces. This leads to friction, fanaticism and intolerance. If they understand that their basic source is one and the ultimate ideal is also the same, then we can have as we have in India a tolerant attitude towards other religions, and towards the various denominations within one religion itself. Wars and riots started only when politicians began dabbling with religion. This is true in India as well as in medieval Europe and Arabia. Religion by itself never brought any sorrow to mankind. Religious wars were all due to the unholy mixing up of religion with politics. When politicians entered religion they brought all their ambitions and frictions into it. Religious people rarely enter politics. In ancient India whenever they entered politics they were forced to do so as raj-gurus. Even then they tried their best to mitigate quarrels and bring more peace, happiness and prosperity to the country. But as soon as the politicians felt that these raj-gurus were a nuisance and a curb on their personal ambitions, they were pushed out and ignored.

It was suggested by one of the participants, Sri Goray, that people associate religion with the colour of my clothes [the monk's robes], and that if I were to cast them off and wear ordinary clothes, sixty per cent of my followers would leave me. I may tell you that by the same logic if Nana Sahib Goray were to take up my colour he also would have no less followers in the country! The point is, it is not merely the colour of the cloth, Sir, it is the man behind the clothes. It is the fragrance of the individual's personality that attracts people. Even if you wear my robes you will still be followed by the people because they know you as a sincere, honest politician. If I were to take up white clothes still these boys will be with me because they know what I am and what I have to give.

Religion is inspiring, great and noble because it has an intrinsic worth. There have been weak points and even now there are many. I think all religious people will admit this. But if on this basis you advocate that we should reject it, then in this country no institution can live, because each institution has innumerable weaknesses which have led to dire consequences in our society. What you must do as the creative thinkers of society is to remove the weaknesses and try to build up healthier institutions which can serve society in a better way. I personally think that we never needed religion so much as we do today. Men today are so confused. The increase of population has led to tremendous social pressures. There is so much insecurity. The rich man is worried, the middle-class man is crushed and the poor man seems to have no hope at all. At this moment all the help and solace they can derive is only from religion. But you say religious masters and institutions are not wanted; we need only look up to Delhi! In Delhi what do we see? Do you mean to say that religion has fallen lower in this country than politics in the last twenty years? Would you dare say that we don't want any more politics and political parties? Surely not. Weaknesses are there. We must fight against them instead of despairing. I am still optimistic. This is the glory of the intelligent man; he can still see the essential goodness in humanity. He knows that people are compelled to behave badly because of the conditions around them. Religion has been helping mankind from time immemorial to relinquish weaknesses and compromises. Therefore, I don't think we can substitute so-called human values for religion.

To illustrate how human values alone are necessary Mr Bedekar gave an example of a boy being helped by a man to cross the road. It was called a perfectly human action born out of a sense of human values. We were also told how a religious person would interpret the situation. Instead of thinking that a kind human being helped another, the religious person would say, 'I prayed to God and He came in the form of that man and helped me to cross the road.' Mr Bedekar has objections to this idea of bringing in God in such a simple everyday human situation. Now what is wrong with this attitude? Let us see how this religious attitude influences that old man's behaviour. Instead of being under an obligation to the other person by always being constrained to greet him and smile at him whenever they meet in future, instead of having the sense of obligation till death, the old man sees the presence of the Divine in all such loving acts of charity. This gratitude is not confined to an individual, but is an adoration of the Divine Truth dwelling in all hearts. Tomorrow when he helps another, he has no sense of vanity about his act of charity, but again it is Narayana, the Divine in him helping another in distress. This attitude diminishes his egoistic vanity. Neither does he expect the other person to repay him with a greeting or smile in future, nor does he curse him for ingratitude. The act and the person's ego are all submerged in that adoration of the Divine who is ever ready to help people in distress.

Someone said that all of us feel human values. But how am I to know whether what I feel is right or wrong? Religions are supposed to have brought into society the burden of sin and merit. But this concept is unavoidable as long as we have ideals to which we aspire. In the primary textbooks of religion this concept is only stated in the form 'Thou shalt' and 'Thou shalt not', not much logic and reason is given for these injunctions. But there are post-graduate textbooks also in religion which explain the logic behind these commands. These are the Upanishads in Hinduism. A doctor cannot, for obvious reasons, afford to discuss with a patient all the symptoms and causes of a disease in the general ward of a hospital. But he may discuss it with the medical college students or other doctors and to the patient he only says, take this medicine or that medicine. Similarly, to intellectually mature students the religious textbooks and masters do explain the 'why' behind the dos and the don'ts. Actions, which after having been performed, come into my mind repeatedly as thoughts that create agitations of shame, regret, etc., are called sins. So the sum total of this theory of sin and virtue is that when I act in the world I must keep a larger vision before my mind, the presence of a greater and diviner Reality in all things, and not act from an impulse of the moment. This will completely transform my whole relationship with the world and make me really live human values in everyday life. This is how true religion can really generate human values.

It is not possible to develop this sense of the sanctity and sacredness of life pulsating everywhere all of a sudden. Hence we have idol worship, the symbolic aspect of all religious life. Through a symbol or idol we come to adore and be aware of the Ideal. Whether the symbol is a sickle and hammer, the Ashoka Chakra, or the stars and stripes, it does not matter. They represent the ideals each country stands for and thus invoke certain feelings and consciousness in those who salute them. The piece of cloth is not my country. The idol is not the Ideal. The wedding ring is not my wife. All these help to remind me of the noble ideals which they symbolize. But alas! We usually forget the ideals and forget the true significance of the idols. This has happened in religion, in its temples, rituals and ceremonies. Most of us have not been educated in the ideals behind all this apparently meaningless paraphernalia. So they have become meaningless formalism and mechanical routine. Thus religion and religious practices become meaningless because the philosophy behind them is not realized by or known to the modern man. Swami Vivekananda expressed this fact succinctly: 'Religion without philosophy is superstition and philosophy without religion is madness.'

In this dialogue my friends here all accepted that they have no quarrel with the philosophical truths which form the basis of religion. So I am saying that a philosophical understanding must be with us when we enter religion, that is, its applied technique. With this basis, religion becomes meaningful. It can then serve us, help us in overcoming the entanglements of the ego and the short-sightedness of the egocentric viewpoint of things. It will elevate us to an awareness of universal oneness beyond all petty desires and passions. Then alone can we be fit servants to serve humanity selflessly. So human values and their fragrance emanate from us when we try to live religion with this philosophic understanding. The question is raised then, can't we live the human values without religion? We can. But we can do so more effectively, without frustration and disillusionment, if we do so within the context of religion. It will give us inexhaustible hope and tireless enthusiasm to serve humanity. Religion will help us to tune our emotions and intelligence to the right degree to make our service effective. Philosophy gives us the ideal. Religion can give us the training to express these values in life. It is this intrinsic value lying shrouded by so many outgrowths that gave religion its vitality down the ages. Many a time in history the then existing religious practices and techniques have been broken and discarded. The Vedic gods and rituals are almost unknown now. The Pauranic practices are still alive. They also need change. Today we are confronted with a situation where society has undergone tremendous change during the last century, but religion has not readjusted itself. When I say religion is still necessary, it does not mean that weaknesses like untouchability must remain. They must go. To be shocked that despite twenty years of legislation untouchability has not gone is unrealistic. It is a custom that has been with us for at least three thousand years. Even in a country like America, where no tradition is even two hundred years old, where everything new is taken up quite fast, they have not yet been able to eradicate the segregation and persecution of the Blacks. The country is considered an advanced and progressive society! It is considered the citadel of democratic consciousness—of freedom and liberty! Yet the social stigma on the Blacks is still quite strong. We must realize that in twenty years we have already achieved much in eradicating this social evil. Hindu society is indeed progressive by this standard. Those who suffer are impatient and the reformers are also equally impatient. But a cultural revolution takes time. Even a single individual takes time to give up an evil habit, though he knows it is ruinous for him to continue it. As far as the educated classes are concerned, untouchability is almost gone. We find it only in rural areas where new ideas and new laws take time to penetrate.

The difficulty in India is that anybody can lay anything at the door of religion because it has penetrated all levels and aspects of our living. Your reverence for your father and mother is religion. Your attitude to your wife is religion. Your food and eating habits—religion. Your clothes and the way you wear them—religion. Religion has seeped into every aspect of life so that it is easy to lay any weakness in society at the door of religion. Religion is capable of accepting these criticisms. Religious people admit that what we see in the name of religion is not the true thing. But the question is whether we shall renounce it altogether or change it by eradicating the evil parasitic growths on its body. Our intelligent forefathers changed religion and so even today our country is known the world over as an inheritor of a great spiritual culture. But if modern Indians democratically decide by a majority vote that we do not want religion and this spiritual culture, that we want a new non-religious culture, Hinduism will welcome it. This is the greatness of this culture. It is totally democratic. It accepts its own suicidal self-destruction.

II

VEDANTA: CORE CONCEPTS

From time to time an ancient philosophy needs an intelligent reinterpretation in the context of the new times; men of wisdom, prophets and seers must guide the common man to effectively apply the ancient laws to his present pattern of life. Whenever such a great Master arrives to re-establish the old truths and teach his generation to efficiently face the present with the values of the old ideals, that great person will be considered by his generation as a God-Man or an Avatar.

—Swami Chinmayananda

FIVE

~

The Vedantic Explanation of Creation[*]

Nothing new is ever created by anyone. The change of form, name, nature, and condition is all that creation is about. Reconversion alone is creation. In thus creating a thing three essential factors are necessary, and they in their aggregate are called the 'cause'.

In any creation these three fundamental and separate causes are: (a) the material cause or the raw material, (b) the instrumental cause, the equipment with which the object is created and (c) the efficient cause, the intelligence that creates or works at the material with the instrument.

Generally, the three causes exist separately, but in the case of the creation of the world, the objects created are *not* different from the Creator. The material cause, the one supreme Paramatman, manifests as different objects, for, in the infinitude of Its existence, there cannot be a second Infinite.

The waves in the ocean cannot claim an existence apart from the waters of the ocean. Likewise, this outer world, and our own world of experiences in the physical, mental, and intellectual spheres rise from, exist in, and merge into that one supreme Awareness, which glows in everyone, and like the bubbles that form and burst

---

[*] From *The Mystery of Creation*, Central Chinmaya Mission Trust, Mumbai, 1986.

upon the surface of water, different experiences in different bosoms rise and fall on that one Consciousness.

Similarly, behind this seeming multiplicity of existence and the manifold nature of our experiences, the one unchanging Substratum persists in all Its splendour. This we variously call the Brahman, the Paramatman, *sat-cit-ananda*. This supreme Being alone is the dynamic Truth, and no differentiation is possible in this state of absolute Reality.

How then do we come to feel the plurality in the outer world of innumerable objects, which we experience now as so very real? If the spirit that pulsates through all the objects in and around us is that One-without-a-second, why is there a conflict created in the perception of plurality by us?

Theories of Creation

The Nyaya-Vaisesika school propounded a theory that 'atoms' (paramanu) are the cause from which the created world has come. They accept 'atoms' to be inert. However, from an inert cause, sentient effects cannot be expected to arise. It is further observed in the universe of happenings that the qualities that are not in the cause are not found in their effects. Therefore, this theory is to be rejected by all sincere students of philosophy.

Another theory is that the world has arisen from the *Pradhana*, (Unmanifest), which is termed in Vedanta as the *Mula Prakriti*. No doubt, the manifested is a projection of the Unmanifest, but to declare that the Unmanifest is the very cause of the dynamic manifested world of expressions is an obvious fallacy. There must be some vital positive substratum even for the Unmanifest to exist and function. Therefore, this theory is not satisfactory to a diligent student.

The Nihilists (Asad vadins), a major school of Buddhists, declare that this existent world has arisen from non-existence. This also is to be rejected. If I am invited to the marriage of the eldest brother of a barren woman's son, obviously I cannot attend the function! No student of philosophy can accept that an existent world has emerged from a non-existent cause.

Thus, by rejecting the different theories propounded by various schools of thought, the Vedantic teachers here directly indicate the nature of the positive divine Substratum over which this delusory world of phenomena can be superimposed—a world of things and beings going around in a game of perpetual change! According to the Advaita philosophy, this substratum is Existent (*sat*), Unconditioned (*akhanda*) Consciousness Absolute (*bodha*), which is subtler than the subtlest, or the Highest (*paratpara*).

Then, how has the world come about? What exactly is this process? Many thinkers have concluded that it must have happened through a process of modification (parinama vada) of the Infinite Truth. If the world is created by God, Himself becoming the world, as milk modifies itself to become curd, it will suggest a great tragedy. In becoming curd, milk has irretrievably lost its properties. So too, if God Himself has modified Himself to become the world, the very God Principle would have ended.

Thus we have reached an unenviable dilemma. The world has for its cause the Infinite Consciousness. Yet the Infinite itself has not become the world. At the same time, the world of plurality is readily available for our experience. What exactly then is the relationship between the Infinite and the finite? According to Acharya Shankara and others of the Advaita school of thought, it is only a delusory misapprehension (abhasa vada) caused by avidya, the non-apprehension of the Reality. Sri Swami Tapovan in his *Hymn to Badrinath* says: 'If this world is the modification of the *sat-cit-ananda* Consciousness, as in curdled milk, the very nature of the Supreme would end to become something else. Therefore, That which in delusion is misapprehended as the world, like mirage waters, to that Lord of Badri, my salutations' (Section 1:25).

This delusory projection is compared in the ancient Vedanta shastra to a mirage, which cannot satisfy anybody's thirst. The desert alone is the reality, but because of thirst, the wayfarer projects his own desire for water and sees an apparent lake of shimmering water at a distance. Once the mind has projected to conceive that there is water, it is the experience of many a desert traveller that he sees ripples and waves, even ships moving on it, and the sun reflecting upon its disturbed surface! Similarly, when pure Consciousness is not apprehended, the mind projects in its place a world of change and, identifying with it, the ego comes to live a life of pain and sorrow.

Vedanta considers the world to be unreal because it is in a state of constant flux. That which exists in all periods of time, in the past, present, and future, without any change, is called the Real (*sat*); and that which did not and will not remain the same, but is seemingly available for our present experience, is called the unreal.

That which is changeless alone can be eternal. Real. Vedanta explains that the world of plurality, which in fact is not real in itself, is superimposed upon that which is Real. Such delusory superimposition takes place only when the real substratum is not comprehended. For example, due to the ignorance of the garland we misunderstand it to be a serpent. Non-apprehension of Reality gives rise to many misapprehensions: on apprehending the Reality, all misapprehensions disappear.

It is an experienced fact that, unconditioned by any of the essential scientific primary factors, such as time, space, and objects, we create for ourselves a world of experiences in our dreams. It is evidently clear that we can, in our imagination, project forth a world of plurality and thus create situations, identifying with which we live through a life of joy and sorrow.

Time is a relative, subjective experience. The dreamer in the dreamworld might live through ten years of life very vividly, and yet when he wakes up he realizes that according to the world's chronometers, only a few insignificant minutes have passed. The dream was projected in the mind where certainly there is not enough space for towns and fields, for houses and mountains, for the sun, the moon, and the stars, and yet, the dreamer dreamed all of them. No doubt these were all real to the dreamer. Within the dream-space and the dream-time, the dream-objects are created. However, to the waker, all of these are empty delusions.

The waking-world—held within the web of our present concept of time, space and objects—is also, it can be realized, an equally imaginary projection from the standpoint of a higher plane of consciousness. This can be realized only if we awaken ourselves into it, and that state of experience is the experience of Truth, the Self.

After projecting the dreamworld, completely forgetting his waking identity, the waker himself becomes the dreamer, the dreamed, and the dreaming, and thereafter continues to experience the joys and sorrows of that realm. On waking up he understands that this triple factor—dreamer, dreamed, and dreaming—is but one homogeneous whole: the waking mind. The waker's mind itself becomes the objects of the dreamworld; the waker's mind in another aspect becomes the dreamer; and the dreamer, drawing vitality and dynamism from the waker's mind, establishes his own relationship with the endless objects and their arrangements in the dream, and acts. This process is called dreaming.

By a similar process of forgetting our eternal, divine nature to be the non-dual Consciousness, we project the misconceptions of a pluralistic world of objects and play the game of experiences through the triple factor (triputi): the knower, the known, and the knowing.

From what we have discussed so far, can we say that the world of plurality has emerged out of Truth—the world being unreal? But though unreal, it has such a similitude of reality that it can choke us with its bondages and can give us a semblance of sorrow and joy!

47

How is it? Every philosopher finds it difficult to explain how the unreal has seemingly come from the Real. Therefore, the great Acharya Gaudapada admits in his *Mandukya Karika*:

> When Consciousness is associated with the idea of activity, the appearances that are seen in it do not come from elsewhere. When Consciousness is inactive, appearances do not go elsewhere from passive Consciousness. The appearances never go into the Consciousness, nor do the appearances emerge from Consciousness since they are not real entities. These are always beyond our comprehension, because they are not subjected to the cause-and-effect relationship. (Alatha Shanti: 51–52)

These verses plainly declare that it is inexplicable how the finitude has come out of the Infinite. The great thinker Gaudapada himself admits that, 'It is not because of any intellectual idleness on the part of the philosophers, but it is because of the very inability of the science of logic.' He says that since causation is but a myth, the law of causation does not function in this particular instance, and evidently no scientific explanation can be given without seeking and discovering the Reality behind the seeming finitude of the eternal Infinite.

Science can function only in a field of cause and effect. But when the intellect and the mind transcend the lower realms of causality and are away from the jurisdiction of delusion, they rise into the world of Truth where causation is not observed, as nothing is ever caused in pure Consciousness. Nothing can be produced there wherein the Truth is One-without-a-second.

We must carefully note that in these two verses Gaudapada hints that Consciousness associated with activity is the consciousness available for us in both the waking and the dream states. When he says that Consciousness is inactive, it is meant to indicate the deep-sleep state of consciousnesss wherein the whole world of plurality that was available for us in the dream and the waking states is no longer with us. It does not mean that the worlds of dream and waking states have gone elsewhere; nor can we say that they have entered into the deep sleeper. The real difficulty is our inability to give a complete intellectual explanation for the 'how' and the 'why' of these false appearances. Why have they emerged out of the Consciousness and how do they come about?

This difficulty in its turn has produced in our philosophical literature various theories about creation. For example:

> Some creationists believe it to be the projection of the glory of God's own superhuman power, while others consider the world to be of the same nature as dream or illusion. The creationists consider this manifestation as having been caused by the mere will of God, while there are others who, looking upon time as real, declare that time is the cause for the manifestation of all things.
>
> Others think that the world is being created for the purpose of God's enjoyments, while still others attribute it to a mere play of the Lord. But it is the very nature of the effulgent being, the Atman, for what desire is possible for Him, whose desires are always in a state of perfect fulfilment! (*Mandukya Upanishad*, Agama Prakarana: 7–9)

Enumerating the theories that existed then regarding the creation of the world, the teacher says that some of them hold that the creation of the world is caused by the determined will of the Lord, while others hold that the world was created with a set purpose behind it, the purpose being either the enjoyment of the Lord, or as an afternoon diversion for the Lord. There are some who hold that the time-factor is a real entity and that the creation of the various names and forms depends entirely upon time.

The non-creationists explain the world as a long dream. According to this school of thinkers, a dream is literally real while the dreamer dreams it; and the magician's illusion, or the illusions such as the serpent on the rope, are all real as long as the illusion lasts. They argue that if a thing is unreal, it cannot impinge upon our cognition and make us perceive it. According to them, wherever an object is cognized and some feelings generated thereby, such objects have a reality, however short-lived they may be!

Theory of Non-creation

After thus enumerating about six theories in all, Gaudapada gives his own reasons why Vedanta does not believe in a created world. According to him, the supreme Reality is non-created and there is never a world created by a Lord. The world of objects recognized by us is nothing but a mental projection made by ourselves. This is called the theory of non-creation (ajatavada). Early Vedanta, mainly represented by the *Mandukya Karikas* and *Yoga Vasishta*, believes in this theory of non-creation while modern Vedanta, represented mainly by Sri Shankaracharya, allows a relative reality to the world of objects seen in our everyday life. In fact, there is no fundamental difference between these two theories, if we correctly understand them. Thus, according to Vedanta, the only logical explanation that can be given for the creation is that it is the very nature of the supreme Reality. Nothing can ever remain apart from its own real nature; it is the nature of Infinity to play the finitude.

The supreme, all-perfect Reality cannot be attributed to entertain any desire. Desire for a thing is experienced only when the absence of it is felt by the entity. If I had just finished a full lunch and someone were to invite me for a second lunch, however tasty it may be, I would cry 'No, no! Not for me, not for me!' For the time being, the desire for food is impossible, since there is no absence of it felt. Similarly, the supreme Reality in its fullness, paripurnata, cannot feel any desire to create the world.

The emergence of the finite world out of the Infinite is a phenomenon that is perceived and felt by us in our present condition of misapprehension. But when our intellect with its sharpened discrimination comes to inquire into it logically, it, the object of our inquiry, somehow escapes even our most diligent pursuit. From the Infinite, the world could not have emerged; yet, at the same time, here is a world of finite things and beings staring at us so vividly—who can deny it? 'This field of "action-and-result", created by none and yet ever experienced by us, is indeed a great magic-play. Therefore, O Badrinath, "This can be only a great play of magic of Thy own Maya"—so say the great men of wisdom' (*Hymn to Badrinath*, Section 11–15).

In Vedanta, this power in an individual to delude himself and to perceive a world of plurality is called maya. This term is one over which a lot of unnecessary discussions have taken place. Also, other schools of philosophy have cast aspersions on Vedanta saying that they cannot subscribe to what maya is. This line of argument is pursued by them because of the misunderstanding in them that maya is a positive cause and not a hypothetical negative supposition.

In all delusory superimpositions there is the ignorance or non-apprehension of the real substratum (a post, a rope, or a garland of flowers), and out of this rise the endless misapprehensions of unreal experiences (ghost or serpent). This ignorance or non-apprehension of the real is the power of maya.

Apprehensions and non-apprehensions and the quality of the misapprehensions depend upon the nature and quality of the thoughts. Logically, therefore, maya is nothing other than ignorance, avidya, which is nothing other than the mind itself. Where the mind is transcended, the imperfect world of sorrows and forms, lived in and experienced by the individual through such experiences as a ghost on a post, or a serpent on a garland, due to maya, also disappears.

'Therefore,' the teacher concludes, 'men of inner experience declare that this universe experienced by us is nothing but an expression of maya.' Maya expressed in an individual is avidya, which is nothing other than the individual mind. The total mind is called maya, and the Infinite functioning through the total mind is called the Creator, Ishvara.

The Truth about Maya

The objects of the world exist and play about only in the observer's mind, and yet, due to maya, they are seen as though they are outside—as the reflection of oneself in a mirror.

> The divine Teacher makes an individual, at the time of realization, experience his own immutable Self, in which the Self alone plays as the universe of names and forms, like a city seen in a mirror, due to the maya power, as though produced outside, as in a dream—to Him, that divine Teacher, Sri Dakshinamurti, is this prostration. (*Dakshinamurti Stotram*, Verse 1)

By using the above example, it is pointed out that the reflected image has no reality apart from the object reflected. Though the reflected image is of the same form as the object reflected, there is a lateral inversion of details in the reflection. This 'lateral inversion' in our personality, causing confusions and sorrows in life, is called the samsara. The supreme Existence-Knowledge-Bliss, when reflected in the mind, is expressed as the non-existent, inert, and sorrowful world.

'If the world has an existence only as a reflection in the mind, then it should be experienced only as an inner emotion. How is it then that we constantly experience the world of objects as outside ourselves?' Acharya Shankara answers, 'It is because of maya,' the non-apprehension of the Truth. In order to elucidate this assertion, he gives the analogy of the dream.

Even though all of us know that happenings in the dreamworld, peopled by the dream-crowd, are all experienced within the mind, while the dream lasts, the dreamworld is definitely outside the dreamer himself. It is only on waking that he realizes that the entire dream and its happenings were but figments of his own imagination, having an existence only within himself, and that his mind was the very substratum upon which the dream was being experienced. In the same way, though the world of plurality exists only in one's own mind, it is experienced as real and substantial, independent of the experiencer.

There is another school of thinkers who consider that maya is an incomprehensible concept of Truth or God. They argue that since they perceive the world, the world must be real. However, this cannot be arrived at logically.

Human perceptions are often false. We see the sun moving, yet we know that the sun is not moving; we perceive the earth as steady and motionless, though the earth revolves around its own axis. The mere movement of air warmed up by the midday sun is perceived as patches of water with waves and ripples in it, though it is only a mirage. Very often an ordinary post is misunderstood as a ghost, a rope as a snake, a bit of seashell as a piece of silver.

In all these examples, the non-apprehension of reality is the cause for the misapprehensions. When we realize that it was only the rope, the snake disappears; when we realize that it was only the post, the ghost vanishes. The non-apprehension of Truth causes the misapprehensions of a pluralistic world.

At this moment, an intelligent student may find a doubt arising in his mind: 'The non-apprehension of Truth may be due to the play of maya, but what power creates the world of perceptions?' This possible doubt is answered in the verse by the statement 'by maya'. The power of maya inherent in the Reality has two definite expressions. It expresses knowledge (vidya) and ignorance (avidya). Of these, the ignorance manifests in two subjective mischiefs, 'the veiling of the real' (avarana) and 'the projecting a show of the apparent' (viksepa).

When the veiling power clouds our intellect, the mind starts projecting its imagination in place of the real object. When the intellect cannot detect the post, the mind projects the ghost. Where avarana plays, viksepa also asserts itself. To control viksepa is to remove the veiling power, and to the extent the veiling is removed, to that extent Reality is unfolded.

In the Upanishads we find positive evidence in the declarations of the Rishis that the world has risen from the Supreme. The Upanishads stress that 'before creation there was only pure Existence'. They also assert that 'verily from This alone all creatures were born'. Further, from this Omniscient (sarvajna), All-knowing (sarvavit) One, whose intelligence itself is thought, and through thought, all these names and forms of the world of matter were born.

According to Vedanta, creation could not have taken place from the Infinite, nor could it have happened from anything other than Brahman. It cannot be that the changeless Infinite has itself become the created world. And yet, there stands in front of us this world of objects and beings. The Vedantic philosophers were never blind to these facts, nor did they close their eyes to the brilliant expositions of Truth by the ancient Rishis.

Sri Shankara's Explanation

Sri Shankara's theory of superimposition (vivartavada) alone satisfies all the statements of the Upanishads. In the absence of the true knowledge of the nature of an object, the object's true nature is misunderstood, and when the real nature of the object is discovered—

when ignorance is ended by the right knowledge—all the misinterpretations end. This is the theory of superimposition. As long as the post is covered by our ignorance, the ghost vision seems real. Under a beam of light when ignorance of the post comes to an end, in the newly dawned knowledge of the post, the false superimposition of the ghost form also ends.

The nature of Reality is not experienced by us, and therefore, in its place we recognize the world of names and forms, of cross-purposes, of negative tendencies, of sorrows and mortality. When Truth is known, the perceived world of plurality itself is reassessed and experienced as nothing but the Infinite Consciousness. However, it is true that the Vedantic theory accepts a relative reality to the world of forms, inasmuch as, though it is unreal from the standpoint of the Supreme, it has a temporary reality as long as the limited ego recognizes it.

In fact, there should be a Reality that exists behind the world of objects, or else, instead of our present experiences such as 'the pot is', 'the chair is', 'the table is', we would have had an experience of 'the pot exists not', 'the chair exists not', 'the table exists not'. The existence of things is experienced by all, since the cause from which every object has emerged is an existent Being. Thus Vedantic philosophers directly bring home to students that all things in the world have risen from the Reality, which is the nature of pure Existence.

Continuing this logical inquiry they arrived at some very important conclusions. When the common experience of 'the table is', or 'the chair is' is analysed, we find that the experience of 'the pot is' comes to us when we are *conscious* of the *existence* of the pot. Similarly, the experience of 'the table is' becomes ours only when we are conscious of the existence of the table. In other words, the existence of an object is recognized only when Consciousness illumines it.

In light of the above, if the common experience of everybody that 'the world exists' is analysed, we shall find that it is because we are *conscious* of the *existence* of the world. Just as a pot has no existence apart from the mud, its material cause, so too, the world has no existence apart from the supreme Existence (satta) and the supreme Consciousness (spurana). Hence Vedanta declares that the world is the effect of Existence and Consciousness (satta spurana karya).

In case we accept that the world of objects has an existence of its own and that existence and awareness are both the very inherent nature of matter, it will be contradicting our experiences in life. According to the objective scientists of modern times, the world *is* existence, while to the subjective scientists, the philosophers of India, the world *has* existence. There is a lot of difference between the assertion that the ever-perishing world of matter *is* existence and the declaration that the changing phenomena *have* existence, that the phenomenal world is a play of matter upon Existence and that the eternal principle of Existence expresses itself in and through all changes.

This world of plurality, with different names and forms that seem to rise and fall like waves in the ocean, is an illusion experienced upon the substratum (adhistanam) painted by the confused ego. Just as the waves are on and of the ocean—they do not stand even for a moment apart from the oceanic waters—so also, the waves of creation are in and of that absolute Supreme and have no separate existence in themselves. This supreme Being is the Atman, who stands unaffected in the least by the changes caused in the arena of time, space, and causality.

Now the student, in trying to understand the Vedantic point of view, may ask, 'If, as you say, O Vedantin, both the objective and the subjective worlds in us are mere imaginations of the mind, what is the source of these imaginations? It cannot be merely the mind, because the mind is nothing but matter: inert, insentient and lifeless. Nor can this be the Atman, since the Atman is knowledge and in knowledge there cannot be any delusion.'

Answering this question, Adi Shankara gives a beautiful example to show how this delusion is maintained. The answer is, 'Like an iron piece appearing to be fire when in contact with fire.'

Enquiring into this phenomenon, Sri Shankara says, 'It is mutual superimposition (annyonyadhyasa).' Any superimposition is always mutual; it cannot be one way only. On a rope we cannot have the delusory misconception of a cow. The superimposition can reflect some or all the qualities of the substratum.

Therefore, not only does the rope borrow the properties of a snake, but the snake also borrows some properties from the rope. The snake is spotted, slimy, long, and has a hood; these snake-properties are not in the rope, but they cover the rope. And the rope lends its *existence* to the fancied snake. The rope exists, the snake exists not. The non-existent snake exists for the deluded man. The imaginary snake borrows its existence from the rope; to the rope the snake lends its spotted slimy appearance; together he sees the rope as non-existent and the snake as existent. The snake-properties he sees and the rope-properties he does not see. So our conclusion in delusion is 'The snake *is*, the rope *is not.*'

Today we *see* the body, the mind, the intellect, the ego, and their sorrows and say that these exist; the reality of God, Consciousness, exists not for us.

When I apprehend the pure Consciousness in myself, all the qualities of the body, mind and intellect and the world of objects, emotions and thoughts disappear. Alone the *Reality exists.*

When the body, mind and intellect are transcended, the individual apprehends the pure, infinite nature of Reality, wherein in its non-dual existence, no such distinctions as world, individual or God can ever arise. Having seen and experienced the post, there cannot remain the ghost vision to give us a share of the old dread or sorrow. This is the result of realizing the Infinite Self, and to reach this desirable Godhood, we take shelter at the feet of the Lord of Badri, who is none other than this Atman Divine.

SIX

THE FALL OF MAN[*]

In the following verses of the Bhagavad Gita, Vedanta's theory of the psychological fall of mankind from a divine status is explained: 'When a man thinks of objects, attachment to them arises. From attachment desire is born, from desire arises anger. From anger comes delusion, from delusion loss of memory. From loss of memory comes the destruction of discrimination, and from the destruction of discrimination he perishes' (III:62–63).

The path of destruction for a seeker is so elaborately detailed in these two verses that, fallen as we are, we shall know how to get back to our intrinsic perfection. The source of evil begins with our own wrong thinking or false imagination. Thought is creative. It can make us or mar us. If rightly harnessed, it can be used for constructive purposes; if misused, it can totally destroy us. When we constantly think of a sense object, the consistency of thought creates an attachment for the object of our thought, and when more and more thoughts flow towards the object of attachment, they crystallize to form a burning desire to possess the object of attachment. The same force of emotion, when directed towards obstacles that threaten the fulfilment of our desires, is called anger (krodha).

An intellect coloured with anger comes to experience delusion. The deluded intellect has no power of discrimination because it

---

[*] From *The Choice is Yours (Ethics in Vedanta)*, Central Chinmaya Mission Trust, Mumbai (reprint, 1991).

loses its wisdom gained from memories of the past. When a person is filled with anger, he or she is likely to commit regrettable acts, having totally forgotten himself and his relationship with others.

Thus, when an individual, through wrong channels of thinking, becomes attached to an object, the attachment grows into a burning desire to possess that object. The mental disturbance caused by the emotion deludes the intellect and makes the individual forget his sense of proportion and his sense of relationship with things and beings around him. Such a deluded intellect forgets its dignity of culture and loses its discriminating power, its conscience. Conscience is the knowledge used to differentiate good from evil and to warn the mind against sensuousness and animalism. Once the conscience is dulled, the human being becomes a two-legged creature with little sense of proportion, and with no ears for the subtler call in him. Thereby he is guaranteeing destruction for himself—destruction, in so far as an impure heart cannot come to perceive or strive for the higher and nobler in life. However, the person who can go with perfect self-control through life and its infinite number of sense objects, each trying to bind him with its charms, and who can approach them with neither love nor aversion comes to enjoy peace.

Desire

Desire cannot arise in the mind of one who is fulfilled. Desires can arise only in one who fails to feel his infinitude and consequently expresses himself as the limited ego (jiva). Forgetting one's own divine nature and identifying with the unreal values of life, one develops a hunger for peace and happiness. Numerous desires arise in him and, seeking a fulfilment of desires, he indulges in sense gratification.

Desire is an expression of the finite ego when the seeker seeks satisfaction and fulfilment through sense enjoyments. Negative tendencies such as greed, hypocrisy and conceit naturally arise, and the individual ceaselessly strives to satisfy the unending demands of his own unbridled desires. The ego, desperately struggling to gain inner peace, forsakes all consideration for others, ignores all the noble values of life, and enters into the fields of activity shamelessly intolerant, inconsiderate, and even brutal. Thus Lord Krishna answered Arjuna's original question of 'what impels us to commit sin' with the assertion: 'It is desire, it is anger born out of all-sinful *rajas*. Know this as the foe here' (Bhagavad Gita, III:37).

Desire for the possession of anything becomes an obsession when it grows out of proportion. When this desire is thwarted, the desire takes the form of anger towards the obstruction. Anger has the capacity to distort our vision of life, and noble traits such as justice, honesty and uprightness cannot express themselves. We then become ready to compromise and even justify our default with a hundred hollow arguments.

Desire and anger arise from *rajoguna*. A sense of incompleteness makes the mind restless to acquire, possess and enjoy the objects of the world in a futile attempt to discover a sense of fulfilment in life. These desires to possess and enjoy are by their very nature insatiable. The more we satisfy them, the more they multiply. There is no end to the mind's demands and desires. These desires and subsequent anger prompt individuals, communities, and even nations to commit crimes against one another. It has made history a meaningless and shameful story of the destruction of mankind.

This obsessive desire, otherwise expressed as anger, is the greatest enemy of humanity. Every cultured individual strives to live a noble and great life as he or she understands it. He wants to live in love and peace, distributing and sharing cheer and service with everyone around him. But when he allows himself to be conquered by the lower desires, his life soon becomes a compromise, a mere caricature of what he knows and believes. Therefore, the Satan in us is not some terrible inexplicable force, lying in wait before us, but our own animal urges expressing themselves as the desire in our hearts.

All human beings have these desire-prompted urges in them. That is the work of nature. When desires mount to an excess, they obscure our thinking power and veil the wisdom in us. This veiling of intelligence by desire is of varying thickness; sometimes it is thin and misty, but at other times it is thick and dark. 'Enveloped, O son of Kunti, is wisdom by this constant enemy of the wise in the form of desire, which is as difficult to appease as fire' (Bhagavad Gita, III:39).

Every human being has some notion of what is right and wrong. Though we may have the knowledge, we still grope in darkness, because the light of wisdom in us is often shrouded by the clouding intensity of our own passions. Furthermore, the unending psychological demands are insatiable. The more we gratify our desires, the more they multiply. Never can desires for things end by accommodating and fulfilling them; they only multiply in quick succession each time they are satisfied.

Passion has its headquarters in three main centres—in the sense organs, in the mind, and in the intellect. Desire does not itself execute its follies; it deludes the sense organs or the mind or the intellect and orders them to do the mischief in our lives. The sense organs, the mind, and the intellect always function in the light of the rational knowledge we have. As long as our discrimination is alert, these instruments cannot function to the detriment of the individual ego. But the mist of desires has the capacity to swirl around the wisdom in us and veil our light of discrimination. In the resultant darkness, under the heat of the prevailing passions, man acts as an animal, without any discriminative intelligence to guide his life and direct his behaviour.

Passion veils wisdom, and the resulting darkness confuses the sense organs, the mind, and the intellect and forces them to act in a manner detrimental to themselves. This desire in us springs mainly out of the conflict of the sense organs with their respective sense objects. We perceive a thing and our sense organs are tempted: feelings of desire arise in our mind and we start contemplating the means of acquiring and enjoying the object of temptation.

Attachments and aversions of the sense organs for their respective sense objects are instinctive and natural. But the sense objects by themselves are incapable of bringing any agitation to the mind. We get agitated and disturbed not in the sense organs, but in our minds. The mind gets disturbed because when the sense-stimuli reach the mind, it accepts certain types of stimuli as good and their opposites as bad. Thereafter, it gets attached to the stimuli it experiences as good and develops an aversion to the stimuli it experiences as bad. Now the mind is forced to suffer the agonies of the world of plurality. Whenever it comes in contact with the infinite number of objects outside, it pants to court the objects of its desire and labours to run away from the objects of its aversion. This excitement of the mind is truly its tragedy.

Lack of Discrimination

'Bewildered by many a fancy, entangled in the snare of delusion, addicted to the gratification of lust, they fall into a foul hell' (Bhagavad Gita, XVI:16). When an individual's mind, as a result of its false philosophy, gets dissipated in dreams, his intellect also falls into a deplorable condition. His power of judgement and discrimination gets ensnared in a web of delusions and false values. Cut off from its permanent moorings, the intellect has no platform of its own by which to judge correctly and evaluate life. It fails to recognize the permanent harmony of life and, instead, recognizes only its own egocentric vanities. Life looked at through such disturbed equipment appears distorted. When an individual's intellect is thus clouded, his mind gets agitated and his sense organs, which are the instruments through which the mind–intellect has to express itself, behave erratically. Naturally, therefore, such an individual becomes a victim of passion and sense gratification.

We need not be great philosophers to understand that such an individual, tired physically, upset mentally, and confused intellectually, lives in a self-created hell, distributing his woes to others around him. A man can make a heaven of hell or a hell of heaven by the harmony or discord in his mind. A subjectively shattered personality cannot find peace or fulfilment in any situation. Even if the environment is conducive to harmony, his mental sufferings create dissonance wherever he goes.

If a single individual who has these false values discovers for himself a world of sorrow, even in the midst of happy surroundings, we can understand what the condition of the world would be when a majority of us have, in varying degrees, the same false values. Hell and heaven are simply the proportion of discord or harmony that we cultivate in our inner personality.

Maya

Essentially godly and divine, the human mind seems to fall under a self-delusion, which, when analysed, becomes perfectly evident by its effects. The cause of delusion is conceived of as the indescribable power called maya. Like unmanifested electricity, maya in itself is not perceptible except in its various manifestations. It is a phenomenon that can be fully estimated and accounted for only through its varied expressions.

Observing and analysing the effects of maya within the constitution of all individualized and embodied souls, the Vedantic masters concluded that it comes to play in two distinct modes of expression, at two different levels of the human personality. Thus, at the intellectual level it expresses itself as a film of doubt and hesitation;

the intellect's capacity to understand or experience the higher is thwarted. This expression of maya is termed by the masters as the veiling power (avarana shakti).

Due to this mist of ignorance that envelops the intellect when it is unconscious of the spiritual reality behind it, the mind starts projecting forth the world of the not-Self and superimposes upon it two firm ideas: (a) that 'it is real' and (b) that 'I am nothing but the body, mind, and intellect.' This is maya's expression as the 'projecting-power' (viksepa shakti). Because of these two effects of maya, the intellect, ignorant of its spiritual destiny, surges forward seeking satisfaction among the finite sense objects of the world. When we act in the world, the resulting reactions and impressions get stored as vasanas in our subconscious personality. The vasanas manifest as our individual habits and desires, and they perpetuate our continuous struggle of seeking fulfilment in an unpredictable world.

But when the intellect discovers in itself an ability to pierce the veil of ignorance, it comes to live its own real nature of infinite bliss. Each fleeting moment of joy in the sense-world only sharpens its appetite for the infinite bliss that is its real nature. When the clouds have moved away and the sun has emerged, he who is warming himself at the fireside moves away from the fireplace and walks into the open to bask in the all-enveloping warmth of the blazing sun. Similarly, the illusion of ignorance melts away in an integrated intellect, and wanderings in the sensuous world are curtailed.

Ordinarily, our entire attention is always engaged with the sense organs and their respective objects. When the intellect is purified and withdrawn from its preoccupation with the world outside, the Self shines forth in its own resplendency. That which makes us strangers to ourselves is our preoccupation with our false identity and our wasteful play with the senses. Once we emerge from that preoccupation, just as the sun emerges from behind the clouds, the Self shines forth to assert itself.

Mind is maya at play. Therefore, conquest of the mind is the conquest of maya; and unless one constantly turns one's attention to the higher Self within, unless one has a deep devotion to the Lord, unless one learns to glimpse His glory in the world of beings around, one must necessarily succumb to the enchantments of one's own mind. But when one is inspired with deep devotion to the Self and pursues the Self alone, one is no more a victim of sensuous pleasures and worldly preoccupations and all the illusions created by the mind.

Vedantic scriptures teach that the purest form of ethical living can exist only when an individual has understood the root cause of social disharmony. The ancient Vedic masters were very much concerned with the question of social happiness, and their inquiries took them to a deeper level. Social happiness is attainable only where individual happiness exists, and individual happiness is assured only when one discovers the intrinsic harmony of the higher Self.

~

SEVEN

Free Will versus Destiny[*]

The study of ethics presupposes that we can assert our will over our lower impulses. We cannot be held morally responsible for actions that are out of our control or not within our capacity to change. A moral system must be based upon an understanding of the nature of mankind and its capacity for change. Vedanta's theory of karma examines this issue of free will versus destiny.

The Law of Karma

The law of karma has often been confused with the law of destiny, when actually there is a great deal of difference between the two. Had the Vedantic law of karma been equal to the law of destiny, Hindu civilization would have long ago perished, as have all the ancient civilizations through history. The law of destiny has a corroding effect upon the human heart, and those who depend entirely upon it to guide them become weak-minded, passive human beings.

Those who believe in predestination, or that all actions and events have been determined since the beginning of creation, deny any personal responsibility for their actions, hiding under the cloak of fatalism—asserting that since they were fated to act thus, they are

---

[*] From *The Choice is Yours* (*Ethics in Vedanta*), Central Chinmaya Mission Trust, Mumbai (reprint, 1991).

not to be held morally responsible for their low actions.

On the other hand, a people believing in and living up to the law of karma become dynamic citizens and spiritual giants. The law of karma is based upon the conclusion that this life is not an end in itself but is just an incident in the eternal existence of each of us. Each one of us is unique and each one's life is different from another's. The destiny of one is obviously different from that of another. Had this been the very first and the last of our births and had we all entered the world as equal, justice would have necessitated that we all have a similar experience of life.

Whenever we inquire into the differences among human beings, we arrive at the conclusion that, having risen from different causes, each of us should manifest as a different effect. Effects depend upon their causes. This life which we live is only one of our incarnations, according to the law of karma. From birth to death and from death to birth, the cycle goes on, but we do not appreciate it or understand it because we view life from a very circumscribed point of view.

We think that life means only the period spent by us from our birth to our death, and what we experience during this interval is the sum total of life. But let us for a moment take the example of a picture painted on a canvas. In order to see the entire picture painted on it, we have to step back some distance and only then can we get the entire view, the rhythm of the colours, the beauty of the shapes, and so on. Similarly, when life is viewed from a close perspective, we feel that it is illogical and unrhythmic. But when we stand back from our present life in detachment and try to view the whole of life in its entirety, we can begin to perceive a vast harmony and perfection.

Some of us blame the Creator for the sorrow or sin in our lives, and despair by saying that the sorrows have been fated to us. The Vedantins teach differently. It is important that we understand that there is a rhythm in the universe, that the planets move regularly, that the stars ride in their appointed paths, and that the natural laws never deviate from nature. Everywhere we can discover the law of rhythm (rtu), and everything conforms to that law. Why then, in the case of human life, do we say that there is no logic or reason in it?

Destiny (Prarabdha)

Each human being represents the various effects arising from different causes. The causes being different, the effects are different. Thus, every action of the past has its own reaction, and each of us must have a treasury of all these past reactions. This accumulation of reactions is called the sanchita karma. We should understand that after having lived the fruits allotted for the present life, called prarabdha, each person, while departing from life, takes the next form according to the pattern ordained by the ripened karmas in the total sanchita karma.

Let me explain it more clearly. Suppose I have a plot of land divided into orchards. In one, I plant coconut seedlings; in the second, apples; and in the third, mangoes. In order to germinate, grow and yield fruit, each seed must take its own time. Similarly, each action takes its own allotted time to fructify. Every action has its own reaction; certain actions give their reactions immediately, while others give their reactions after an interval.

To live out the reactions of our past actions, each of us needs to experience certain joys and sorrows, and in order to bring forth these required experiences, each must have a definite field, or loka, of his own experiences. The generally accepted meaning of the word loka is 'the world'. Etymologically, loka means 'a field of experience'. In the discussion of karma, loka means the special, private realm in which I live my subjective experiences.

Again, people misunderstand the real meaning of prarabdha when they use it to mean all the failure, impotence and selfishness in their character. If we are to be guided by this delusion that all our actions

69

are predetermined, then in every act of ours there is no room for self-improvement through effort. There are some who justify their actions by saying, 'I have no faith in a Higher Good, and it is my prarabdha, so why should I try to live a noble, moral life?' This is a self-defeating concept based on a defeatist mentality.

But then, where does this self-effort, purushartha, come in if prarabdha orders every situation? We have been given limited freedom by nature. For example, we cannot bend a piece of thick metal, but supposing the metal is beaten out and made into a chain—it then becomes pliable. Similarly, when a cow is tied to a rope in the centre of a pasture, it is not free to graze the entire field but can move freely only within the circle drawn by the rope. Similarly, although we have taken this form to live out a fixed prarabdha, we can reach the supreme goal of life by applying our pure motives and intelligent discrimination to harness the freedom allowed us from moment to moment.

We have come into this world to enjoy and suffer for our past karmas, through the circumstances ordered by our prarabdha. There is provision for us to discriminate and act rightly. For example, is there not a certain amount of freedom of choice involved in deciding whether to go to a cinema or to a temple? At every moment of life there is a challenge posed by the question, 'Shall I do this or shall I do that?' Two distinct paths are open to us, the path of the good and the path of the pleasant. We find ourselves at every moment standing at the junction of these two paths. Often we are at a loss to decide which path to pursue. There is a tussle between the devil and the God in us at such a moment of trial. By adopting the path of the pleasant, we can get immediate but short-lived rewards, whereas by adopting the path of the good, we can gain the long-term goal, our full satisfaction.

Imagine the mind to be made up of soft matter. As each thought passes through it, an impression, like a scratch, is left on it. When similar thoughts are repeated, the small scratch deepens into a channel. Every subsequent thought has a tendency to flow through that ready-made thought-channel. Thus, if the impression, or the channel, was produced by good thoughts, then a good character is maintained and strengthened by the subsequent thoughts flowing irresistibly in that direction.

Let us take another example. Examine the working of the human mind. If you have a tendency to get angry and want to overcome that tendency, you should first of all feel repentant about it. Then you will have already suppressed the anger to some extent. Of course, pent-up anger will burst forth at a later date if you merely suppress it. But if you are intelligent, you should divert that energy to some other profitable direction. You should not succumb by meekly saying, 'It is my prarabdha to get angry.'

Carve out a new channel in your mind with repeated good thoughts. Repeat to yourself, 'I love all,' or 'I am very tolerant.' Go on repeating the suggestive thoughts, and in a short time you will observe that you have no anger at all in your mental make-up.

First of all, we should be aware of our weaknesses. We must be fully aware of them. We are essentially the very composition of our minds. When we perform some actions repeatedly, our minds get fixed with certain impressions. The quality of our experiences depends upon the quality of the mind that undergoes the experience. The mind, being what it is, is conditioned by the various impressions that it has gathered in its different stages of life. Thus, when we control and chasten the motives and thoughts in our minds, we purify the mind itself.

Free Will (Purushartha)

At each moment of our life, we are not only living the fruits of our past actions, but also creating those for tomorrow. Similarly, at each moment we are preparing ourselves for the lives yet to come. Prarabdha is caused by the actions done in the past. Thus, if our prarabdha is a sorrowful one now, let us perform such acts today that can determine a happier life for us in the future.

The law of destiny does not explain to us how, even while we live the preordained and prarabdha-controlled pattern of circumstances, we can have in the immediate moments a freedom to create afresh (purushartha). This positive approach is an essential part of the law of karma.

A happier tomorrow is built only when we assert our will to live a divine life today. Religion asks us to entertain and live such values of life so that while living them we are able to create an ordered life, full of joys, in the future. Follow the righteous path of the good; avoid the by-lanes of the crooked, the unrighteous path of the pleasant. We must start and constantly keep on the right path to reach the goal of supreme good. If our course is in the right direction, we shall certainly reach our destination.

Yet another way of looking at the question of free will versus fate is by reviewing life in the light of the flow of time, wherein the future, through the present, is ever becoming the past. Anything that is now in the future must in time arrive to become the present and before long will pass on into the past.

We have already noted that the human intellect cannot rest without seeking the cause of things, but we generally do not take full advantage of this causation-hunting urge in us. If we search for the causes of our present life, we shall discover certain facts that reveal to us the inner meaning and the deep significance of the law of karma.

From the seed the tree grows; the seed is the cause and the tree is the effect. From cotton cloth is made: cotton is the cause, and cloth is the effect. Now, in all conceivable examples, the cause is anterior with reference to time, like the father of a child, and the effect is posterior, like the child born. The father was in existence before the child was born. Cause is thus that which was, and the effect is that which is. The past causes the present: the present will, therefore, cause the future!

In short, it is said that the future is not a mystery, an unknown miracle, that we must wait to see unfolded. The past modified in the present alone is the future. The things to come are not ordered by a mere continuity of the past. This freedom to modify the past and thereby create a future for better or for worse is called purushartha, or self-effort.

To illustrate: a log floating down a river will move at the same speed at which the river flows, but if the log is fitted with a motor and manned by an intelligent driver, the log will have an independent movement of its own, although conditioned by the flow of the river. Let's assume that the waters of the river are moving at two miles an hour. When the speedometer on the log shows ten miles an hour, the log will move at twelve miles an hour down the river, but only eight miles an hour if it goes upstream. The flow of the river will always be there; but because of the motor and the intelligence of the driver, the log has a limited freedom of movement now.

The plant and the animal kingdoms move just as the log that floats down the river, directed and guided by their inborn instincts and impulses. But we, having reached the human level, have acquired a reasoning capacity and a discriminative faculty. Using these two we can steer the ship of life safely to our destination, the higher goal we have set for ourselves.

To consider therefore, that the present is but a product of past actions (prarabdha) is undignified: to recognize that the future is only a product of present actions (purushartha) is equally unintelligent. There is no slavery, nor is there complete freedom. There is however, a limited freedom, which, if used intelligently, can redeem us from all entanglements.

73

Thus, the law of karma, when understood correctly, is the greatest force of vitality in Vedantic philosophy. It makes us the architects of our own future. We are not helpless pawns in the hands of a mighty tyrant. If we are weak or sorrowful, it is solely because of our own wilful actions. In our ignorance, we may have pursued certain negative values of life in the past, and their fruits have reared up now to give us the pattern of circumstances we are living today.

Still, take heart. By living rightly today the divine values of love, kindness, tolerance and mercy, you will ensure a more noble pattern for your future. By honest introspection, you can detect your wrong tendencies and eliminate them through constant, deliberate effort. Develop positive thinking and thus come to be the creator of your own future life. Then only will lasting success be yours.

EIGHT

REFLECTIONS ON LIFE AND DEATH*

There are some schools of thinkers who have established that death is the end of everything and there is nothing beyond it. There are others who accept, argue and heartily proclaim that there is existence even beyond the grave. Most of us also show a keen interest in wanting to know what lies beyond. But only few of us apply ourselves to the practice of how to make our lives more fulfilling in the present moment. Yet, understanding our present life is much more important than trying to discover what is after death. How to experience undisturbed peace and happiness in ourselves, and how to bring this newfound peace and harmony back to the world is of vital importance to us all. Nevertheless, in this modern era, where people consider themselves to be highly intellectual, there is great curiosity and preoccupation to know what lies beyond the death experience. This shows that what we cannot see or experience has significantly greater attraction for us. Before entering into the subject, we should first analyse the following questions. What is life? What is death? And who dies?

Q: What is life?

A: From the point of view of the materialist, life is an illogical and

_____

* From *The Sages Speak about Life and Death*, The Mananam Series, Chinmaya Mission West, Piercy, California, 1995.

meaningless procession from birth to death. One who is constantly engaged in the pursuit of earning, procuring and hoarding material wealth cannot have the required subtlety of mind to inquire into the possibilities of the hereafter. As long as the mind and intellect are drowned in the base values of life, which are built upon thoughtless conclusions and instinctive identification with one's body, one will not easily entertain the urge to go beyond the shackles of mortal limitations. The materialistic person seems convinced that there is nothing after death, and firmly believes that death is the end, as no one has ever come back to talk about it.

But for spiritual students, life is a continuous process with a great purpose, a glorious pattern, and full of meaning. They understand that the life which they are living today is an effect, and since every effect must have a cause, their lives must have their independent causes, even though they may not be visible today. Spiritual life is a continuous attempt to live a divine life. Thus, the spiritual student tries to live up to certain higher values, such as tolerance, love, kindness and mercy.

Q: What is death?

A: Viewed from a scientific perspective, a person is considered to be alive when he is able to respond to certain stimuli that he receives through the sense organs. When an organism or individual stops responding to the stimuli, we say he/she is dead. Now let us analyse this, please. Who exactly is dead? We see that the body is still there; no part of it has gone away. The same body is lying there which was there before death. Yet, when we say Mr X has died, what we really mean is that the mind and intellect which were receiving and responding to the outer stimuli have left the body. [The mind and intellect are expressions of thoughts in two different functions: feeling (mind) and thinking (intellect).] Hence, we conclude that Mr X, the person who called himself 'I' or 'me', is other than the body. Though the physical body is still there, the mind and intellect have left it.

This physical body is composed of the five great elements: space, air, fire, water and earth. It is the nature of the body to merge with the same five elements when it is dead, meaning, when the mind and intellect have left it. Therefore, I must conclude that I am the possessor or the indweller of the body. The body is just like a tenement for which I pay rent in the form of food, three or four times a day. If I forget to pay the rent you can imagine what a tragedy I will have to meet with!

Similarly, this 'dwelling' is but an instrument through which I express myself in this world, just like my car. If my car is destroyed, why should I think that I am destroyed? I am not the car. I am only the owner of the car. In the same way, if the body is destroyed, I am not destroyed. I am other than the body. My senses are only those instruments through which I receive stimuli from the outer world. Therefore, it is the mind and intellect which is the real individuality of a person. When we say we must develop the personality, we denote that the mind and intellect are to be developed. A truly cultured or civilized person is one who has a sharp and integrated mind and intellect. Due to our unintelligent ways of thinking, however, we do not look beyond the body.

Q: What is the difference between life and death? Matter activated by Consciousness is a living body. If Consciousness is not activated in a dead body, what happens to that Consciousness? Is it all-pervading? But if Consciousness is not present in a dead body, how can we say it is all-pervading?

A: Consciousness reflected in the mind and intellect (subtle body) is the consciousness of things. When the mind and intellect leave the gross body, it is the condition of death of the gross body. Since the subtle body alone can reflect infinite Consciousness, there is no apparent feeling, thinking or perception for a dead physical body.

When, with a mirror, we reflect a pool of light A at a point on the wall and then tip the mirror, the specific pool of light A moves to B. We can now say the special individuality at A has gone (death) and a special individuality has come (been born) at point B. But remember, the general sunlight that is on the wall has never 'come' or 'gone'. When the special light created by the mirror at point A has moved away, the general light on the wall is still there, pure Existence (*sat*) is in the dead body, but Knowledge (*cit*) and Bliss (*ananda*) are not manifest in the dead body, as the subtle and causal bodies have left it.

The Question of Identification

Q: The sages proclaim that death is an easy and simple process, that it does not demand any effort on the part of the dying. They have told us that it is like going from one place to another. However, if this is so, why do we feel so sorry about an impending death, which is but going from one body to another?

A: This sorrow is due to our attachments to the objects of the world which we do not want to leave behind. Suppose I am sitting in the dining room and I tie myself to the table, chairs and cupboards with a rope. If I then leave the dining room for the bedroom, I naturally invite discomfort, pain and sorrow for myself.

One can frequently observe scenes of attachment at railway stations just before the time of the train's departure. A few persons will have tears rolling down their cheeks, some will have melancholic faces, and you may even see some of them running along with the train shouting, 'Please write every day.' This is all because of attachment.

Possessiveness or attachment is due to identification. In the waking state you identify yourself with the gross body. Therefore, you are conscious of it, and you think that happiness and sorrow of the body are *your* happiness and sorrow.

When you withdraw your identification from the gross body and identify with the subtle body, you are in the dream state. You do not experience any happiness or sorrow of the gross body, but you are happy or unhappy in the dreamworld of experience, which was created by your mind and intellect.

When you have withdrawn your identification from the gross as well as from the subtle body and have identified with your causal body, you are in the deep-sleep state and do not experience any happiness or sorrow of the gross or subtle bodies. There you experience undisturbed peace and bliss, but you are not conscious of your experience of peace and happiness. When you reach the fourth state of consciousness, called turiya, you have conscious experience of happiness which is your own nature.

As we have already discussed, when the subtle body takes the pilgrimage from a given physical body to another, we say that the person has died. Yet, each will continue to go on to such bodies as controlled by their desires, demands, or cravings. We remain in a certain place until our particular demands are met, and afterwards we leave that place and go to another where our next predominant desires are to be fulfilled.

You could say that the mind and intellect's relationship with the body is something like that of a bird with its nest. The nest is safe as long as the bird continues to visit the nest to feed its young. But as soon as its purpose to visit is over, it flies away, never thinking about the nest. And without the bird, the nest perishes. There is no sense of possession or ownership in this.

Similarly, until the subtle body exhausts its desires, loves and hatreds, and likes and dislikes, the physical body is safe. When the purpose of the subtle body is exhausted, it leaves its physical frame.

Without the subtle body, the physical body must perish. But actually we have not perished, for we are something other than the body.

Q: Why do we fear death?

A: Whatever be the span of life allotted, there is death lurking at the end of it all. Death is equally painful whether it be today or a thousand years from now. Everything that one has gathered, for which one has worked many hours each day, three hundred and sixty-five days of the year—the house, wife, children, name and fame—he must leave one day. Because we lack the correct knowledge of our real nature, we unintelligently create wrong relationships with the objects of the world. These relationships are called attachments.

But suppose there had been no death and only birth. What a tragedy! There would have been no more space available on the earth. An increase of only a few million people creates a headache for the government. Whether we like it or not, it is the benevolent law of nature that brings death. When we agree that death must come, why should we fear it?

We fear death because of our identification with the gross body and of gathering the qualities of the body on our Self. Our identification with the body is so strong that we apprehend destruction of ourselves whenever we think of the death of the body. Now the question is: can the mind and intellect remain without the body?

Let us take the example of the relationship of the bullet and the gun. A bullet or a gun alone cannot frighten or kill us because by themselves they do not have any power. But when the bullet is in the gun, it certainly can frighten us. And when fired from the gun it can bring death. A bullet can only travel in the direction in which the gun is pointed. As long as the bullet is in the gun, the gun has control as to which direction the bullet will travel. Once the bullet is shot or has left the gun, the gun has no control over it.

Similarly, while our mind is in the body we have control over the mind. But once the mind and intellect have left the body, the body has no control over them. The mind will be shot in the direction decided by the sum total of our thoughts and activities in our entire lifetime.

Q: Why should we not indulge in the objects of the world during our lifetime, and contemplate the Lord only at the time of death?

A: This proves impossible, for how can we think of God in our final hours after focusing a lifetime of thoughts on the external world? It is therefore suggested that we should begin to contemplate God right here and now, for it is not certain when death will come. It is necessary for us to think of the Lord at the time of death because these thoughts provide us with a certain atmosphere and a proper vehicle to accomplish our voyage to perfection.

Therefore, to the intelligent person, death is not painful, but a new experience. If a candle is burned, nothing is lost. There is only a change in name and form. Similarly, nothing is lost in death to the person of wisdom. For him it is but a change of body, place and time.

Q: Is there an interval between the departure from one body and entry into another?

A: This can be explained by the following example. When an officer is transferred from one city to another, say from Bombay to Delhi, he must first give up his charge and leave Bombay and then reach Delhi in order to take up his new appointment. He has handed over his duties at Bombay and is on his way to Delhi. If he is asked on the way if he is an officer, he will certainly confirm that, but when he is asked if he is an officer of Bombay or Delhi, he cannot answer, for, at that moment, he is neither in Bombay nor in Delhi. Yet he is still the officer inasmuch as he is also getting paid for the interim period. Therefore, the interval can be called the joining time.

Similarly, when the subtle body leaves a given physical body in order to assume a new one, there must be an interval between the two events. The duration of this interval depends upon the relationship that you have with the body that you are shedding and the urgency you feel for the next embodiment.

Q: Can we contact the dead?

A: In our scriptures it is said that we can contact the dead, but the Rishis strongly advise against it. They say that by calling our loved ones back here, we are perhaps asking them to come down into a lower world. If, at that time, our loved ones are at higher realms of experience, we stop their pilgrimage by calling them down, and instead of sending their blessings they will curse us.

In this world also, no one wants to come down from a higher to a lower state. If one is forced to come down from a higher state he will be cursing those responsible for his fall. Similarly, why should the spirits respond to our call when they are in a higher realm? They do so because they are overpowered by their love and attachment for us. Some spirits, however, refuse to come down because they are not overpowered; thus they continue their pilgrimage to a higher plane.

We can observe similar incidents right here on earth as certain parents sacrifice their own principles in order to make their children happier. Say a young man wants to marry a particular girl, but his parents do not like the match. If, after much persuasion, the son still wants to marry the girl, the parents, though not happy, will sacrifice their happiness in preference to that of their son. This is because of their attachment to him.

Therefore, by calling the spirit of a dead person, we are not going to do any good for our dear ones. If we are not able to do something good for them, at least we should not harm them. It is now left to each individual to think these ideas over and act intelligently.

NINE

THE FLIGHT OF THE SUBTLE BODY*

The cardinal philosophical idea in Vedanta is that an individualized ego continues to identify with a given physical body only as long as it needs that particular instrument for gathering its desired quota of experiences. Once it is over, it 'kicks the bucket' as it were, and walks off forgetting all its responsibilities, relationships, and the vanities of that particular existence. With reference to the body, this condition is called death. But the ego-centre, although not manifest and functioning through the body, continues to exist in its subtle form.

This ego-centre set in the subtle body is conveyed to its next field of activity (loka) by the energy called udana. Udana, which is one of the five upa pranas, is that energy which supplies the motive power for the ego-centre, with its subtle body, to move from one physical structure to another at the time of death.

When the subtle body thus divorces itself from the physical body, it is logical to believe that its thoughts would revolve around the most predominant desire or aspiration in it—either gathered in its past embodiment, or acquired in its present life. This last powerful will, determined by the last thought, decides its destiny in the future.

We are now going to discuss the routes in which evolutionary pilgrimages can be undertaken by the subtle bodies of those individuals who performed self-evolving actions and therefore, were essentially good.

---

* From *The Sages Speak about Immortality*, The Mananam Series, Chinmaya Mission West, Piercy, California, 1995.

The following verse from the *Prashnopanishad* indicates what would be the direction of this flight: 'And there are two paths: the southern and the northern. Those who follow the path of Karma alone, by the performance of sacrificial and pious acts, obtain only "the world of the Moon" and certainly they are born again ... This matter is verily "the path of the ancestors" (Section 1:9). The 'Path of the Ancestors', also known as heaven, is considered to be the path of return, and presided over by the Moon, which represents the world of matter. Those who leave the world after spending their lifetime in doing good and performing rituals, unaccompanied by meditation and worship, are those who go to the world of the ancestors.

Vedanta, being thoroughly scientific, has systematically divided every conceivable noble action capable of contributing to the evolution of humankind into two groups: istam and purtam. Istam comprises those noble acts sanctioned by the scriptural texts called srutis. Purtam are the noble acts of kindness and charity sanctioned by other subsidiary texts of dharma called smrtis.

Istam includes all Vedic rituals, self-control, truthfulness, the study of the Vedas, disseminating Vedic knowledge to deserving aspirants, serving unexpected guests, and tending continuously to the sacred fire in the house. Purtam includes constructing village tanks, public wells, bathing ghats, maintenance or construction of temples, feeding the poor, constructing new roads, parks, feeding places, watersheds, and so on. If you analyse these classifications and understand them from the level of the mental condition of the devotees, you will certainly understand how and why they follow two different paths in their evolutionary progress.

Two Classifications of People

Those who perform istam are individuals of high culture with well-developed intellectual discrimination, who also have a great amount of self-control over their sensuous desires. They are mainly people with a contemplative nature, whose only demand in life is to gain greater mental and intellectual perfection. They direct all their efforts towards reaching the final goal of life. Naturally, when they depart from this life, having all the time meditated upon the universal energy aspect of life, their minds identify with the Path of the Sun. And reaching the source of *prana*, they cross it to go beyond.

Those who perform purtam actions are also highly cultured members of society. But they are, to a large extent, still entertaining desires for wealth or progeny, or glory and position in life. They are trying to fulfil the small desires of many people through purtam. Through that they expect to be blessed by these satisfied members of society, and ultimately obtain fulfilment of their own desires.

Thus, though they live a noble life of charity, purity, benevolence, and so on, there is always an undercurrent of desire deep within their apparently noble hearts. Their demands are mainly on the material plane. Naturally, when they depart they go to the world of matter, the Moon. Thus, following the southern route they reach the Moon and, crossing it, go to that plane of consciousness technically called the pitriloka, the world of the manes. There they enjoy supersensuous objects with supersensitive apparatus.

One who has thus gained the heavens as a result of his meritorious acts, after exhausting his merit balance, will have to return to the lower planes of consciousness. And there, pain and struggle, loss and gain, and birth and death will again be his experience. Therefore, the Rishi says in the *Mundaka Upanishad*: 'Engrossed in the ways of the ignorant, these people childishly think that they have gained the end of life. But, being subject to passions and attachments, they never attain Knowledge, and therefore, they fall down wretched, when the fruits of their good deeds are exhausted' (Chapter I, Section II:9).

In the earlier part of the Vedas, in the Karma-Kanda, there is a sincere advocacy of the performance of karmas. Later, in the Upanishadic portion we find, in stanzas such as these, a vehement condemnation of them. This would look as though it is a palpable contradiction, but it is not.

When children are in an elementary class, you have to insist upon their learning the multiplication tables by heart. But when they come to pure mathematics, it would be absurd to insist that they practise multiplication tables every day.

Similarly, rituals have an elementary purpose, without which nothing higher is possible. Yet to continue to devote one's entire life to mere ritualism would be a terrible waste. Therefore, sruti (scripture) is critical against such wasteful policies in spiritual seekers.

It is desire that generates the flow of thoughts in the mind. And it is the quality, texture, quantity and direction in which thoughts flow, that determine actions. Thus, karma cannot be where desires have ended. Thoughts cannot end where desires have not ceased.

Therefore, annihilation of the mind is possible only when desires are annihilated. This amounts to saying that these wise, energetic, devoted, and sincere people, in whom ritualism has fulfilled itself, pursue this wrong path of wasteful activity only because of the germs of desire that still breed in their hearts. Thus, the Rishi continues: 'These ignorant men, who regard sacrificial and charitable acts as most important, do not know any other way to bliss. Having enjoyed in the heights of heaven, the abode of pleasures, they again enter this world or even inferior worlds' (Mundaka Upanishad, Chapter I, Section II:10).

Never was the world without this controversy between the two principles of life, namely, laborious extrovert action (karma) and peaceful introvert seeking (jnana). Karma and jnana have forever been at a tug-of-war, unbroken at all times. This endless controversy itself, we may say, was the main force that gave Hinduism such a perfect and exact science of spirituality. In the history of the world we find periods of karma yielding place to periods of jnana. Which in their turn, give place to karma again after a period of retirement and renunciation.

Meritorious acts are divided into two groups by our ancient Rishis, as we have already seen. In the above verse, however, scripture refuses to define the heavens, which are obtained by doing these two types of noble actions, as positive places of happiness. It only says that it is a plane of existence where the soul-killing sorrows of life are not present. It wants us to understand that, though in heaven there are none of the pains of mortal life, it is only relative happiness. The denizens in heaven are only creatures in pain when their state is compared with the absolute state of perfection, which is the theme of the Upanishads.

In the above verse we also have a positive declaration against the optimistic view held by some of our pundits as well as the most sympathetic of gurus. According to them, once the ego receives the form of a human being, one can never go down to any lower plane of existence, whatever one's actions are in life. This idea is being blasted in this mantra. It is also interesting to observe that a person can go down on the ladder of evolution to the existence of even a worm if he engages in deliberate criminal activities.

The Supreme World of the Creator

On the other hand, scripture promises perfect evolutionary success to those rare few who have gained the required spirit of renunciation. As the following verse states: 'But those who perform tapas and shraddha in the forest, having control over their senses, who are learned and living the life of mendicants, go through the orb of the Sun, their good and bad deeds being consumed, where the immortal and undecaying Purusha is' (*Mundaka Upanishad*, Chapter I, Section II:2).

It is a Vedantic theory that those who merely perform karmas, on departing from here, take to the southern path to live in pitriloka. And after enjoying it for a period of time they come back. Those who not only perform the yajnas and yagas, but also meditate upon the great Truth of Vedantic philosophy (that is, those who perform karma and upasana), leave the body and take the northern route. Through the corridors of the Sun they go beyond and enter Brahmaloka, the supreme world of the Creator.

It is the belief that they along with the Creator, at the end of the yuga, during the pralaya (dissolution), become merged with the supreme absolute Awareness. This method of liberation is technically called krama mukti (gradual liberation). But in the case of the Buddha, Shankara, Ramakrishna Paramahamsa, Ramana Maharshi, Aurobindo and other masters, there is no coming or going; they reach what is called pure liberation (kaivalya mukti) or immediate liberation (sadyo mukti).

The theory of gradual liberation accepted by Vedanta, says that ritualism (karma) accompanied by meditation (upasana) takes the ego to the realm of the Creator (Brahmaloka). This is where, at the end of the kalpa (the cycle of creation and dissolution) it merges with the Supreme. Even in Brahmaloka it is necessary that the ego must, through self effort, live strictly all the spiritual directions of the Creator, and through constant contemplation upon the Self, come to deserve the total liberation, by ending all its connections with ignorance. Those who have not reached the realm of the Creator, may not come to enjoy the supreme merger. They will, at the end of the cycle, have to come back and take their manifestation in embodiments, ordered by the remaining vasanas. Keeping this principle in mind, Lord Krishna says in the Gita that rebirth is for everyone, even for those who have attained the higher planes up to Brahmaloka. Having reached Brahmaloka, however, there is no return and the jiva rises to merge with the Self. 'Worlds up to the world of

Brahmaji, are subject to rebirth O Arjuna, but he who reaches Me, O Kaunteya, has no birth again' (Bhagavad Gita, VIII:16). To those who have awakened to the rediscovery of their eternal nature, and realized themselves to be the one, all-pervading Self, there is no return to the plane of limited existence. To the waker there is no more readmission into the dreamrealm. To awaken is to drop forever the joys and sorrows of the dream. After attaining the wakerhood (Me) there is no return into the dreamland (samsara).

TEN

~

SELF-REALIZATION[*]

It is interesting how, in the history of thought in the Upanishads, the goal of life, which in the beginning was considered to be a state of deathlessness, later became known as the absence of rebirth. At first, the anxiety of the seeker was to end the unavoidable and most horrid of all experiences, death. As knowledge increased, through the right evaluation of life, it soon became clear that death had no sting at all for those who understood that it is but one of the different experiences in life. Death can in no way clip off the continuity of existence. The sages came to the conclusion that birth was the beginning of all pain. Therefore, the goal of life, if it were at all possible to achieve, should be the state of no more rebirths.

Estimating the benefits enjoyed by a person of perfection, through the realization of the Self, it is said in the following verse, 'Having attained Me, the great souls (mahatmas) do not again take birth, which is the house of pain and is non-eternal, they having reached the highest perfection, moksha' (Bhagavad Gita, VIII:15). The dream of rebirth and its destinies belongs to the delusory ego, which is nothing but the Self identifying with Its delusory matter envelopments. Electricity conditioned by the bulb is the light. When the bulb breaks, the light that is an effect merges with its cause, the electricity that is the same everywhere.

---

[*] From *The Sages Speak about Immortality,* The Mananam Series, Chinmaya Mission West, Piercy, California, 1995.

Similarly, the Self conditioned by a particular mind and intellect is the ego (jiva) which suffers rebirth, the agonies of imperfection, disease, decay and death. Once the mind-intellect is transcended, the ego comes to rediscover that it is nothing other than the Self.

One who experiences the Self as his own real Nature, realizes that he never had any relationship at all with the equipment of feeling and understanding, just as an awakened man no longer has a relationship with his dream, wife and children. When thus the ego awakens to the spiritual cognition of the Self, it ends its march through the thorny path of pain and finitude. Such great souls no longer have any need to manifest in the plane of plurality.

In all other states of existence there is the experience of return. Just as sleep is not the end of life, but a refreshing pause between two spans of activity, similarly, death is not an end, but often only a restful pause in the unmanifested existence between different embodiments. It was already indicated that, even from higher realms of consciousness, ego-centres will have to return to exhaust their unmanifested cravings (vasanas). Birth, we have already been told, is a house of pain and finitude and therefore complete satisfaction can be reached only when there is no more rebirth, or no return.

Educated students often ask: 'Why, after realizing the Self, should there be no return?' Here, in the following verse of the *Mundaka Upanishad*, we have a clear statement explaining the law behind rebirth: 'Whosoever desires objects, and broods over them, is born again for the fulfilment of those desires. But in the case of a seer whose longings have found their final consummation, who has realized the Self, desires vanish even here in this life itself' (III, Section II:2).

We have already discussed the genesis of action elsewhere. We found that ignorance of our real Nature, which is all perfect and all-full, generates vague and fantastic desires in us. This ignorance also makes us feel that it is virtually impossible for us to accept our own real Nature. We found that desires are like a hornet's nest of stinging thoughts, and those thoughts manifest themselves in the outer world as the selfish actions of an individual. The individual ego naturally has to seek conducive fields of activity for the expression of its desire-prompted actions.

The State of Perfection

Self-realization is the ending of every trace of ignorance in us. In the vital moments of experiencing Selfhood, the God-man drops forever his unawareness of his all-perfect Nature, and after that he cannot have any more desires in him. Desirelessness is generally misunderstood as a negative state. Some think of it as a mental coma, into which a person falls when his disappointed desires begin to pollute him. If this were the case, the great masters of wisdom would not have recommended it as the supreme state of perfection.

Desirelessness, with its accompanying state of mental poise, is attained by a master because of his realization of the Self, the state of absolute Bliss. After a complete dinner and plenty of dessert a fully satisfied person will certainly refuse an offer to take another slice of bread. Similarly, total satisfaction comes from experiencing the perfection of the Self. To the master of realization, sense objects are considered as the little toys of life when they are compared to the infinite treasure of joy that has already become his. A millionaire will never be tempted to go to a soup kitchen hoping to get sumptuous food, even in his dream.

Thus, if the Hindu philosophers glorify the state of desirelessness as the be-all and end-all of life, it is because they know a technique that will make us reach a greater state of perfection. And when we look down from there, the flimsy joys of life would look ridiculous, stupid and childish. To be desireless is certainly a much more glorious state of fulfilment than trying to chase every changing object and being. Our fulfilment lies in knowing that we already have with us all the happiness that we seek. Therefore, when the great masters talk of the state of desirelessness, they mean the state of full and conscious awareness. In this state there are no longer any regrets at not having things that one had previously longed for. Ignorance was the cause of the desires: once the cause is removed, the effect will no longer be there.

In short, according to the texture of our desires we think, and these thoughts ensure that we are born into various situations identifying ourselves with various forms—born, dying, and the reborn. The seer, who has rediscovered his true identity, leaves all desires. Therefore, for him there is no longer any reason for making his appearance again in the world for gaining or fulfilling any of his unfulfilled desires.

III

EMBARKING ON THE SPIRITUAL PATH

Spiritual life is all inclusive. A mere part effort with one aspect of your personality is not good enough to register progress. Your physical, psychological (mental) and intellectual involvement is unavoidable. At each level [of] the sadhana [the] emphasis is different.

—Swami Chinmayananda

ELEVEN

THE THIRST FOR TRUTH[*]

If the realization of the Self is the end of our bondage and of the thraldom of birth and death, naturally students of the scriptures would be anxious to know how this state can be attained. The first instinct might be to try to reach the Self through the study of the Self. But the ancient masters of Self-knowledge have negated all such paths that our intellect would ordinarily suggest to us. In a verse from the scriptures it is said that no scholar should think that because he can give elaborate and learned discourses upon Self-knowledge he can realize or has realized the Supreme. 'The Self is not attained through discourses nor through memorizing scriptural texts, nor through much learning. It is gained only by him who wishes to attain it with his whole heart. To such a one, the Self reveals Its true nature' (*Mundaka Upanishad*, II:3).

The Self can be gained only by one who yearns for it with his entire inner personality. Realization is possible if we pursue the methods advocated by the Rishis, or sages, with sincerity, faith, and consistency. Here, the sruti (Vedic scriptures) says that to the aspirant, who seeks the Self diligently, the Self reveals Itself.

According to the sruti, even though the path to Truth is an open way for all sincere seekers, the pilgrimage to Truth can be easy for those who have the basic divine qualities. The quality of emotions

---

[*] From *On the Path: Preparing for the Spiritual Quest*, Central Chinmaya Mission Trust, Mumbai, first Indian edition, 1989.

and the texture of the values of life respected by an individual will determine his cultural progress and spiritual evolution. In the absence of this wealth, any amount of external show of orthodoxy and formal obedience to the rules of conduct cannot by themselves help a seeker. As Swami Tapovan expressed it:

> The path to reach the Truth can indeed be walked by all those who have the divine accomplishments. In reaching the Truth, caste and status in life are no bar at all. He who has the thirst for the nectar of Truth, whoever he be, may drink freely at the well of knowledge and become contented. O mind, contemplate constantly upon the well of Truth, the Lord of Badri. (*Hymn to Badrinath*, III:4)

The divine virtues enumerated in the scriptures are all ways of controlling the false channels through which positive vitality gets drained off into unprofitable activities. By controlling the thought-forces from dissipating, a new column of reserve potential is discovered, which can easily be tapped for self-development and spiritual progress. Any individual who has discovered in himself this secret reserve of strength can walk the path of Truth with confidence and the assurance of success.

Every individual has the right to walk the spiritual path. It is not a monopoly of any caste, creed or community. The spiritual path can be walked by anyone who is sufficiently rich in the inner wealth indicated. Whoever has the urge and the thirst for it can freely come to the eternal spring of spiritual life to drink to his heart's content. Self-realization is not an impossibility. To realize the Godhood that now lies dormant in each one of us is the heritage of mankind.

From the shells of our limitations we can, through a scientific process of self-purification, grow in divine stature and dimension, wisdom and perfection. Reaching this state of perfection is the accomplishment of the goal. Any person who has the basic qualifications, that is, the mental instruments necessary and the powers of application required, can hasten nature's process of evolution and reach this supreme goal.

The Basic Qualifications

When a spiritual aspirant finds that his mental avenues are blocked and his progress is slow, it is meaningless for him to sit in disappointment and curse the entire hierarchy of masters of the science of Vedanta. Instead, one must look within to see the adjustments to be made. For the seeker's guidance, the scriptures give a description of the necessary qualifications, so that he may know what common troubles arise in the inner vehicle during the flight to the Beyond.

There are some seekers who wait for better circumstances to do their sadhana, a more suitable time, or a great master to initiate them. No doubt, time, place and circumstance are important, but not unduly so, for they are only subsidiary requirements. Without the necessary inner adjustments, even if a seeker is placed under the best conditions of time and place, he will not be able to make use of them. On the other hand, a true seeker will turn even adverse conditions to the best advantage and will progress unhampered. These prerequisites are described in detail in two verses from the *Vivekachudamani*. 'He who has a keen memory with enough knowledge of the world outside and understanding of the world within, and who can argue for the scriptures and refute arguments against them, is fit for receiving the knowledge of the Self' (*Vivekachudamani*, verse 16).

Here the seventh-century Vedantic teacher, Adi Shankaracharya, mentions some of the essential qualities needed for the student before he can successfully undertake a journey on the spiritual path. The power of memory, which is indicated as a basic requirement, does not merely refer to the prodigious capacity that some have to memorize an impossible number of scriptures in a very short time. By 'memory', Shankara means a capacity on the part of the student to react intensely to an experience at the time of its occurrence, so that later it automatically springs forth to the level of conscious awareness.

A student attending discourses given by a master is required to react intensely to his words and thus make the ideas and theories explained his own, at the very time of listening. There is no question of writing down notes and learning them later as present-day students do. The study of Vedanta insists on immediate understanding. He who has this capacity is fit for the study of Vedanta. If there is a student who did not understand what the master said on a previous occasion, as the lessons proceed the master will not be able to give his discourses freely, since the student at every moment will voice his misunderstandings, doubts and confusion. Every time the teacher will have to go back to the portions finished earlier, and that would mean no progress at all. Such a dull-headed, wool-gathering mind is not a fit instrument for the subtle study of the science of Vedanta.

Again, a fit student for the study of the scriptures must be learned or well-informed (vidvan). This does not mean already well-versed in the scriptures, because without listening to the teachings of a master, no amount of self-study in the scriptures will make one a true vidvan. What is meant here is that the student must have a good general knowledge of the outside world and also a certain degree of insight into his own psychological and intellectual composition. The more general knowledge an aspirant has, the easier it will be for the master to make him understand the subtle truths through a variety of examples, parables and metaphors.

An argumentative spirit of inquiry and understanding is also absolutely necessary to walk the path of knowledge. In the other paths of Self-discovery, this spirit of independent inquiry is not emphasized because the seekers do not demand an explanation for personal conviction. But for the one who wants to walk the path of knowledge, a blind faith in the scriptures or in the teacher cannot supply a sufficient motive force. One needs a conviction that arises from within, born out of one's own intelligent thinking and intellectual absorption of ideas.

Similarly, a student of Vedanta must be an individual with a receptive and agile intellect, ready to catch every subtle idea given out by the master and, through a process of intellectual assimilation, arrive at its true significance. If this agility of the head and heart is lacking, one cannot hope to have a steady and unobstructed progress in spiritual sadhana.

Four Requirements

After giving the broad characteristics of those who are fit receptacles for knowledge, Shankara continues with a clearly etched specification in the following verse. 'He alone is considered qualified to inquire into the supreme Reality who has discrimination, detachment, the six mental qualities, and a burning desire for liberation' (*Vivekachudamani*, verse 17).

These terms have often been found to frighten away students with severe orthodox interpretations. But upon a closer analysis, they are found to be healthy instincts present in every bosom. Only a few, however, are conscious of them, and even fewer consciously develop these qualities in themselves.

Viveka is the capacity to discriminate between the real and the unreal, between the true and the false, between the permanent and the impermanent. It is the faculty that we employ in almost all our day-to-day decisions, but when it is brought to play upon the inner constitution of the individual it is called viveka.

Vairagya is commonly translated as detachment. For many it holds an uncanny fear, for it seems to point more to a condition of living death than to a state of better and fuller living. When one employs the discriminative capacity to differentiate between the real and the unreal in the world outside or in the world within, all false values automatically drop away. Once anything is understood to be full of bitterness, pain and imperfection, rare is the one who will continue to court it. Invariably, we run after a thing only when we hope to get a greater fulfilment of joy and peace out of it. When we come to the intellectual appreciation that the object is riddled with sorrow, the immediate attempt would be to get rid of it.

Thus, detachment born of discrimination is what is meant by vairagya. In fact, detachment is the fulfilment of discrimination, and whenever the former is strong, the latter gains in essence and efficiency. Therefore, when Shankara defines vairagya as detachment from all the fruits of one's actions here and hereafter, he only means that a spiritual seeker must come to a sufficiently strong intellectual conviction that fruits born as a result of actions cannot be infinite.

It is the nature of the mind to entertain thoughts, and if it has nothing better to do, it will dwell on one or another of the objects of the world. Therefore it is enjoined in all the yogas that the mind should be immersed with an ideal greater, nobler and more divine than thoughts of sense objects. Unless we train the mind to revel in a subtler field, it cannot redeem itself from the field of ordinary pursuits.

In bhakti yoga, the path of devotion, the devotee employs the mind constantly in the meditation of his beloved Lord, and therefore the mind is automatically drawn away from its pursuits of sense objects. Similarly, in the early stages of the path of knowledge, the intellect is to be given a divine field for its occupation, because ultimately an intellect basking in the contemplation of the all-pervading Consciousness, Brahman, alone is the instrument that can successfully detach the mind from sense objects.

Not only should the mind steep and maintain itself in Brahman by meditating upon the glories of the goal, it should also be whipped away from its mischievous fields of false entertainments by making it constantly aware of the weakness and imperfections of the field of objects. The more one gains control over the mind, and through that control withdraws it from its revellings in the field of finite objects, the more one will become equanimous, peaceful and serene. This mental calmness, consciously brought about by a lived discipline, is known by the term sama. Of this condition, Shankara comments: 'The peaceful state of the mind when it rests constantly upon the contemplation of the goal, after having again and again detached itself from the chaos of sense objects, through a process of continuous observation of their defects, is called sama' (*Vivekachudamani*, verse 22).

Sama is the first of the six mental qualities that are essential to gaining Self-knowledge. These are not enumerated to frighten away the unqualified, but are for conducting self-analysis and adjustment. In the next stanza, Shankara explains two more qualities of the mind and intellect that are essential in an aspirant, that is, dama and uparati. 'Steering both kinds of sense organs (of knowledge and action), away from their sense objects and placing them in their respective centres of activity is called dama (self-control). That condition of the thought-waves in which they are free from the influence of the external objects is the best uparati (self-withdrawal)' (*Vivekachudamani*, verse 23).

Sama is a condition experienced by the mind when it does not function in worldly activities, but quietly contemplates the supreme goal. On the other hand, dama is a system of discipline concerned with the outer fields, since it prescribes control of the sense organs. To withdraw the mental rays that shoot out through the sense organs for the perception of their respective pleasures and to absorb those rays of perception within the sense organs is dama, or self-control. When one has gained a degree of proficiency in self-control and mental calmness, self-withdrawal (uparati) automatically takes place, wherein the seeker's mental condition is such that it is no longer affected by disturbances created by external objects.

When we think of these requirements, it is possible that we think of them as very delicate, distressingly difficult feats, but in fact the more we practise them, the more easily we will understand that this is but a verbal description of the state of mind of anyone who is trying to achieve or execute any great work. Even on a material plane, we find that these qualifications are essential for a person who wants success in his activities. In a successful businessman we can observe a certain amount of self-control within as well as without, and also self-withdrawal, at least while he is at the desk. Of course, the comparison of these qualities with the qualities exhibited by the materialist or the money hunter is not fair, because a spiritual seeker needs a subtlety a million times greater than a materialist. Yet, to a large extent we can appreciate and understand these qualifications within ourselves when we watch for them and experience them in our workaday world.

The fourth psychological qualification of true spiritual stamina is titiksa, the quality of silent endurance. Meek surrender and silent suffering are glorified in all the religions of the world. This quality to endure and suffer for a cause that has been accepted by the individual as the ideal finds a place in every great philosophy, religious or secular. To bring about a revolution in the world outside, the revolutionaries are called upon to make silent sacrifices. How much more essential are they then in the inner revolution of an individual who is trying to free himself from his psychological and intellectual confines? This capacity of the mind to accommodate cheerfully all its vicissitudes and patiently ignore all obstacles that might come its way is titiksa. According to Shankara: 'Titiksa is the capacity to endure all sorrows and sufferings without struggling for redress or for revenge, being always free from anxiety over them' (*Vivekachudamani*, verse 24).

Unfortunately, many people indulge in acts of perversion in the name of titiksa. A number of unintelligent people persecute themselves physically and mentally in the name of spiritual seeking, and as a result of their self-persecution, all they gain at the end is a crooked, ugly, deformed mind! They do not ever achieve the least amount of inward beauty or perfection.

Discarding clothes or starving oneself, denying the body its bare necessities or giving unnecessary pain to the mind, running away from life or preserving oneself on inhuman diets in solitary caves, living an animal's life exposed to brutal climate or breaking the body in an effort to make it endure more discomforts—none of these is true titiksa. True forbearance is a result of the mind being governed by an intellectual conviction that is complete and self-ordained, divine and noble. When the intellect is fully convinced of its accepted values of life, the mind cooperates and faces all difficulties and obstacles. Such a firm person alone is fit for realizing the immortality of the Self.

Since every situation, of its own nature, must keep on changing, it would be foolish to get upset at every change. It is wisdom to suffer adversities meekly, with the comfort and consolation of the knowledge of their finite nature. It is the attitude of the wise to go through life, both in joy and sorrow, in success and failure, with the constant awareness: 'Even this will pass away.'

The Role of Faith

As long as we live as the body, we are not able to ignore or calmly endure the sorrows of the body. But when we are fired by a sentiment of love or hatred, we make ready sacrifices of bodily pleasures. Because of my love for my son, I am ready to make any sacrifice of my physical needs so that I may give him a good education. When intellectually one gets fired by some idea or ideology, for the satisfaction of it one readily ignores and overlooks one's own comforts. The martyrs and revolutionaries in the world could with pleasure face physical persecution and mental agonies for the satisfaction of their intellectual demands and for the fulfilment of their ideals and ideologies. This strong faith in an ideal is the fifth qualification necessary in an aspirant.

This shraddha is not blind faith, as it is generally understood by those who have not carefully analysed it. Shankara is very clear in his definition that shraddha is a healthy attempt to gain a clear intellectual appreciation of the secret depths of the significances underlying the words of the scriptures and the teacher. Thus we read in the *Vivekachudamani* the following definition of shraddha by Shankara: 'That by which one understands the exact import of the scriptures as well as the pregnant words of advice of the preceptor is called shraddha by the wise; by this alone does Reality become manifestly clear' (*Vivekachudamani*, verse 25).

Indeed, shraddha is an essential requisite for anyone trying to master the truths of the scriptures. The scriptures give us, through a technique of suggestions, as clear a description of the infinite Truth as is possible through finite sounds and words. Pure Consciousness, which is the core of Reality, cannot be defined or expressed in words; therefore, this supreme goal of human evolution can only be indicated by the scriptures. So, an honest and sincere effort on the part of readers and students is absolutely necessary if the words indicating the Truth are to be correctly interpreted, understood, and efficiently made use of. This capacity to realize the words of the scriptures in all their suggestiveness is termed as shraddha.

Cultivation of Inner Poise

Whatever be the path of divine self-development that he may follow, it is an unavoidable necessity that the seeker must give his undivided attention to it and must on all occasions maintain in his mind a continuous consciousness of the Divine. A mere intellectual study of the scriptures will not help in purifying the mind; it is necessary to pour out the mind and intellect into the scheme of living that the Upanishads advise.

The qualities explained above will not sustain themselves, and no seeker can consistently hope to entertain them, unless he is constantly striving his best to live in a spirit of self-control. It is the sense organs that seduce one into the life of excessive sensuousness, and when one has entered into the troubled waters of a sensuous life, one has no chance of floating quietly in the higher values of life. To walk the Path divine is to get out of the gutters of sensuousness. Excessive sense-life and absolute God-life are antithetical to each other: where the one is, the other cannot be. Where the light of inward serenity and deeper peace have come, the darkness created by sense passions and animal appetites must depart. It is imperative therefore that a seeker should learn to live in steady and constant sense-control and thereby gain a certain amount of inner poise, called samadhana.

The last of the six great qualifications that are essential for a true spiritual seeker is samadhana. As it is understood today, samadhana is an indifferent attitude towards both good and bad, especially toward insults and failures, threats and despair. It is believed that samadhana is the mental attitude of an individual who has completely hardened himself and has grown to be insensitive to the lashes of failure and the arrows of insult.

But Shankara's definition does not sanction such an unfounded belief. Shankara is quite emphatic when he defines samadhana as a

107

state of poise and tranquillity that the mind gains when it is trained to revel continuously in the concept of a perfect ideal, at once universal and omnipotent. He says: 'Samadhana (tranquillity) is that condition in which the mind is constantly engaged in the total contemplation of the supreme Reality; and it is not gained through any amount of intellectual oscillations' (*Vivekachudamani*, verse 26).

This tranquillity, samadhana, is not the state of mind in which the individual sits quietly in cowardice, not daring to face life and its challenges, but at the same time lamenting the scheme of destiny that he has to face. The tossings of the mind created by his passive revolts against life are his only gains, and if physically and intellectually he accepts them all silently, in consummate cowardice, it is not samadhana. Samadhana is the state of mental equilibrium that comes to one when intellectually one has unshakeable foundations and when mentally one soars to the highest pinnacles of greater visions.

When we are on the ground, our neighbours may be nuisance to us. There may be bitter hatred between us. We may even be arguing over some land. But when we take off in a plane, these bickerings seem to have no meaning, from these tremendous heights my property and my neighbour's property seem to merge into one unbroken expanse of beauty. In an aerial view of the world, there are no mental agitations, because in that vision of oneness, the differences of opinion about a boundary line pale into insignificance.

Similarly, when a spiritual aspirant raises himself into the greater ambits of spiritual vision, his mind can no longer entertain any agitation at the ordinary level of likes and dislikes. This inner poise, gained as a result of constant contemplation on the Supreme, is indeed samadhana. This becomes a special qualification for every seeker on the path.

So sama, dama, uparati, titiksa, shraddha, and samadhana are the six great qualifications that are essential in the psychological make-up of a fully evolved seeker, who alone can walk the last lap of his journey with hope and success.

Desire for True Wisdom

However, there are many seekers who, having long practised these six requirements, complain that they have not progressed at all. Such people claim 'true living' for themselves in their honest endeavours in life. They say, 'I am very dutiful; I earn my living honestly. I look after my home and dependents, and to the extent I can afford it, I share my wealth with others in a spirit of charity. I believe that I am a nobler soul than those who practise the so-called spiritual disciplines.'

While it is true that these great qualities are intended to create an ethical and moral atmosphere in the psychological field of the neophyte, Vedantic practices are not merely a training in ethics or morality. There are many spiritual cowards who ask, 'Merely by living an honest life can we not reach the perfection that is explained by Vedanta?' This question has become very common these days, asked by people, in confusion and perhaps intellectual fatigue, who refuse to make a thorough study of the scriptures. This wrong notion is being criticized by Shankara in this stanza: 'Calmness and other practices have their meaning and bear fruit only in he who has an intense spirit of renunciation and yearning for liberation' (*Vivekachudamani*, verse 29).

These qualities of self-restraint, self-control, purity, and so on can bear fruit only when they are in an individual who has a complete sense of detachment born out of discrimination, and a burning aspiration to surmount the limitations of his mortal existence. The destiny of some of those we meet who are living an 'honest life' is indeed heart-rending. They live in the world in sensuous excess, running after the mirage of wealth, power, popularity and enjoyments. Although their means are fair, their goal has always been low and finite. So in their pilgrimage through life, whenever they come across a 'ditch' of hatred or a 'mount' of competition they sit back, fatigued and weary, and blame religion and their own philosophy, based upon hollow and meaningless ethics. Since spiritual evolution is not the outcome of their 'pure' living, whenever the scheme of things around them changes, they find themselves lost. Without spiritual stamina, no one can stand up to the threats and the onslaughts of circumstances in life. The six qualifications cannot bear fruit unless they grow in a heart watered by detachment and ploughed with an intense wish for liberation, or mumuksutva.

This burning aspiration of a seeker should not be an idle enthusiasm to gain an unknown goal through some mysterious intervention of a God or a teacher. The seeker should definitely know his limitations and the causes behind them. One must be clear about the goal and the various techniques and paths by which one can attain it. It is only when an individual develops his sensibility until it is subtle enough to recognize the weaknesses in his life that he comes to feel a pressing urgency for liberation.

Therefore, it is evident that a mumuksu is not a seeker vaguely wanting some unknown pleasure or development within himself by the practice of some pseudo-spiritual activities, pursued only at a given time during the day. To be a seeker only for half an hour each evening is not to be a right pursuer of Knowledge. Therefore, Shankara describes true mumuksutva thus: 'Mumuksutva is the impatient and burning desire to release oneself from all bondages of egoism created by ignorance, by realizing the real nature of one's Self' (*Vivekachudamani*, verse 27).

To rediscover ourselves is to invite into our life the cognition of a greater intellect and divine Consciousness. In order to turn the entire beam of my consciousness upon myself, I need to purify my mind and intellect and then slowly and steadily give them a turn so that they may come to contemplate only upon themselves. This inner revolution cannot be accomplished as a half-hearted hobby, it can only be the result of a life-long dedication and full-time endeavour. Such a true seeker who is ready to live every moment of his life in diligent pursuit of the Real is a mumuksu.

In the ignorance of our real nature, we start identifying with our egocentric concepts such as 'I am the body', 'I am the mind', and 'I am the intellect', and thereafter the conditions of the body, mind and intellect, in our stupidity, become *our* conditions. To end this ignorance is to gain the wisdom of Reality.

Because of the non-apprehension of our real nature, misapprehensions about ourselves arise in our mind. The identification with the body, mind and intellect, together called the ego, is what gives us our sense of limitation. The limitations do not belong to the Self, for the Self is perfect, infinite and absolute. While forgetting our real nature, we come to look upon ourselves as something other than what we actually are, and this misconstrued personality is the sufferer, the finite, the mortal. To rediscover ourselves is to end all sorrows. This is the consummate peak of evolution.

TWELVE

Spiritual Unfoldment—How?*

For one who accepts this world of names and forms as the *only* reality, the idea of the existence of a Greater Reality is very difficult to conceive. And such a person should not be blamed for not being able to accept the grand mystic conclusion of the Rishis: that there is a Greater Reality beyond the seen, that the seen is nothing but a false perception of that Great Reality, and that, that Great Reality alone is the only existent essence. This incapacity on the part of some individuals to conceive of the Great Reality is called 'atheism' and it is due to the total extrovertedness of their minds. This spiritual ignorance (ajnanam) darkens an individual's bosom, veils (avarana) his intellect's ability for subtle perceptions, and creates agitation (vikshepa) in his mind.

Knowledge in man never remains the same. The outer environment impinges upon his mind and intellect at every moment in an endless variety of patterns. It beats out new channels of thoughts, brings fresh streams of ideas and results in an ever-changing set of conclusions. This happens to everyone, all through life. Based upon this reaction to the ever-changing outer world, a man's beliefs, ideas, views, opinions, are in a constant state of flux. An atheist of today can become a theist of tomorrow, and in a few weeks he may even become a great devotee. The biographies of many saints and sages

---

* From *Tapovan Prasad*, Vol. XV, No. 1, Chinmaya Mission, Chennai, January 1977.

around the world, witness the truth of this miraculous phenomenon. That which turns an atheist into a theist, is the technique called sravana (listening) in Vedantic science.

In the material world, a mere description of a thing and an enumeration of its qualities, cannot ever give us a clear experience of the thing. We can at best only get information about it. But in the spiritual science of the Supreme Reality, words of the scriptures when properly 'listened to' with the necessary quality of attention, can actually lift the listener into worlds of experiences in a new dimension of consciousness. Sravana, or attentive listening (to words from the scriptures), is the means by which one who has had no experience of His Presence within, can recognize this divine presence everywhere.

The objects of the world have names and forms, qualities and functions. The theme of the scriptures is God, the light of consciousness in us, which lends its sentiency to all inert matter-made equipment: our body, mind and intellect. This Self is beyond the instruments of perception (body), feeling (mind) and thinking (intellect). The world of the scriptures, when properly 'listened to', sets the listener on an adventurous voyage through strange possibilities to the very frontiers of the perceived. It gives him his first glimpse of the beyond. Thus, one who is at present in a lower plane of consciousness, where he is in tune with only the gross world of names and forms, can by sravana awaken to a dynamic set of creative thoughts which uplifts his mind into a higher state of awareness. This is the true fulfilment of sravana.

In Sanskrit the term 'sravana' means merely 'hearing' which is, of course, the physical function of the ears. In the science of Vedanta, the use of this term implies 'listening' and not merely 'hearing'. While 'listening' we are actually hearing with full attention. During sravana our intellect strives to grasp the arguments and lift itself in the direction indicated by the pregnant discussions contained in the scriptures. In short, sravana in the context of Vedanta suggests 'experiencing His Presence through the ears'.

What has been experienced can never be denied. When 'sravana' is properly pursued, the non-believer, the atheist, slowly becomes a believer, a theist; for, how can he deny what he has already experienced during his alert 'listening' as a humble seeker? Thus, effective sravana leads the individual to an understanding of the deeper truth of life and makes him question the validity of the perceived world of names and forms, quaking so constantly in its inevitable convulsions of perpetual change. He becomes aware of the changeless substratum, subtler than, and distinct from, the world of beings and things. It is that changeless substratum that illumines the flood of constant change. It is the sole KNOWER everywhere! That is the Lord, the god of the theist, the Self Supreme of the Vedantin.

This is the stage when you get convinced of the play of the one infinite consciousness, the Self, behind the universe of names and forms; nobody can, in any way, shake this conviction, as it is born of your own understanding and experience. Yet, at this stage you cannot convince others, nor communicate your feelings. You appreciate the arguments of the atheists, and at the same time you see the hollowness of their laborious logic. Still, you cannot express your own deep thoughts and present the theme of your belief in an efficient manner capable of convincing the listener. However, when this, as yet dim, understanding, gained through enthusiastic and attentive 'listening' is again and again reflected upon along the arguments supplied by the scriptures, the clarity of your vision increases and your ability to express your conviction to others improves. This process is called mananam (reflection).

The term 'mananam' literally means 'mental reflection upon a theme all by oneself'. But in Vedantic science, mananam also signifies experiencing the Self by the mind. If sravana is experiencing God, the Truth, through the ears, mananam is experiencing God, the Truth, with the mind. In sravana your 'participation' is required: in mananam your 'involvement' is unavoidable.

We all realize that the mind is many times more powerful and efficient than the sense organs. If while 'listening', one can come to gain glimpses of a divine Presence and one's atheistic concepts can get blasted, one can then get a measure of the avalanche of experiences that can flood one's inner being when one gains this fuller confirmation through mananam. The belief that the world of plurality—perceived by the body, felt by the mind and comprehended by the intellect— alone is real is a false conclusion maintained by us through millions and trillions of our lives all through the march of our evolution. This crumbles like mud-walls at mere sravana. Through mananam the experience becomes a thousand-fold stronger and deeper.

If thus through 'listening' and 'reflection' we are convinced that the world of plurality is false and the pure Self alone is the 'real', we still are confused because we cannot live in this world without depending upon the things and beings around us which are understood as illusory. This inherent sense of contradiction apparent in Vedanta, can really discourage, confuse and bewilder any intelligent seeker. It is nididhyasana (meditation) that can clear this confusion for us.

Nididhyasana or meditation is the intellectual insight and constant awareness at the intellectual level of the Truth which the ears 'heard' and which the mind through 'reflection' confirmed. Nididhyasana, in Vedantic Science, is the experiencing of God at the intellectual level. At each level of understanding, the experience grows in clarity and depth. The sense organs are the grossest; the mind is subtler than the sense organs and has a wider reach; the intellect is the subtlest equipment in man and it is the instrument by which man crashes down the present frontiers of his thoughts and reaches out and conquers new arenas of knowledge. Sravana gives just a vague vision of God through the ears. Mananam gives a clearer vision as it is the experience of god with the mind. Nididhyasana necessarily gives the clearest vision of the Self. This fact is confirmed by Adi Shankara in his *Vivekachudamani*.[*]

During the jnana yajna sessions[†], we have an intense course in sravana. But that is not sufficient. It must be followed by independent regular weekly sessions of mananam among serious students. This is achieved in the Chinmaya Mission Study Groups. Later, really sincere students should strive at nididhyasana all by themselves, regularly and daily. The cumulative effect is a total transformation of one's own inner personality: the Spiritual Unfoldment.

---

[*] See *Talks on Shankara's Vivekachudamani* (Text with Translation and Commentary), Swami Chinmayananda, Central Chinmaya Mission Trust, Bombay, first edition, 1970.

[†] Swami Chinmayananda established the tradition of week-long discourses on a particular text or a particular portion of a text. This tradition is continued in India and around the world by the many swamis and brahmacharis trained in the Chinmaya Mission Ashrams and is often the first introduction to the systematic study of the scriptures for the public.

THIRTEEN

COMMITMENT TO THE IDEAL[*]

The path of sadhana (spiritual practices) must be intelligent and also within the ability of the average person to practise. The results may not come easily or quickly, but when the practices are continued sincerely and heroically, there must be some rewarding results, otherwise the average seeker will leave the path in disappointment.

Our Upanishadic seers have discovered a very attractive path to help us get established on the road to Reality. They seem to point out a steadily rising path up to the summits of the mystic peaks. Thereafter, each may find his way clearly to the crown.

Study of the scriptures, in a spirit of total participation, directly through books—augmented with frequent listening to the learned exponents and a few direct contacts with the authoritative masters is found to be very helpful in the beginning. This regular study of the Upanishads, the Bhagavad Gita, and other such spiritual literature is called svadhyaya.

Repetition of a sacred word (mantra), with or without the help of a rosary or beads (mala)—continuously fixing our mind on the divine and spiritual suggestions of the 'mystic word'—is called japa. This technique keeps the mind uplifted, away from the world-of-objects and their distracting fascinations, on to the reviving climb to the final spiritual illumination. The mind becomes quiet and gets

---

*   From *The Razor's Edge*, Central Chinmaya Mission Trust, Mumbai, first Indian edition, 1991.

more and more introverted.

When the thoughts have been nourished by study (svadhyaya) and rendered quiet and peaceful by japa, meditation (dhyanam) helps to rest this hushed mind at the altar of the Self in a joyous mood of choiceless contemplation.

The Rishis encourage us to combine these three main paths judiciously and thus deny the mind the least chance to wander into the spiritually unhygienic fields of sense gratification. The great Acharya Shankara advises, 'After listening, study and japa, practise meditation. After emerging from meditation, engage in listening, study, and japa. After japa, meditate again. At the end of meditation, pursue japa. One who is thus well trained with japa and meditation, on such a steady seeker the supreme Auspiciousness (Para-Siva-Paramesvara) showers His Grace.'

While listening (sravanam) we only *participate* in spiritual life. When we study (svadhyaya) we get *involved* in the ideas that we had listened to. In japa our involvement deepens, and in meditation we come to get ourselves totally *committed* to the ideal, which is the goal of all spiritual seekers.

The agitations of the mind and intellect in us create an impenetrable thought-barrier between our sense of ego and our divine status as the infinite Consciousness. All spiritual practices (sadhanas) are training by which the disturbances of thoughts are brought down to a minimum.

Turning Within

When our minds have thus become relatively quiet, our meditation gathers an extra flight and efficiency. Our minds get filled with peace, and an unearthly joy comes to spread in our hearts. This state of expansion within, which invokes an unusual quality of inner joy leaving behind for some time a subjective sense of holiness and contentment, is the first experience that assures us of a richer reward that awaits us at the end of our journey. Once this is experienced, we will no longer be irregular in our meditation. All other external obstructions get rejected and ignored. Nothing can any longer entice us away from our regular meditation sessions.

We come to regulate, reorganize and readjust our daily programmes. Items of interest, contacts, engagements, duties, and even our professional responsibilities will all irresistibly undergo a salutary reorientation. Till now, our activities and relationships were based upon our maximum physical comfort and sense gratification. Now our lives become oriented for meditation.

We come to live a pure life of dedication, truthfulness and deep devotion. We engage ourselves only in peaceful, God-centred activities. All the promises of joys, which we had pursued so long, can no longer carry any attraction for us. We retire from all such contacts that might bring the slightest mental fatigue or mystical disturbance, for a fatigued mind cannot reach and maintain high altitudes of meditation, and without the mystic vitality poise in meditation will be totally absent.

The more the mind retires from its direct involvement with sense objects and from attachment to things and beings, the more it develops, what is technically called in Vedanta, retirement (uparam). As the mind retires from the world outside, it enters more and more into the subtler realms of the Essence. Those subtler realms are the mystic regions of unearthly brilliance, of heavenly melody, of supersensuous joys. Retirement of the mind leads it to extreme peace.

In the scriptures, the masters of meditation have no hesitation in openly and distinctly declaring that retirement is extreme peace. Those who practise it shall experience that their spiritual unfoldment is directly proportional to their success in retirement from mental engagements with the outer world. The more we take ourselves away from worldly, lust-prompted activities, the closer we move towards the culminating goal of meditation—the total quietude of mind, the still intellect, the transcendent experience—called samadhi.

No progress in any walk of life is possible without leaving the present state and moving forward to win the new state of greater glory. No growth is possible unless there is a willingness to drop out of our previous conditions and accept the ampler status of the new conditions. Childhood must end in the youngster: the youth must end in the old man. If a bud is not ready to end its present state, how can it grow and unfold itself to become a flower?

Our mental power, so entirely invested in our outward life, must be curbed in order to turn it within. When we have successfully curbed the mind from its play in the lower planes, it will naturally discover itself revelling in its own meditative flights in the higher planes of Consciousness.

Remember always to sincerely hasten, but slowly.

FOURTEEN

DEVELOPING A RELATIONSHIP WITH GOD[*]

In the early stages of evolution man worshipped trees, animals, and the departed ones, as can be seen even today among tribal civilizations. As man grew under the pressure of his needs and the visions of his intellect, he came to make his gods out of stone, clay, wood or metal. Idol worship then started. Even here, at the earliest stages of his history, man seems to have worshipped his god as Mother. In this Divine Mother concept, the goddess is supposed to love Her children just because they are Her children and for no other reason. The divine Mother is all-loving, and whatever we might do we have only to cry out for Her and She is supposed to forgive everything and gather us into Her protective, nourishing bosom.

From the mother-centred days, religion slowly moved to the father-centred attitude, wherein God was considered as a strict, but kind, father. He expects us to obey His laws, to live as His 'image,' and to fulfil what He expects of us. In case of default in any of His expectations, He inflicts severe punishment; but if we are obedient and industrious, humble and productive, He makes us His successors!

In general, most religions are now at this stage. Yet, it must be admitted that the concept of God as the supreme mother will never leave the world as long as man craves for the mother's unquestioning and all-giving love.

---

[*] From *The Power of Prayer*, Central Chinmaya Mission Trust, Mumbai, first Indian edition, 1987.

Thus, there was a movement from the matriarchal to the patriarchal view in religion. Even in patriarchal religion, as man grew into a fuller awareness of his independent and separate existence and as he explored more of his own capacities in the consciousness of his fuller stature, his concept of God also gradually changed. From that of the unrelenting disciplinarian, the concept of the Lord evolved into a divine power of absolute mercy, love, and justice.

This growth corresponds to the growth of the child into his adolescence, and from the adolescent stage, with its fears of authority figures, his growth into the responsible status of young adulthood, when he matures and recognizes the reasonableness of his father's authority, the blessings of his rules, and the justice of his laws. He is now able to recognize the anxious, loving, dedicated benefactor in his apparently fierce father.

The final stage is when the youthful man reaches full maturity, and the son begins to identify with his father. Religion at its highest recognizes this noble relationship between the devotee and the Lord—a relationship of agreement, a sense of supreme nearness. Ultimately, he discovers his total identity with the Lord: the one infinite Reality, the Self in All.

This is not a mere hypothesis or an idle supposition. According to the kind of people that constitute a community in any given period of history, these different types of relationships between man and God are found emphasized. Sri Madhavacharya emphasized the view that the devotee and the Lord are ever separate—the Dvaita philosophy.

Sri Ramanujacharya declared that man is not totally different from the Lord, but that he and his Lord have a part-and-whole relationship. The Lord is the whole while the devotee is a part of Him—the Visishtadvaita philosophy.

According to Acharya Shankara, identification is the yardstick of bhakti. When identification is complete, love is fulfilled. On identification of the ego—and all its weaknesses, imperfections, and limitations—with the absolute Reality, Perfection or Bliss or supreme Knowledge is achieved. Through a constant remembrance of the nature of the Self, the finite ego gets released from its false notions of limitations, and discovers itself to be nothing other than the Supreme. In this Self-discovery it experiences complete identification with the Self. Then alone is bhakti entirely fulfilled. To live as the Self and to meet others in life while standing up on this solid foundation of the true nature of the Self is the culmination of knowledge, and this is termed by Acharya Shankara as bhakti. He defines bhakti as the means and the end, where love and knowledge merge together to become the Experience-Divine. 'Among the instruments and conditions necessary for liberation, bhakti alone is supreme. A constant attempt to live up to one's own real nature is called single-pointed devotion' (*Vivekachudamani*, verse 31).

Acharya Shankara says that bhakti is the path, but he adds a codicil explaining the term bhakti. According to him, bhakti is not a practice of beggary at the feet of the Lord, but is a constant and consistent effort at raising the ego-centre from the welter of its false values to the knowledge of the Self.

Offering Up One's Anxieties

'No worry or anxiety should be entertained at worldly losses, as it is the nature of a true devotee to surrender constantly his limited self and all its secular and sacred activities to the Lord of his heart' (*Narada Bhakti Sutra*, VI, 2:61). 'Never entertain anxiety. Don't worry. Never mind whatever happens'—this is the attitude that a true seeker should cherish, explains the sage Narada. There is the Lord; He is the Reality. All these worries and anxieties are only mere bubbles—even their threats and dangers are from the All-loving Lord alone—that somehow hold on!

The cardinal attitude of heroism in Vedanta is 'Refuse to weep; keep smiling.' Then even the sorrow that reaches you gets ashamed and retires in its incompetency to make you suffer. It has to go away; it cannot stand against such a heroic heart.

'O Lord, this is all your maya. O beloved, I know You are just behind this very sorrow I am now facing'—this is the attitude of a true devotee in all his experiences, good or bad; and true enough, just behind the experiences is ever the Consciousness divine, the effulgent One, constantly beaming forth Its irrepressible glory.

'Apart from Him, I don't exist,' declares the devotee of the Lord. 'Everything of me is already laid at the feet of the Lord. I do not exist, so I cannot worry about anything. It is all now His worry. I am but the "witness" of the sorrow; as such the sorrow itself cannot be mine.' Constantly the bhakta lives in this attitude, dedicating himself, the world, the Vedas, and everything to the Lord.

By this attitude, the bhakta cultivates in himself the spirit of renunciation, the joy of surrender, and the constant sense of self-offering. To give is ever the expression of love. Love is measured by the very joy of sacrifice—of giving one's self and one's all to Him, the Beloved. How can one take back what has already been offered in love? When one's anxieties have been offered, whose worries are these? When one's self has been offered, who then exists to worry? 'O Lord, it is all yours.'

Living and Growing In God

In the world we find that some of us are in unhappy circumstances while some of us are in relatively happy surroundings. Joys and sorrows cross the paths of our lives, creating endless situations. A true devotee never allows his mind to worry over them. For the bhakta (devotee) who has already surrendered himself and all his profits, losses, successes, failures—in short, everything—unto the Lord, anxiety cannot exist. But as long as this great Reality has not been apprehended or such an all-consuming devotion has not been developed, our worldly duties are not to be given up. It was on this principle that Lord Krishna did not allow Arjuna to leave the field of his action.

As long as we are sadhakas (seekers) cultivating and developing devotion to the highest, worldly activities of material nature, our duties towards home, society and nation, should not be given up. Until one reaches the highest, one must continue the dynamic life of activities, fulfilling one's duties and responsibilities. As long as we practise, we must live fully the life of responsibilities provided for us by the Lord. Nothing need be renounced. Each should pursue his life in the field where the Lord has placed him, because the Omniscient One knows exactly what is needed for our inner unfoldment. It is for the exhaustion of the existing vasanas in us that we have been given this equipment, and we are placed in the right kind of environment. It is useless to protest or weep about it. It is for the doctor to decide if the patient should be admitted to a hospital and what kind of treatment he should undergo. Therefore, the advice of Narada is: 'Until a consummate love is gained (or even after attaining the consummate love), worldly activities are not to be abandoned. Certainly, we must diligently pursue love and learn to renounce our anxiety to enjoy the fruit of our actions' (*Narada Bhakti Sutra*, VI, 2:62).

So then, are we to continue living the same wretched life that we are now living—with a mere added prayer on our lips? No. Since we have started sincerely cultivating devotion for the Lord, whose expression is this entire world around us, we will, with joy, continue to go to our fields of activity, but with a difference: our attitude to work will now be totally transformed. Now that we constantly think of Him and habitually surrender everything to our beloved Divine, it becomes easy for us to renounce the anxiety for the enjoyment of the fruits of our actions. We must do our best to fulfil our duties in whatever field He places us. For, as we act on, we now recognize the field of action—nay, the whole world—as the Lord Himself in another form. Our work then becomes our worship of Him who is the Self in us.

Constantly the devotee's mind turns more and more towards the Lord as he learns to withdraw himself from the sense appetites and the anxiety to hoard. Simultaneous with the change in the inner attitude, the devotee's daily sadhana deepens in ardour, broadens in love, and expands to touch new realms of spiritual experiences. He finds greater pleasure in his daily prayers, and gradually he comes to understand that the very environment wherein the Lord has placed him is the most conducive one for him to grow, and that it is most necessary and almost unavoidable for his development. Therefore, joyously the true devotee goes through the muddy pools of life constantly remembering Him and waiting eagerly for the day when he would be leaving the 'hospital'—the life in the field of plurality.

When an aspirant has not yet attained pure love, a cheerful life of selfless activities dedicated to God should be the sadhana. One must learn to detect the ego whenever it rises and surrender it unto the Lord, renounce all anxieties for the fruits of action, and act sincerely with all one's heart, with a serene mind, and with complete dedication—wherever one has been placed.

Even those who have already gained the highest devotion should not give up their duties, but thereafter their obligation should be not to their home, but to spreading the culture, whereby their own perfect living will uphold the spiritual ideologies. When a Self-realized person works in the world, he will have no anxiety for the results, for he is not working for glory, achievement or success. He is not concerned whether his work is appreciated or recognized by others. The fruits of action belong to the Lord.

The life of such a selfless seeker becomes a life of sadhana. He should not give up the spiritual practices he observed before he gained his devotion. He should continue with them as vigorously as before. There is always the risk that if he overlooks them when he is dealing with the world, maya might encumber him once again with its limitations, or at least, it will try to dim his vision of the Reality. Therefore, the advice to all sincere seekers is: 'Virtues, like ahimsa (non-injury to others), truthfulness, cleanliness, compassion, and faith in the Lord should be consistently cultivated' (*Narada Bhakti Sutra*, VIII, 2:78).

It is a law that one can never unfold and develop spiritually if one's conduct is bad. Even sadhana is impossible for such an individual. Virtues such as non-violence, compassion, faith in the Lord and in the existence of a higher Truth, and righteous behaviour must be scrupulously observed and cultivated.

To come to live a virtuous life is to study the scriptures regularly and reflect deeply upon what is righteousness, so that our belief and faith may deepen and we may come to live up to it and experience it more and more. Such a total involvement in the higher way of life is true spiritual pursuit and evolutionary living.

The Four Conditions of Prayer

While thus cultivating the spiritual beauties in one's personality, unintentionally some people find themselves empty, exhausted, sunk back again into their crude animal urges. Such falls happen to the mind when it loses its firm hold on His feet and consequently gets dragged into the swirl of samsara.

Hence sage Narada, the immortal preacher of devotion, advises us in the following verse, giving us the entire essence of all sadhanas, as it were: 'Always, free from all mental anxiety, the Lord alone is to be invoked and sought after, with all factors of our personality' (*Narada*

Bhakti Sutra, VIII, 2:79). At all times, in all conditions, in all places, with all one's heart, in perfect devotion, let the Lord be worshipped quietly, serenely, and with a composed mind by those who have given up all worries and anxieties. This is Narada's advice to seekers. Go in full surrender unto Him. Invoke Him. But there are four conditions to be scrupulously practised: (i) at all times, (ii) in all conditions, (iii) in calmness and serenity, (iv) as the sole source of your seeking.

Even today many of us pray, but it is only a prayer of the ego, 'I, I, I'—a worship of the perceiver-feeler-thinker 'I'—so naturally, instead of becoming calmer in mind, we are ever in agitation, continuously persecuted by our own mind with its endless hungers and demands.

The seeker who understands this will not say that these four conditions of sadhana are very difficult. He will only have to redirect his present preoccupation which keeps his mind distracted in a thousand channels, agitations, worries and sorrows. From the attitude of constant adoration of the body and the ego, the seeker must take on a spirit of surrender to and worship of the Lord. This capacity to invoke (bhajana) is already in each one of us, but we are misusing it. We unintelligently employ it for achieving the wrong ends in the lower fields of sense pleasures. Rightly used and properly employed, the powers of invocation can uplift us, and we can thereby reach the Infinite Truth—the Lord.

Prayer or invocation should be from all the levels of our personality. It must be an outpouring of all our faculties in glorifying Him who dwells in us. At the physical, mental and intellectual levels we must be able to put forth all the best in us as an offering unto Him, in the service of all around us, and at all times. Let our actions sing His glory. Let our feelings waft with the fragrance of His eternal purity. Let our thoughts gurgle out, expressing His dynamism and divine will. Such a total God-centred life is a true hymn in praise of the Lord. Let our life be a devotional song, sung in praise of Him who is ever in our heart.

Transformation of the Devotee

When the whole being of the devotee exposes itself in ardent invocation of Him, the bhakta, through such intense association with the Infinite, is gradually transformed to discover that he has attained the very divine attributes he is worshipping. 'When invoked, He indeed reveals Himself and makes the devotee realize His absolute nature divine' (*Narada Bhakti Sutra*, IX, 1:80). When we worship the Lord, invoking Him by our constant contemplation upon His glories, our mind is cut loose from its fanciful attachments to the pluralistic world. When the mind is turned towards the Higher, through our earnest identification with His glories, the Truth that is already within us unveils and reveals Itself.

Truth is not anything separate from us—it is already present as the Illuminator behind every thought in us. Ere long, indeed, very quickly, as soon as the mind is hushed, Truth is recovered, just like a lost key, having been long sought for in futile excitement, is at last discovered in one's own pocket. The key was already there, but not being aware of its presence the owner searched in vain everywhere. Truth was with us all the time, but we did not know it, and only when we invoke It, we experience It as a divine revelation.

The Self is ever with us, but because It is veiled from our direct perception we do not apprehend It. Apprehension of the Truth takes no time; the Self is revealed immediately when the non-apprehension is removed. Turning our mind towards Him through constant contemplation of His glories will lead us to apprehend the Reality, the Lord.

It is the Lord Himself who gives His faithful devotee the experience of this absolute, unchanging Truth. The devotee cannot say 'I know God', or 'I saw God', for Reality is beyond the triple distinctions of the experiencer, the experienced and the experiencing. At that stage there is no instrument for us to perceive or feel or think of Him! The knower, the known, and the knowing are all merged into One, the pure Consciousness.

When the equipment is transcended, there is no instrument with which to know. Then how does one understand Reality? The Lord, out of His own compassion, makes the devotee experience Him. To realize is not the seeker's responsibility—his is only to experience. Eating is our job; to remove the hunger is the Lord's work.

Even in the world outside, an object may sometimes be veiled from our perception when there are unfavourable conditions for its perception. In order to hear a sound, the sound produced must be of the right frequency, and the sound waves must reach the eardrum of the listener. Similarly, an object may be in front of the eyes, but it must be bathed in a beam of light before the eyes can perceive it.

The Self that already exists in us, now hidden behind conditions unfavourable for its cognition, gets unveiled when these unfavourable conditions are removed. The negative atmosphere in us that screens the Self is called 'the darkness (tamas) born of ignorance'. Even in the darkness of ignorance the Self abides; only it is not available for our intimate, subjective experience. When a seeker has established himself in the above-mentioned constant invocation of the Supreme, he becomes fit for the final experience of his real identity with the Self.

When a seeker succeeds in removing the veils of ignorance, which are nothing but his mental agitations caused by the cloudiness of his intellect, the self-effulgent Self then spontaneously reveals Itself. It comes not as a result of deliberate action, but as a spontaneous revelation, as though by the intervention of the divine Grace.

When ignorance is destroyed by Self-knowledge, the Self stands revealed in Its own glory as One-without-a-second, all-pervading and all-full. This act of Self-revelation is undertaken and performed by the Lord, the Self, who ever abides in the heart of His devotees. This kindly act of revealing the Self is undertaken in a spirit of compassion—in fact, towards Itself. When I am tired of walking during my pilgrimage, I may sit on a roadside stone to rest, out of compassion for myself.

This compassion cannot be directly invoked unless the seeker pays the price for it. In daytime when I open the windows of my room, the sunlight, 'out of compassion', illumines the room for me. We know that the sunlight has neither the freedom to withdraw this compassion as long as the windows are open, nor has it the ability to show its compassion before the windows are opened. In short, the sunlight is 'invoked' the moment the obstruction is removed.

Just as darkness is instantaneously removed by light—however thick its density—so also in one who gains knowledge of the Self, beginningless ignorance (avidya) is at once lifted, and within a lightning flash it ends. When ignorance is ended there is the immediate apprehension of Truth, the supreme Brahman. 'To those whose ignorance has been destroyed by the knowledge of the Self, knowledge like the sun reveals the Supreme' (Bhagavad Gita, V:16).

When a dreamer wakes up, he ends his dream personality and discovers himself to be the waker. The waker is never considered an object attained by the dreamer on his waking. The dreamer himself transcends the dreamworld and enters the realm of the waking, wherein he knows himself to be the waker. In the same way, when the deluded ego walks out of ignorance and enters the realm of pure Consciousness, it becomes that Consciousness, which is the Self (Atman). This relationship between the ego and the Atman and the technique of rediscovery of the Atman by the ego are beautifully described by the example given in this verse. Generally students fail to understand how the Self can be experienced when the experiencer, the ego, and the instruments of experiencing have all ended.

Foreseeing this possibility, Lord Krishna tries to explain here how, when the ego has ended, knowledge becomes self-evident, by the example given in the second line of the verse: 'like the sun'. To see the sun we need no other light; to experience the Self we need no other experience. The Self is Awareness. It is Consciousness. To become conscious of Consciousness, we need no separate consciousness; to know knowledge we need no knowledge other than knowledge; knowledge is the very faculty of knowing. Similarly, when the ego rediscovers the Self, it becomes the Self.

FIFTEEN

PRAYER AS INVOCATION[*]

The Power of Prayer

The scriptures declare that the grace of the omnipotent Lord is functioning through us in all our activities. If this be true, there can then be no limit to the abilities and capacities of man. Since the Infinite is functioning through us, infinite are our potentialities. We see this demonstrated in a few people's lives. A worker during moments of inspiration is capable of excelling his normal performance. At times we also have experienced an excellence in our work that we cannot reproduce at will. At such moments, we ourselves become excited onlookers at our own splendid performance. Such spontaneity is not always with us: it comes of its own accord, we seem to have no control over it.

To many of us it is an accidental mood, and that rare moment yields us deep fulfilment inasmuch as in that mood we excel in our actions and are rewarded by a sense of joyous satisfaction. Scientists, artists, and men of all occupations have climbed to the peak of their individual achievement during such accidental moods of inspiration and unearthly spontaneity. But according to Vedanta this is not an accidental happening. There is an infallible law behind these so-called accidents and there is also a definite discipline by which all

---

[*]   From *The Power of Prayer*, Central Chinmaya Mission Trust, Mumbai, first Indian edition, 1987.

can come to live continuously in the spontaneity of inspiration. Great saints amply demonstrate this possibility in the dynamism of their actions and in the magnitude of their life's achievements.

The Secret of Success

A verse from the Bhagavad Gita discloses the secret by which success can be assured for spiritual seekers. 'To those who worship Me alone, thinking of no other, ever self-controlled, I secure that which is not already possessed (yoga) by them, and preserve for them what they already possess (ksema)' (IX:22). If we consider this as a tip for the people who are sweating and toiling in the world, the verse yields a code of instructions by which they can assure for themselves complete success in their life. If a person is capable of maintaining self-willed thought (sankalpa) consistently and with singleness of purpose, he is sure to succeed in any undertaking. But unfortunately, the ordinary person is not capable of channelizing his thoughts. Therefore, his goal seems to be ever receding. Since his goal seems to be ever changing, his determination to achieve a particular goal constantly changes. To such a man of weak determination no progress is possible in any line of undertaking.

The greatest tragedy seems to be that we ignore the fact that thoughts alone create. Activities gain a potency from the power of thought that feeds them. When the feeder is choked and dissipated, the executing power of the external activities becomes feeble. Thoughts from a single-pointed mind must flow steadily in full inspiration, enthusiasm and vigour towards the determined goal that the individual has chosen for himself in life.

Channelizing the thought power towards the goal is the first step for gaining success in one's endeavours. But mere thinking is not sufficient. Many of today's youths, though capable of consistently maintaining a chosen goal, are not ready to enter the field and invoke the possibilities dormant in the situation. Hence the need to do upasana (worship). Through worship we invoke the 'deity', meaning 'the potential in any given field'. This should be a total effort for carving out one's victories in one's field of endeavour.

The Power of Faith

Lord Krishna says in the Bhagavad Gita that everyone, be he a sinner or a saint, dull or energetic, cowardly or courageous, must invoke God, and when invoked, He is ready to bless one and all, irrespective of the manner or the motive with which they invoke Him. 'In whatever way men approach Me, even so do I reward them. My path do men tread in all ways, O son of Pritha' (IV:11).

All people do not worship at the same altar. Each approaches the one Truth by worshipping the idol of his own heart. Lord Krishna declares here that in all churches, mosques, or temples, in public places or in private institutions, in busy homes or in silent caves, in the open or in privacy, wherever and in whatever form a sincere devotee seeks to worship, it is He, the Self, that constantly supplies him with more and more faith to nourish the devotion in his heart.

It is well known that the greater the consistency with which an idea is maintained by an individual, the more he becomes fixed in that temperament. The more often a particular type of thought is entertained in the mind, the deeper that thought channel becomes. These deep patterns of thought indicate the pattern of desires which the individual entertains.

It is a psychological fact that when we are determined to achieve a goal, we develop a faith in the goal and a confidence in ourselves. This faith is what ultimately takes us to success. The Lord explains that He rewards supplicants only by making faith in His devotee more firm.

Faith is a growing belief that is rooted in understanding. As faith increases, the mind becomes more and more efficient. A single-pointed mind is a mighty force against which no obstacle can stand for long. Success is directly proportional to the depth of faith we have, both in ourselves and in the goal.

Imbued with faith, man invokes the potential in the activity of his choice and gains the fulfilment of his desires. Lord Krishna adds that in all cases these desires are being verily dispensed by Him alone. The Self is the force in all activities, gains, fulfilments and despairs. Faithful activity always brings about success, but the very existence of the field of activity, the ability to act, the fervour of faith that supplies consistency to all efforts—all these are possible only in the medium of supreme Consciousness, the Self. Lord Krishna, identifying Himself with this spiritual centre of the universe, declares here that He alone is the One who supplies an ever-growing faith in all activities, and ultimately when the laws of action are fulfilled to the last degree, it is He alone who dispenses the result of each action. Thus is the power of invocation.

Impartiality of the Divine

Complete happiness and satisfaction lie only in the innermost precincts of the bosom and not in the external fields of profit and success, glory and fame. Unmindful of this enduring profit that lies within himself, man, bitten by desire, runs wild, bringing about chaos and sorrow not only to himself but to others walking on the same path. Seekers of happiness in the external world of sense objects can gain only insignificant success in the fields of sense enjoyments, whereas if the same effort is applied by them in the lines of constructive living, they can come to discover their identity with the Self. But due to the extroversion of the deluded ego, it identifies itself with the finite matter envelopments and revels in a world of countless objects, called jagat in Sanskrit.

Discriminating and careful seekers, who understand the utter uselessness of the pursuit of finite pleasures, detach themselves from their false egocentric lives, and through the process of devotion to the Self come to rediscover their real nature in the sunny fields of bliss that lie unrolled beyond the by-lanes of all physical, psychological and intellectual pursuits.

It is the law of life that as one thinks, so one becomes. The thoughts entertained at a given moment get crystallized to form the blueprint for the individual's character formation. In emotional literature expounding bhakti (devotion) there is always the sentimental explanation that only because of the Lord's direct grace some manifest a greater amount of divinity. This theory is perhaps satisfactory to the few who do not bring their reasoning ability into the field of religious discussion. But to the intelligent ones, this explanation should appear unsatisfactory inasmuch as the Supreme would then have to be considered as exhibiting partiality. To negate this unsatisfactory explanation and to express the purely scientific theory, Lord Krishna declares that the Self is the same everywhere and always, and that to the Self there is no distinction between the good and the bad; the Self entertains neither a particular love nor hatred for any living being.

The idea implied here can be better understood by studying the phenomenon of reflection. Though the same sunlight gets reflected upon the different objects in the world, the quality and nature of the reflecting surface only will determine the clarity and the intensity of the light reflected. On a piece of rough stone there will be the least amount of light reflected, while in a clean and polished mirror there will be maximum reflection.

Because of this difference in the intensity of reflection, sunlight cannot be accused of having a special love for the mirror or a disgust for the rough stone. Applying this analogy to the subjective life, it becomes clear that if spiritual strength and beauty get reflected more from the hearts of the rare few and not at all from the rusted hearts of the many, it is not because the Self entertains in Itself any preference for or any prejudice against anyone, but it is only a natural phenomenon happening with perfect obedience to the law of the universe; a prayerful mind invokes its divine qualities.

Even though the Self has neither any favour for nor any prejudice against devotees, to the extent they 'worship Me with devotion', they are 'in Me and I, too, am in them'. Those who worship the Self with devotion come to rediscover that the worshippers themselves are none other than the Self that is worshipped. Realizing the spiritual implications of worship calls for a deep study. Worship is a technique by which the entire thought forces in the worshipper are mobilized and directed to flow towards a divine point of contemplation, seeking a total identity with the Truth contemplated upon. When this is done in a spirit of devotion, the worshipper comes to realize his total oneness with the object of worship.

With this implied meaning in mind, when we reread the verse, what Lord Krishna means becomes clear. Even though truth has neither a preference for nor a prejudice against anyone, some noble souls come to experience and exhibit in themselves the effulgence of divinity, because, as the Lord says, they, through their devoted worship, have sought and discovered their oneness with the divine Principle, the Self.

Of all the spiritual practices, the most efficient is the constant remembrance of the Lord with a heart overflowing with love and devotion (upasana). It is the Vedantic declaration that through upasana the mind gets purified, and Lord Krishna assures us that with a purified mind devoted to the Lord 'we attain the supreme Goal'.

SIXTEEN

HOW TO RETAIN GODHOOD[*]

The attitude of individuality—the perceiver-feeler-thinker-am-I sense—arises as a result of one's ignorance of the Self. It has been maintained by each one of us over a long period of time, during our slow scrambling up the ladder of evolution from the beginning of time. Hence, this ego cannot be totally annihilated all of a sudden, nor is it at any time easy. Except those who have become steadfast in the experience of nirvikalpa samadhi (absorption in Brahman), even the great learned and wise men cannot end their ego suddenly and fully.

This is due to the residual vasanas in the spiritual seeker. Hence Sri Shankara warns in his book *Vivekachudamani* that even though you have ended the ego, it can again revive and rise up to tyrannize you.

The Ego Reasserts Itself

'Even though completely rooted out, this terrible ego-sense, if revived in the mind even for a moment, returns to life and creates hundreds of mischiefs, like a cloud ushered in by the wind during the rainy season' (*Vivekachudamani*, verse 309). If you allow your mind freedom, then the play of the ego-sense will start again. And when the ego is

---

[*]   From *The Razor's Edge*, Central Chinmaya Mission Trust, Mumbai, first Indian edition, 1991.

reborn and starts reasserting itself, agitations will immediately rise up. As long as you have the ego, the world of objects-emotions-thoughts can never be satisfactory by itself. A thousand varieties of agitating desires and worries must necessarily come into the mind. When the ego thus reasserts itself, peace will be lost.

In the rainy season the clouds are all driven away in a moment, and yet the next moment we find the sky cloudy again. The breeze that removed the existing clouds brings in its next windy dash a hoard of new ones. The sun shines brightly at one moment and the next moment it is hidden again behind the newly gathered clouds.

So too, the mind is at one moment steady in prayerful meditation. Next moment, there is a rush of thoughts which dash the brilliant poise of the mind at meditation and make it full of agitations. You feel more distracted when you come out of the prayer room than when you went in. All this is because of the devastating play of the ego. Therefore, beware! Conquer the ego and continue with the alert vigilance of a successful conqueror. Never think that the ego has left you permanently. It must have only receded; it can come up again if you slacken your diligence. Therefore, 'Having once overpowered this enemy, the ego, not a single moment's rest should be given to it to ruminate over sense objects. That is verily the cause of its returning to life, just as water is the cause for the flowering of a citron tree that has dried up before' (*Vivekachudamani*, verse 310).

If a chance is given to the mind and its passions to express themselves, there will be no end to their destructive floods. Therefore, having destroyed the ego, which is your sole enemy, never give the mind the slightest chance to think of the objective world. Attachment for even the most innocent-looking, insignificant thing will pull you down to endless bondage. The story of the sadhu illustrates this point clearly.

A sadhu who had an attachment for his loincloth could not tolerate the rats that gnawed it. He brought a cat to keep away the rats. The rats no doubt disappeared, but the cat had to be fed, and hence, he brought a cow to his hut. The cow had to be looked after; hence, he decided to have a wife to look after the needs of the cow. After some time they had children, followed by their naming ceremony, the nourishing and educating of them, their marriages, and so on—disastrous!

Therefore, never give a chance to the mind to ruminate over sense objects. Sense objects will come your way with all their irresistible enchantments. It is absurd to say that they will not come into your mind. They will and they should; it is natural. But let us not encourage them and commit ourselves to thoughts of them.

Sensuous thoughts are the elixir that revives the once-annihilated mind. This is the miracle that revives the dead ego. An apparently dried-up citron tree when regularly watered for a few days revives and flowers again. The tree that looked dead gets revived by a little water. Similarly, the apparently dead ego revives the moment you take an active interest in maintaining sense thoughts.

When a dried tree is revived, the tree will produce millions of seeds. If the tree is destroyed, there will be no crop of seeds emerging from it. Stop the cause, and the effect also ends.

We all have lower tendencies in us. If these are given a favourable chance, watered by our egocentric thoughts, the seeds, the urges for sense gratification increase, grow, flourish and multiply. Then the individual helplessly confesses, 'I cannot get out of it.' Therefore, when the low, base, and extrovert vasanas spring forth to expression, curb them, crush them, and do not allow them to stem forth and yield more of such poisonous vasanas.

Don't Look Back

Even though the ego has been apparently annihilated, the vasanas, which are the cause of the ego, are dormant, and so if we allow sense thoughts a free play in the mind, those vasanas will revive and the ego will necessarily manifest. Therefore, 'Thinking of sense objects and selfish actions leads to an increase of vasanas. Thus, in order to snap the bonds of the ego, one should burn to ashes these two' (*Vivekachudamani*, verse 314). The two main causes for the increase in vasanas are continuous thinking of sense objects and acting upon the sense objects in the world outside. Both subjective thoughts and objective actions create vasanas, which drag the ego into new births and deaths. These two are to be cut asunder in order to end the tragedy of an egocentric existence.

These forces prompt each individual to take up again and again an appropriate physical body, to continue the stupidity of living for sheer sense gratification. He who wants to cut off this endless stream of sorrow, the nonstop dash from stupidity to stupidity, has to end these two prompting forces.

Thinking about and doing selfish activities are themselves, no doubt, the effects of powerful vasanas, and they create a fresh crop of more vasanas. If you want to get away from these powerful vasanas, you must destroy these two.

In the spiritual path there are moments when one has the feeling, in fact a hallucination, that one has reached some heights. These are, no doubt, great peaks, but in those apparent heights we cannot permanently remain in perfect safety. We may slip again if we look back even once. 'Back' means towards the object-emotion-thought world. When the mind and intellect have turned towards Reality, never look back again. Once you become extrovert, the ego at once precipitates; the sense objects crowd around for attention and terrible vasanas are created. You fall again into samsara. All sadhana becomes impotent, futile, and a great waste. So without looking back, go ahead with a constant forward gaze.

Sometimes the seeker feels very lustful. This is caused by himself: there is no other cause. He himself allows a lustful thought to rise up in him and encourages it. Then this thought forces him into lustful activity, and the two together create lustful vasanas. Tying him down, they blockade his march and he gets helplessly stranded. When a lustful thought comes, do not encourage it; maintain the attitude of a witness towards it. Be fully conscious of it and chant ardently, 'Narayana, Narayana'.

Seeing the pure body and serene face of the Lord Buddha, a prostitute felt tremendous attachment. She went with fruits and other offerings to the place where the Buddha was resting for the night. When she knocked at the door Lord Buddha opened it and stepped out. He saw a beautiful, richly dressed girl standing with offerings of fruits at that untimely hour. Obviously she had come to offer them to the Lord . . . but at midnight? Without any hesitation Gautama said, 'Mother! What can your son do for you?' The poor woman, who came with burning passion, froze to the spot.

Similarly, a lustful thought might rise up in your mind. Do not encourage it. Beware of low thoughts at all times; carefully sublimate them with divine thoughts. But how? Sri Shankara advises: 'Augmented by these two, the vasanas produce one's egocentric existence. These three, however, are destroyed by looking upon everything, under all circumstances, always, everywhere, and in all respects, as Brahman and Brahman alone. Through the strengthening of the longing to be one with Brahman those three will be annihilated' (*Vivekachudamani*, verses 315-16).

The only method of destroying thoughts, actions, and vasanas is to recognize nothing but Brahman everywhere, under all conditions, at all times, in all circumstances. 'Oh, that thing is beautiful,' thus when the mind craves for it, immediately tell it that its beauty is because of Narayana. How beautiful the Lord must be Himself to impart this much of His beauty to this insignificant thing! Passionate lust transforms itself into pure devotion by such a divine attitude. The lustful love for the world of objects when turned sincerely towards Narayana is called bhakti.

Those who do sadhana will understand this; others will not understand. 'Seeing Brahman everywhere' is not merely saying that everything is Narayana. It is much more serious than a vocal declaration. 'All this is nothing but Brahman. It is all my own Consciousness playing in eternal variety as objects.' Such a feeling and understanding will come as a result of developed and deepened spiritual vasanas.

Constant Remembrance

The continuous attempt to hold on to Brahmic Consciousness is Brahmanishtha. Let not this constant awareness, this remembrance of the Lord, ever fall away from your intellect even for a short time. Then there shall be no forgetfulness. Remember Him constantly. 'Him' does not mean the one who is worshipped in the temples. He is your Awareness, the brilliant light of wisdom, expressed in all creatures. This Life in your bosom, which is Life-everywhere, is He, the Supreme. Let there not be any carelessness and consequent forgetfulness and oversight in the constant practice of contemplation. You should never forget this great Reality under any circumstance, at any place, at any time. Constantly remember Him in your heart. Just as you never forget that you are an ego, that you are a man or a woman, so continuously and constantly assert that your real nature is the Self.

Forgetfulness of the essential divinity in us and our sense of holiness is death itself. In fact, this is real death. Living in forgetfulness of one's own divinity is spiritual death, because thereafter, man can live only as a biped animal. Therefore, 'No greater danger is there for the man of wisdom than carelessness about his own real nature. From this comes delusion, thence egoism. This is followed by bondage and then by misery' (*Vivekachudamani*, verse 322).

To a spiritual seeker there is nothing more tragic than this forgetfulness of his own real nature. Inadvertence erupts the volcano of all other sorrows. Forgetting our real nature means non-apprehension of the Reality, which can create misapprehensions. Therefore, for a wise man there can never be any other tragedy greater than Self-forgetfulness, as this can breed a chain of terrible consequences, each replete with insufferable agonies.

From Self-forgetfulness starts delusion; from delusion comes the ego. This ego sense leads to bondage, which breeds misery. When one forgets one's real nature, the infinite Brahman, one deludes oneself into thinking that one is the limited ego. This delusion gives birth to the concept 'I am'. Then one starts considering oneself to be one's own body, mind and intellect. Naturally, conditioned thus by the body-mind-intellect, one comes to suffer limitation—bondage. In order to release oneself from it, one runs after the world of objects-emotions-thoughts: this exertion is sorrow ridden.

In order to fulfil our desires we strive; the desiring produces more sorrow and sweating agony. When the desires are fulfilled, there are even more worries—the struggles that are required to preserve the objects gained. But finite worldly objects definitely perish in time, and therefore, they produce more agony. If our desires are not fulfilled, certainly, we are unhappy: if we get them, we want more. This is how the fall comes. For all this, the initial cause is Self-forgetfulness—the non-apprehension of Reality.

The forgetfulness of the divine within is natural to any ignorant, deluded man. But how can a wise man forget his real nature? How is it so difficult to remember the Lord? How is it that the Lord made us so?

The truth is that the Lord never makes us forget our real nature. When the mind is turned outward, we forget our divine nature and come to play the fool—a limited ego. 'Finding even a wise man hankering after sense objects, forgetfulness torments him through the evil propensities of the intellect, as a woman torments her doting paramour' (*Vivekachudamani*, verse 323).

The Lord has created the sense organs to be turned outward, and therefore the foolish ones forget the divine presence of the Consciousness that shines from behind every sense, act and thought. They forget His presence because of their complete identification with their bodies. The sense organs are turned outward, and the foolish ones come to gaze on and see only the objects of the world outside and never the Consciousness, which always vitalizes the sense organs. Some wise, discriminative men, wanting to realize that immutable, eternal Reality, turn their attention away from the objects of the world and realize the infinitude in their own Self.

This idea is expressed here by Sri Shankara. Even a man, well versed in bookish knowledge, will forget his divine nature of Bliss, if his attention is turned towards sense objects. When he forgets his real nature, the imperfections of his intellect make him agitated. Vasanas, desires, passions, jealousies and greed are the ulcers of the intellect, which produce nothing but sorrow. The poor man is led to disaster by the imperfections of his own intellect, just as a paramour tempts and spoils his or her beloved.

A paramour is a secret lover. He uses his partner for his own satisfaction. When one is secretly in love but the beloved is beyond reach, the memory of the sweetheart haunts the paramour and makes him or her miserable.

Similarly, you are wedded to the Self, the Brahman; but you also have a private and secret love with the world of objects. You are constantly fascinated by the innumerable objects of the world. Every one of them causes more and more disastrous, vitriolic sorrows. Normal sorrows can be borne and some sympathy from others can be expected. But these sorrows, one cannot even tell others or expect any sympathy from them. Hence, once you start acting disloyally to your own divine nature, you become miserable, like the beloved, haunted by the memory of the secret lover. Moreover, 'If the mind ever so slightly strays from the ideal and becomes outgoing, then it goes down and down, just as a ball, inadvertently dropped on a flight of stairs, bounces down from one step to another' (*Vivekachudamani*, verse 325).

To drive home the idea this example is given: When a rubber ball inadvertently slips from the hand—meaning not deliberately but only accidentally or due to forgetfulness—and falls from the top of a flight of steps, it bumps down, and we can recover it only on the ground below.

Once fallen from our own essential nature, there is no question of our ever understanding easily the nature of the Self. Thereafter, identified with the body, mind and intellect, we will jump to reach the world of objects and cling on to one object after another. When our real nature is forgotten, there is a deep and precipitous fall. He who has thus fallen, goes down to a sad death, a miserable destruction, an empty end. It is the tragic and total destruction of his spiritual personality. Such a fallen individual is rarely found to rise again. Do not fall, therefore, is the only logical advice.

Directing the Mind

In order not to fall, renounce idle thinking of the world of objects. Refuse to entertain such thoughts. Contemplating the objects of pleasure is the cause for all sorrows and tragedies in life and for all difficulties and falls in sadhana. Renounce, reject and refuse all the idle ramblings of the mind. Cry 'halt' to the wandering mind. When the patient renounces the objects that his doctor has advised him not to eat, he will become cured of his illness easily. When the objects are in front of us, ordinarily we would love to take them. But in order to get rid of the disease, we must reject them. Similarly, let the mind, which is now suffering from sensuality, reject its tendency to contemplate sense objects. Reject and rise above the senses. When sensuous ideas come, let us positively turn our thoughts to the higher and learn to rise above the cheap sensuousness of our thoughts.

Therefore, let us try to withdraw our minds from objects, emotions and thoughts, and contemplate our real nature: the one Self in all. When the mind is withdrawn from the object-emotion-thought world and starts contemplating Brahman, it refuses to initiate any new selfish activity. In the Bhagavad Gita we are similarly advised: 'Having set the mind upon That, thereafter never initiate any new line of thought.' Similarly, here we are told how, when the mind has been withdrawn from its outer wanderings, and held in abeyance at the chosen point of contemplation on Brahman, one gains the goal. Therefore, withdrawing from the external activities of physical, mental and intellectual imagination, let us teach ourselves to bring our entire attention to the Consciousness within.

Contemplate the Self *with great care*—meaning slowly. You cannot force-open a bud and make it a flower. It must take its own time. A forcibly opened flower will not have real beauty or true fragrance. Never make haste. Let it take its own time. All that we have to do is to put ourselves on the right track, running in the right direction. We all shall reach our coveted destination in time.

IV

GURU AND SHISHYA

Self-redemption must come ultimately from ourselves. The external props such as temples, idols and gurus are all encouragements and aids. They must be intelligently used to help build up inner perfection.

—Swami Chinmayananda

~

SEVENTEEN

THE WAY TO FREEDOM*

In the first half of the Vedas, called the Karma-Kanda, the path of ritualism is advocated; yet in the second half, the Upanishads, we find a vehement condemnation of that path. This would seem to be a palpable contradiction, but it is not.

When our child is in the elementary class, we have to insist that he studies the multiplication tables daily. But when the university level of pure mathematics has been reached, it would be absurd to insist on that same routine. Arithmetic tables were certainly necessary in those early days, but in the higher grades they are redundant. Similarly, rituals have an elementary purpose, without which nothing higher is possible; but to stop at that would be a terrible waste.

Approaching the Ideal Teacher

When a seeker learns that yajnas and other rituals cannot in themselves take him to the Supreme state, it is natural that he should wonder what he is to do. The following verse explains the duties of such a seeker in whom the rituals have fulfilled themselves:

Let a Brahmana (an aspirant), after he has examined the worlds gained by karma (action), acquire freedom from all desires, reflecting

---

* From *The Way to Freedom*, Central Chinmaya Mission Trust, Mumbai (reprint, July 1997).

that nothing eternal can be gained by karma. Let him, in order to obtain the knowledge of the Eternal, take sacrificial fuel in his hands and approach that preceptor alone who is versed in the Vedas and established in Brahman. (*Mundaka Upanishad*, I, II:12)

The idea indicated here is that moksha (liberation) cannot be the result of any action performed, for, if it could result from action, it would be a perishable state. The eternal should be—and ever is—the unborn, for, all that is born must necessarily die. When a seeker's intellect realizes the impermanence of the benefits accrued by ritualism, he becomes indifferent to them, and wants to know only that Knowledge 'knowing which everything becomes known'.

In order to realize the Self, a sincere aspirant is advised in this verse to approach a guru. Nowhere else in our scriptures do we have such a clear and exhaustive definition of a perfect guru: one who has both a mastery over the entire scriptural literature and a complete personal experience of the absolute Reality.

These two great qualifications are the essential criteria for becoming a spiritual teacher. In order to realize the Self, mastery of the scriptures is not necessary. It is only to become a spiritual teacher that we need this education.

Unless the guru is well versed in the scriptures he will find it difficult and impossible to direct the gaze of the student towards the Self shining within. If the guru is very learned but does not live constantly in full awareness of the Self, he will be unable to bless anyone. Pundits are apt examples of gurus who are shrotriyas (well versed in the scriptures) but are not Brahmanishthas (established in Brahman).

Likewise, some of the masters of realization living in the Himalayas—adored and worshipped for their perfection—cannot act as a guru to a disciple, since they have no medium through which to express their deep subjective experience. Often such masters guide us through their presence, their ways, and their actions.

A true teacher, however, has a thorough knowledge of the science of religion and is also rooted in his own subjective experience of that state of Consciousness indicated by the scriptures. Only such a master can convincingly propagate the scriptures and kindle the enthusiasm of students to brave the difficulties of life until they reach the eternal goal.

In olden days, students would approach a teacher carrying a bundle of fuel as a symbol of the disciple's readiness to surrender totally to the master and tune himself through continuous and tireless service. The fuel in the student's hand symbolized the disciple's declaration that he was coming to the guru only after burning all his negativities, animal tendencies, egoistic vanities, and foolish attachment to the sense world.

The scriptures dictate that a guru explain to the sincere aspirant the Truth, in all its purity, and consistently encourage the student to live that life which can take him to the goal. 'To that pupil who has thus respectfully approached him, whose mind is at rest, and whose senses are subdued, let the wise teacher truly teach that Brahma vidya (Science of Brahman) through which the Supreme is known' (*Mundaka Upanishad*, I, II:13).

A true guru has no right to deny instruction to any qualified disciple, that is, a disciple with complete self-control and a degree of mental tranquillity. To such a disciple the guru must explain not only the word meaning, but also the indicative meaning by which the limited words of the scriptures explain the inexplicable, thus relieving the student of his mental confusion.

This is not all. The scriptures contain many technical methods by which one can achieve a direct experience of the Truth as described in the Upanishads. The guru must also instruct the student on the processes of self-unfoldment and help him along the path to succeed in his subjective quest of Truth.

The Conditioned Truth

Yet, declarations made by the scriptures and the teachers are at best a vain attempt to define the indefinable. Since the theme of the Upanishads is the subjective Self—which is a realm of experience that lies beyond the intellect—all theoretical discussions must necessarily fall short of the subjective experience. But at the same time, the teacher can instruct only from the level of the intellect. The following story illustrates this point.

The master would often repeat at the end of his discourse that the discussion had been concerned only with 'the conditioned'. 'Remove the conditioning and realize the Self,' he would say. So one day the disciple was compelled to ask him: 'Sir, if this be so, why not remove the conditioning and explain the pure Brahman?'

The student received no direct reply, and the class continued. As the lesson proceeded, the student forgot his doubt. Then, all of a sudden, the teacher said to the disciple: 'Get me water to drink.' Though surprised at this unusual thirst at such an early hour, the disciple brought a glass of water and placed it in front of his master. 'What is this?' asked the guru in an assumed air of anger.

'Sir, this is the water you wanted,' the disciple murmured.

'But did I ask you for a glass, or for water?' roared the master. 'Take the glass away and bring me the water.'

'But sir, how can I serve water without a glass?' the disciple stammered, feeling confused and agitated.

'Never mind,' said the master in a soft, encouraging tone. 'Nobody can convey water without a vessel. So too, absolute Truth cannot be explained in words. Just as you cannot bring water without a vessel, so too we cannot express Truth except through the medium of its conditioning. Hence it is that the scriptures and gurus explain only the conditioned Truth instead of the absolute Truth.' Any amount of intellectual understanding of the conditioned Brahman will not take us to our goal. The spiritual thirst in man can be satisfied only when he breaks away from the shackles of his limitations and soars higher and higher to his full divine stature. And this can be accomplished by the seeker only through an intimate and intense subjective experience of his own real nature as the eternal Existence-Knowledge-Bliss.

Refining the Mind

To gain this intuitive experience, the seeker must have the necessary instruments: a purified mind and intellect. A mind that tosses the least is called a pure mind. Tossings are caused by desire, hatred, lust, and other negativities in our psychological make-up. The mind, goaded as it were by its impressions (vasanas), throws out for us the external world of objects, just as the picture on the film reel gives us the story on the screen. The person watching the show identifies himself completely with the picture and comes to suffer or enjoy the sorrows and joys of the hero and the heroine.

Similarly, our external world is formed by objects and circumstances. Identifying ourselves with this world, torn between hope and despair, loss and gain, we live the pains of a life of limitations. Yet, this world of objects and circumstances is only as true as the reality we claim for the hero in the picture during our stay in the movie theatre.

How then can we remove the vasanas which inhibit the vital, intimate, and subjective experience of our real Self? How can we acquire a pure mind? The only known method of erasing the vasanas is to scrape the mind clean. Imagine holding a piece of sandpaper close to a reel of film in a projection room. As it winds and rewinds itself, the film reveals less and less of the story to the audience. In time, the scratched strip will have lost much of its distinct charm, and be only a blurred vision of filtered light interspersed with patches of darkness.

In the mind-film, the vasana picture can be erased by scraping it with devotional practices consisting mainly of constant repetition of the names of the Lord and remembrance of Him. In a clean mind, divinity comes to manifest in all its absolute glory.

EIGHTEEN

GURUS, TEACHERS AND PRECEPTORS*

Q: Is a guru essential for one to enter the spiritual path and attain the goal? How does one choose a guru?

A: The very fact that you are asking these questions clearly shows that we need teachers to teach us. Think for a moment: is there anything that we do well today with confidence or any amount of mastery that has not been taught to us? If for every perfect act in the world, in any activity, we need the guidance of an instructor, we can very well understand the need for a guru on the spiritual path, for, there we have to deal with the subtlest forces and the enormous confusions of the vehicle called the mind, and with its moods called delusions.

The guru–disciple relationship is unavoidable. Every great master has been under the guidance of a teacher. It is not true to say that we can reach the goal just through books. A teacher is necessary.

But you have to understand very carefully. To say the guru is necessary does not mean that the guru will take the responsibility, that all you have to do is meet the guru and thereafter he will carry you to the goal.

The relationship between the teacher and the taught is exactly like the relationship of the gardener with the flowers on the bush.

---

* From *The Essential Teacher*, Central Chinmaya Mission Trust, Mumbai (reprint, July 1997).

The gardener does not create the flowers from the soil and the manure: the flowers must themselves come from the bush. The gardener can only tend its roots, water it, protect it, see that it has the correct amount of sunlight and shade—all these externals he can provide. But no mere gardener can guarantee the blossom: it can come only from the bush itself.

Similarly, the teacher's job is to nurture the student with right thoughts. The student must be given a conducive and protective environment where he or she need not overstrain to live. But the blossoming—the real fragrance and beauty of the personality—must come from within.

There are some gurus who will say that they will carry you to the goal. Those are all mule gurus. You can ride on them. But the true gurus only show you the way and encourage you.

As the student advances and the mind becomes quiet and concentrated, its subtler powers, called siddhis, come to manifest themselves. If you revel in the play of these psychic powers, you may never reach the goal. Here, too, the guru is needed to knock you down: 'Why are you lingering here? You may enjoy such fascinations in passing, but don't stay and play with these toys, for you are still only playing with the mind. Go forward!'

You ask, 'How does one choose a guru?' It is not a question of the disciple selecting the guru. He gravitates towards a guru, and he will find exactly the guru he needs for his present state of mental development.

So choose whatever guru comes to you. But understand that the only guru is He, the Lord, who finds expression in many forms.

Q: What about the current Hindu pantheon of gurus and godmen who run their private industries, and who often suggest completely different and sometimes contradictory routes to salvation?

A: Have you watched the followers? They all come voluntarily, they are all free, no one forces them. They follow these masters because they find some consolation. So, at different levels, all gurus are valid. I know that there are too many teachers, too many masters, too many gurus. But I would wish there were more.

Q: Sure. As long as they are teachers, not quack healers or exploiters of the innocent.

A: Don't think that all teachers will teach only at the undergraduate level. Or that the graduate-level teacher can teach everybody. There are students who must be taught the alphabet, only addition and subtraction. Isn't this true? In education, there are various levels and various teachers. If the graduate teacher is given an elementary class to teach, he will become confused, go screaming mad. The elementary teacher cannot, similarly, teach graduate classes. So, at different levels, different teachers are valid. They do not know beyond their levels, just as their students cannot understand beyond the levels at which they speak.

The True Preceptor

Q: What are the qualifications of a true preceptor?

A: From the Bhagavad Gita's descriptions of a man of perfection (Chapter II), we know that a man firmly established in wisdom is tranquil, and his equipoise is never disturbed even when he invests his entire energy in the service of mankind.

The Upanishads summarize the qualifications of a teacher in two terms: Shrotriya (one who is a master of the scriptures) and Brahmanishtha (one who is well established in the experience of Truth). Without knowledge of the scriptures, the teacher will not be able to convey his wisdom to the disciples. But a mere bookish knowledge is not sufficient. The words coming from an individual can gather wings only when they spring from a heart soaked with sincere subjective experience.

However, to be a preceptor, he must have two more qualifications. His behaviour in the world must be perfect, since we as students when admiring the teacher will be tempted to imitate him in all his external habits. If his behaviour is not perfect, it is possible that we will copy his bad habits and thus ruin our chances. Secondly, a preceptor must have large-heartedness and be flowing with kindness and patience. This is necessary since in the early stages the students will revolt against new concepts that conflict with their present understanding. To weed out the mind and to replant new ideas is a very painful operation, and this can be achieved only when the teacher has infinite patience, endless love, and supreme affection.

When these qualifications are not there, the preceptor is not a true one. A preceptor is known by his own disciples, just as a good musician is known only by true students of music. Students who have a spiritual urge and have practised a little will instinctively recognize a teacher. Our preceptor is he who inspires us to live a nobler life, and in whose presence we feel elevated. When we compare our life with his we feel ashamed of our own weaknesses; at times of burning passion, by remembering him, we feel cooled down.

In fact, the true preceptor to all of us is the Lord, and the Lord of our heart talks to us very often through His chosen deputy among us, and we revere and worship Him as manifesting through the individual. No individual mortal is ever a preceptor. The Lord alone is the Teacher, everywhere, and at all times.

On Progress

Q: Why has the world made no true progress despite the coming of so many prophets and saints?

A: The answer is obvious. For aeons, waves have been coming and lashing against the shores and still there are waves in the ocean. When will they end? For centuries politicians have been arriving and giving us political philosophies. Believing them, successive generations have sacrificed themselves; yet, where are we today? Medical science has progressed over time. Hospitals have been built, doctors trained, yet, is there no illness now in the world? Would you say, therefore, the world has not progressed? If in these known realms there is progress in spite of imperfections, can you say that man has not progressed in spite of prophets and religion?

No doubt the ideal world has not yet been reached, even with the valiant contributions of politicians, doctors, scientists and economists. But please consider what our condition would have been, had these mighty intellectuals not served the world.

In spite of prophets and preceptors, man has not given up lust and has not learned the art of living in tranquil joy. But consider what our condition would have been, had these benign influences not taken place in our evolution to present civilization.

There is plenty of food in restaurants and stores. And yet, so many people die of starvation. The existence of food in the world is no guarantee against people starving. Even when food is in front of us, unless we take it in, it is not going to help us. Even if we take it, unless we have the strength to assimilate and make the essence of the food our own, health will never be improved.

The religious masters lay down rules of conduct and explain the greater Reality in life. We have to digest these ideas and assimilate them to make them our own. Religion is a subjective science.

In the generations in which many recognized and lived these values, there were more peace and progress. But when, as in our times, moral virtues are discarded and religion is shunned on the false and stupid argument of secularism, we find immorality, corruption and faithlessness in all departments of activity.

Yet, when we look around us, we see how religion and prophets are still serving the world. We need not have another demonstration of how effective they are. Evidences of their contributions are aglow everywhere.

~

NINETEEN

THE TRUE DEVOTEE*

In the concluding verses of Chapter XII of the Bhagavad Gita, named 'The Path of Devotion', Lord Krishna brilliantly enumerates the characteristics of a true devotee. He thereby prescribes with careful detail the correct way of life for all seekers. As a painter would again and again step back from his canvas to judge his own product and then go forward to add a few more strokes, so too does Lord Krishna attempt, in these seven stanzas, to paint the mental beauty and intellectual equipoise of a true devotee and his relationship with the world around him.

In Hinduism, ethical codes of behaviour are not a list of commandments thrust upon its followers by the thunderings of a God. The rules of conduct are based on the behaviour of godly people who actually lived in the world and attained spiritual perfection. A seeker who strives to attain the experience of these saints and seers should start by copying their external behaviour and mental beauties, which constitute the moral and ethical rules prescribed in religion.

The Man of Perfection

'He who hates no creature, who is friendly and compassionate to

---

* From *On the Path: Preparing for the Spiritual Quest*, Central Chinmaya Mission Trust, Mumbai, first Indian edition, 1989.

all, who is free from attachment and egoism, balanced in pleasure and pain, forgiving, ever content, steady in meditation, self-controlled, and possessed of firm conviction, with mind and intellect dedicated to Me, he, My devotee, is dear to Me' (Bhagavad Gita, XII:13-14). Eleven noble qualities are indicated in the above two verses. Each one of them declares a moral phase in the character of a man of perfection. He who has realized that the Spirit everywhere is one and the same, and that the Spirit-in-All alone is his own Self, cannot thereafter afford to hate anyone, because from his vision there is no one who is other than Him. No living man hates his own right hand, because he is in it. Nobody hates himself!

The man-of-perfection's attitude to all living creatures will be friendly, and he is ever compassionate. He offers security of life to all beings. He cannot regard anything as his possession; he is completely free from the notion of egoism. Even-minded in pain and pleasure, he remains supremely unaffected, even when beaten or abused. Always contented, he discovers infinite joy in himself whether or not he obtains even the means of his bodily sustenance. Steadfast in his meditation, self-controlled and firm in his resolve, he lives on joyously, his mind and intellect ever centred in the Lord. 'Such a perfect, devoted yogi,' the Lord says, 'is dear to Me.'

Lord Krishna continues his word picture with three more qualities of the real devotee. 'He by whom the world is not agitated (affected), and who cannot be agitated by the world, who is freed from joy, envy, fear, and anxiety—he is dear to Me' (Bhagavad Gita, XII:15).

He by whom the world is not agitated: A man of perfection is one who will not create any agitations in the world around him. Where the sun is, there cannot be any darkness. Where the peaceful master of equanimity and perfection dwells, by the intrinsic divinity in him, he creates an atmosphere of serene joy around him. Even those agitated by the world will suffer no longer from their agitations when they approach such a master. In fact, the world irresistibly rushes to such a saint to bask in his brilliance and experience the joy that wafts all around him!

Who cannot be agitated by the world: Not only does a man of perfection quieten the very world around him into a dynamic peace, the world too—however chaotic, revolting, boisterous, and vengeful it may be—cannot create any agitation in him. The world of objects will almost always be in a state of flux, and its maddening death dance cannot bring even a whiff of its storms to disturb the serenity of the saint. He is made of stronger mettle and his life is built upon surer foundations.

Floating reeds dance upon the surface of the sea, but the lighthouse that is built on the rocks beneath stands erect and motionless, watching the smooth sea turning rough with the rise of waves. The personality of a perfected person is rooted in his realization of the deeper substratum of life, and since he is not attached to the superficial conditions of matter and its playful magic, any amount of wild agitations outside cannot bring disturbance to his inward equipoise. In and through the battling of life's daily circumstances, he perceives the changeless ground; he hears the harmony that runs through the various discordant notes in the life around him.

'He is completely freed' from all the usual causes for inward agitation such as 'joy, envy, fear, and anxiety'. A devotee of this type, ever peaceful with himself and the world, who rules over circumstances and never yields to be victimized by them, who has crossed beyond the usual weaknesses of the mortal heart, such a devotee 'is dear to Me'.

Adding a few more brush strokes to the picture, the blessed Lord declares: 'He who is free from wants, who is pure, alert, unconcerned, and untroubled, renouncing all undertakings (or commencements), he who is (thus) devoted to Me, is dear to Me' (Bhagavad Gita, XII:16). This verse throws more light upon the picture of the perfect devotee as conceived by the Lord Himself. Fourteen indications were already given in the above three verses. To that picture are added six subtler attributes of the spiritual seeker.

Free from dependence: A true devotee does not depend upon either the objects of the world outside, or their pattern, or their relationships with himself. An ordinary person discovers his peace and joy only in the world of objects, their conditions, and their arrangements around him. When the right type of object is in the right pattern courting him favourably, he feels temporarily thrilled and joyous. But a real devotee is completely independent of the world outside and draws his inspiration, equanimity, and joyous ecstasy from a source deep within himself.

Who is pure: Dirt has no place anywhere within or without a true devotee. One who aspires to reach Perfection will necessarily be so well disciplined physically that he will not only be clean in his relationship with others but even in the very condition and arrangement of his belongings around him. It is well known that the condition of a person's desk and the cleanliness of his apparel can give a great insight into the mental nature, discipline and culture of that individual. Great emphasis has been laid in India on this physical purity, not only of the person but also of his contacts in the world. Without external purity, internal purification will be but a vague dream, an idle hope, a despairing vision.

Alert: To be always alert becomes the second nature of an integrated person. Enthusiasm is the key to success in any undertaking. A dynamic person is not one who slips in his behaviour or action. He is mentally agile and intellectually vigorous. Since there is no dissipation in him, he is ever on his toes to spring forward to activity, once he determines to shoulder any endeavour.

Unconcerned: It is not difficult for one to observe many devotees who have resigned themselves to a state of unexpressed sorrow, because they have been cheated by others, ill-treated by society, and persecuted by the community. If foolish devotees think that they should be unconcerned about these outrages practised on them, their own devotion to the Lord must then prove to themselves a wretched liability, rather than a positive gain! Philosophy misunderstood can easily end in the suicide of the community.

The 'unconcerned' attitude is only meant to economize our mental energies. In human life, small difficulties, discomforts and wants are but natural. To exaggerate their importance and strive to escape from them all is to enter into a life-long struggle of adjustments. In such instances, the student is warned not to squander his mental energies but to conserve them by overlooking these little pin-pricks of life in an attitude of utter indifference.

Free from trembling: Inward tremors are experienced only when a burning desire has conquered us completely. Once victimized by a fascination for an object, the individual personality becomes tremulous in fear that its desire may not be fulfilled. A true seeker is one who never allows the inner person in him to entertain such fears or agitations.

Renouncing every undertaking: In Sanskrit, this could also be translated as 'to end all beginnings'. This literal meaning has made the majority of Hindus incompetent idlers and the religion has been criticized as glorifying idleness as a divine ideal! The deeper suggestions have been overlooked. To perceive any definite beginning in an undertaking, the individual actor must have a solid and gross egoistic claim that he has begun it himself. He must have the strong feeling that he is beginning an activity to gain a definite goal, whereby he will fulfil a specific desire. One who is a seeker of the Divine, striving to reach the higher perfections, must renounce this egoistic sense of self-importance and work on in the world selflessly.

No undertaking in our life, in fact, is a new act that has an independent beginning or end. All actions in the world are part of the eternal pattern of the total world movement. If correctly and honestly analysed, all our undertakings are controlled, regulated and ordered by the world of things and situations. Apart from them all, no independent action is undertaken, or can be fulfilled, by anyone. A devotee of Truth is ever conscious of this oneness of the universe, and therefore he will always work in the world only as an instrument of the Lord and not as an independent agent in an undertaking.

Mental Qualities

Such a devotee who possesses all the six qualifications enumerated above 'is dear to Me'. In addition: 'He who neither rejoices, nor hates, neither grieves, nor desires, renouncing good and evil, full of devotion, is dear to Me' (Bhagavad Gita, XII:17). A perfect devotee is one who has lifted himself from the world of the mind and intellect and has awakened to his inner spiritual nature. Therein, the ordinary experiences of joy and sorrow, of pain and pleasure, do not affect him.

He who neither rejoices: 'Rejoicing' is the feeling of satisfaction and fulfilment that comes on attaining a desired object, which is extremely desirable, and extremely difficult to realize.

Nor hates: The sense of revulsion that one feels towards undesirable things and circumstances is generally hatred. In short, these two terms indicate that there are no objects that a man of perfection would ardently like to acquire, nor are there any occasions that could create anger in him.

Neither grieves, nor desires: Grief is generally experienced while parting with a beloved object, and desires are entertained when one yearns to possess something unattained at present. A man of perfection is one whose beloved object, the Self, can never be apart from him. Having attained the Self, the inhabitant of his heart, he has such a complete sense of fulfilment that he has no desire for attaining anything. He has no sense of attachment to any other object. The

Self being the All, he has at once attained all.

Renouncing good and evil: The happenings in the world around us can fall under these two categories, according to whether they arouse in us a feeling of joy or sorrow. To one who is living apart from the realm of dualistic experiences and who has learned the art of drawing inspiration from something beyond, none of the happenings at the level of the mind and intellect can be of serious consequence.

The above terms, used in this verse to portray a perfect devotee, have a secret import. If we consider only the literal meaning, we will think that such a perfect one is a corpse: 'neither rejoices, nor hates, nor desires; renouncing good and evil, he lies dead!' This is a very striking example of how the literal meaning is not at all what is meant by the scriptural declarations.

When a true devotee, being awakened to God-consciousness, evaluates life from his new height of experience, he cannot rejoice or hate, grieve for or desire anything in this world. He renounces totally the very concepts of good and evil. The divine charioteer Krishna declares: 'He who is such a devotee is dear to Me.'

Ethics in Action

In this verse, the divine Lord enumerates six more qualities that make a perfect devotee. So far we have been told of twenty-six subtle traits that are the intrinsic qualities of a perfect yogi.

> He who is the same to foe and friend, and also in honour and dishonour, who is the same in cold and heat and in pleasure and pain, who is free from attachment, to whom censure and praise are equal, who is silent, content with anything, homeless, steady-minded, full of devotion—that one is dear to Me. (Bhagavad Gita, XII:18-19)

Equal to foe and friend: The estimation of our relationship with another as foe or friend is generally our own psychological reaction towards another. It belongs essentially to the heart. It is experienced by the psychological being in us. A man of perfection is one who does not identify himself with his mental estimation of things, and therefore is equanimous and maintains a uniformity of attitude towards his friends and foes.

And so too, in honour and dishonour: A situation is judged by the intellect as honourable or dishonourable with reference to its own existing values and cultivated habits of thinking. That which is ordinarily considered dishonourable can come to be estimated by the same person as honourable in a new pattern of circumstances, ordered by a change in time and place. On the whole, these are all different tides in the intellect, and those who live in that realm are affected by them.

Who is the same in heat and cold: Heat and cold are only experiences of the body. By remembering the preparation process of nitric acid, my thoughts cannot get corroded; by feeling the smouldering beauty of the burning embers in the fireplace, my mind cannot get blisters. My knowledge of my beloved and my capacity to love cannot freeze at the North Pole, nor can it ever get evaporated in the Sahara desert. Heat and cold affect only the body. Whenever this idiom is used in the context of philosophy, it represents all types of experiences to which the physical equipment is the heir.

The above three terms encompass the entire possibility of experiences in life: physical, mental, and intellectual. In all of them, a true devotee is unagitated because he 'is free from attachment'. Attachment to and identification with the matter equipments—body, mind, and intellect—are the causes by which we are helplessly made to dance to the mad tunes that chance happenings dictate. One who is detached from these is the one who is a master of them all.

To whom censure and praise are equal: To a great devotee, living as he is in a realm of his own, full of transcendental and blissful experiences of the Divine, worldly censure and praise make no impression at all. He realizes that one who has been praised today will be censured tomorrow, and that yesterday's censured man becomes the praiseworthy leader of today! Praise and censure are in themselves nothing more than the passing fancy of those who express them.

He is silent: A true seeker of wisdom becomes a man of few words, not only physically but mentally. Silence within is the real silence (mauna) that the scriptures tell of. Keeping physical silence while letting the mind chatter generally results in repression. Be silent and understand how really silent silence can be!

Content with anything: Contented with anything that might reach him accidentally, unasked, and unexpected is the motto of all serious seekers of inward growth. To entertain the demands in life and to strive to satisfy them would be an unending game, as the mind has a knack of breeding its own demands very fast. The policy of contentment is the only intelligent attitude to be taken by all sincere seekers, or else there will be no time to seek, to strive for, and to achieve the divine goal of life. Self-integration is a reward promised for faithful pursuits. It is said in the Mahabharata, 'He who is clad with anything, who is fed on any food, who lies down anywhere, him the gods call a Brahmana (one of the highest caste).'

Homeless: Home is that which provides shelter from the inclemencies of weather for the resident who dwells under its roof. The person of spiritual realization is one who is trying to pull down all his conditioning and striving to free himself from all sense of possession and material shackles. Living under a roof, in itself, does not make the place a home. To spend a night in a railway station or an airport does not make the place the traveller's home. It is only along with a sense of possession, reinforced by a sense of happiness and comfort, that the place under a roof becomes a home. A true devotee finds satisfactory refuge only at the seat of the All-pervading,

171

and therefore his mental condition is indicated here by the simple, pertinent word, 'homeless'.

Steady-minded, full of devotion: Steadfast in his intellectual understanding of the goal and ever striving to attain his divine ideal, the devotee lives on. 'That one is dear to Me.'

These last two verses represent ten additional qualities. In short, in thirty-six artistic strokes, Lord Krishna has brought about a complete picture of the seeker of Perfection, his relationship with the world outside, his psychological life, and his intellectual evaluation of the world of beings and happenings.

The enumeration of the various moral, ethical and spiritual qualities of a true devotee is concluded with this verse: 'They, indeed, who follow this immortal law of righteous living (sanatana dharma) as described above, endowed with faith, regarding Me as their supreme goal—such devotees are exceedingly dear to Me' (XII:20).

Sanatana dharma: This immortal law, emphasized again and again in the Hindu scriptures, is summarized in the above lines. To realize the Self and live that wisdom at all our personality levels—physical, mental, and intellectual—is the fulfilment of the life of a devotee. It is not sufficient that one understands this law of life, or reads the scriptures regularly, or is even able to explain the ideas intelligently. He must be able to digest them properly and assimilate them fully. Therefore, the blessed one must be 'endowed with faith'. Here the term 'faith' means the necessary capacity to assimilate spiritual ideas into ourselves through subjective, personal experience.

Such devotees are supremely dear to Me: This concluding verse serves as a divine reassurance to all spiritual seekers that when they develop these qualities in themselves, they will gain the supreme love of the Lord.

To read and assimilate the entire twelfth chapter of the Bhagavad Gita, entitled 'Bhakti Yoga', is to cherish true love for the Lord and cure ourselves of the various misconceptions that we have today in our practice of devotion. The path of devotion is not a mere sentimental explosion or an excessive emotional display. It is the blossoming of the human personality through the surrender of all limitations and the acquiring of new vitality during the inspired moments of deep contemplation.

V

SOME SPIRITUAL PRACTICES

Of all the spiritual practices, the most efficient is the constant remembrance of the Lord with a heart overflowing with love and devotion (upasana).

—Swami Chinmayananda

TWENTY

JAPA YOGA*

You may wonder why a student of Vedanta listening to and reflecting upon discourses on the Upanishads and the Gita should care to take up any method of sadhana (spiritual practice) other than pure meditation. It is natural for seekers in their blind enthusiasm to come to question the importance of japa for a Vedantic seeker. This doubt comes out of a confusion in the understanding of Japa Yoga.

Japa is a training by which the ever-dancing rays of the mind are compelled to behave in some order and rhythm, and thereby bring out of their cooperative effort a single melody of repeated mantra chanting. In this manner the mind becomes single-pointed. In fact, japa properly done can more effectively bring about a sustained single-pointedness than all the hasty methods of meditation. A mind seasoned with japa is like tinned food which is ready for consumption after a few seconds of warming on the fire. A short period of meditation can take a japa-prepared mind to unimaginable heights in a very short time.

Japa trains the mind to fix itself to a single line of thinking. We cannot pronounce a word without a thought-form rising up immediately in us, nor can we have a thought-form without its corresponding name. Try! Can you repeat the word 'pen' without its form? Can you? In this close connection between the name and

---

* From Swami Chinmayananda, *Tune in the Mind*, Central Chinmaya Mission Trust, Mumbai, second edition, 1986.

the form lies the underlying principle of the technique of japa.

Again, love is not generated where sufficient thought is not bestowed. You love your near and dear relatives more than your uncle's sister-in-law's nephew, whom you probably have seen and even admired; yet, love is not there, for you have not spent sufficient thought on that child. Thus, training oneself to repeat mentally His name constantly during the waking hours as also to perform japa in all intensity in the prayer room are the sure ways of developing bhakti. It is always the repetition of thinking that brings about deep attachment. The less one thinks of a thing, the less one gets attached to it. The opposite is equally true: the more one thinks of a thing the more one gets attached to it.

The Supreme Reality is experienced through meditation alone. But the boat to reach the goal, that is, meditation, is rigged with the practice of devotion through japa. In meditation one remains wingless if one has not acquired concentration power and a perfect knowledge of how to fix one's mind at will on a single point for some length of time. Meditation is keeping the mind fixed on one line of thought. To succeed in this we must learn to stop at will all other dissimilar thought currents. This mental capacity is gained through japa when it is intelligently practised along with the regulation of daily life.

Japa is a very effective mental discipline for spiritual progress. In recent history there is the instance of the esteemed teacher of Shivaji, Samartha Ramdas, who perfected himself through the Japa Yoga of the Sri Ram Mantra: *Sri Ram jaya Ram, jaya jaya Ram*. Bhagwan Yogeswara Krishna Himself says in the Gita: 'I am, among the Yogas, the Japa Yoga.'

How should I start? By getting down to it immediately. What happened to that holiday-maker who waited on the sea-shore for the waves to subside so that he could take his bath comfortably? Don't waste your time in vain on the shores of life: get into the ocean of Bliss and be refreshed.

Have a special room for your prayers: fix a charming picture of your heart's Lord at such a height from the floor that when you sit in front of it, the Lord's feet shall be at level with your eyes. Spread a plain seat—asana—in front of your ishta, the lord of your heart. Have a mala (rosary) of one hundred and eight beads. Now start the japa behind closed doors please, to begin with. Sitting on the asana in any comfortable posture, gaze at the Lord's face, then body, legs and feet. Now slowly raise the gaze from the feet, legs and body, to the face of the Lord. Close the eyes now: feel His presence within you and try to visualize the Lord exactly as in the picture. This visualization of the Lord should be done within your 'love heart', which is exactly on the right side of the physical heart. This is the spiritual heart centre, where, if you meditate, your success is doubly assured. Feel . . . feel His presence.

Now repeat your ishta–mantra (chosen mantra) a few times slowly, steadily, with all the love you are capable of. This invokes bhakti in you to do the japa most effectively. Take the mala, search for the bead at the tip: this is called the meru. Bring the tips of your ring-finger and thumb together and let the mala be hung at this junction. Repeat fervently your ishta–mantra; at each repetition turn one bead with the middle-finger, always allowing the index finger to stand apart. The index finger is considered to be an 'outcast' because of its 'language'. This finger is generally used to point out the 'other', to accuse 'another', to threaten, etc. Essentially the index finger is used to express duality and the otherness of things and beings!

When you have repeated your chosen mantra one hundred and eight times, you will come back to the meru bead. You have now completed one mala. Now be careful; don't cross the meru. Turn the mala in such a way that the hundred and ninth mantra is counted on the bead with which the hundred and seventh mantra was registered. Thereafter proceed in all sincerity and finish with your second mala of japa. In this manner do twenty malas of japa twice a

179

day—once in the morning and once in the evening.

A mantra is a word symbol or symbols representing and expressing, as nearly as possible, the particular view of God and the universe they stand for. There is nothing secret about these mantras. All of them are in the scriptures, but when the mantra is given to the disciple by an enlightened teacher, it becomes a living seed. The teacher, by his spiritual power, gives life to the word, and at the same time awakens the spiritual powers latent in the disciple. That is the secret of the teacher's initiation.

Just as a mantra is an aid to meditation, the worship of Kali, Durga, and other deities is also an aid to meditation. The latter is called worship of god through a pratika (symbol) or a pratima (image). Mind you, it is not the pratika or the pratima that is worshipped but the God represented by the pratika or the pratima.

These various forms of worship have been provided to suit the needs of different types of individuals at different stages of their spiritual evolution. This is similar to learning writing. The student first forms large letters before he can successfully try a smaller hand. So, too, a person must acquire the power of concentrating his thoughts by fixing the mind first upon Divine forms before he can succeed in fixing it upon the formless Divine.

Start today, right now! There is no moment more sacred or as auspicious as *now* for spiritual practice. Japa is an easy method for people like us kicked about and troubled by the worlds without and within.

A) Vedic mantras:

Tat twam asi—That thou art

Aham Brahmasmi—I am Brahman

Ayam Atma Brahma—This Self is Brahman

Sivoham Sivoham—I am Siva-auspiciousness

Tadeva Satyam tat Brahma—That alone is the Truth—That is Brahman

Anandoham Anandoham—I am Ananda, I am Bliss
Hamsa Soham Soham Hamsa—I am He, He is me; He is me, I am He.

Or

B) Puranic mantras:
Om Namo Narayanaya
Om Sri Rama Jaya Rama Jaya Jaya Rama
Om Namah Shivaya
Om Sri Shanmukhaya Namah
Om Sri Ramachandraya Namah
Om Sri Lakshmyai Namah

Any one of the above mantras can be taken up according to taste, faith and devotion for the purpose of regular, purposeful, intense chanting.

While doing japa, remember that even though the asana, the beads-rolling, the ishta devata and other such equipment for japa are external, japa in itself is a mental exercise and is to be raised to a still higher level. A mere rolling of the beads and non-stop verbal repetition does not constitute japa yoga. It should be an all-out intense and sincere effort on the part of the practitioner to apply all his mental and intellectual faculties—like emotion, discrimination, sensitiveness, will, logic, reason, sympathy, love, faith—to the 'mental chanting' of the sacred mantra, performed at the feet of the Lord's form, which is visualized steadily in the spiritual heart centre.

Initially, japa practice gives rise to a myriad unproductive thoughts. If the student is not diligent enough to detect this and arrest the flow of thoughts, it is possible that his japa will result in frustration and stupor. To begin with, this seemingly simple yoga should not be over-practised. Start with one mala of japa a day. Slowly raise the number of malas. You may start by increasing the number of malas at first on convenient holidays only, and when you are convinced of your mental capacity to sustain your inspired attention for the required period of time then alone should you take to long sittings at japa.

Another difficulty common to ninety per cent of practitioners, is an irresistible attack of sleepiness while doing japa and a shamelessly evident tendency to express bad temper soon after the japa sadhana. The seeker should not get annoyed with himself on observing this. He should learn to fight these tendencies patiently and overcome them.

Sleep comes because a mind in japa is a mind at rest. Train the mind not to sleep in the salubrious climate within. It is natural for children to sleep in a running car and the poor things gain no thrill from the trip. Bad temper comes because of two reasons—suppression of tendencies and fatigue. The former starts with the practitioner's annoyance at his mind's wandering during his japa. This is caused by exhaustion, because to hold the mind in balance in a given line of thought is a great strain for the beginner, and therefore, his mind gets fatigued.

A new driver at the wheel knows not how to relax, and thus, he unnecessarily exhausts himself before he has driven round the next corner of his own street; a novice in swimming will feel tired within a few yards; a young mother gets tired of looking after her first-born. Later on, the same woman easily manages her half a dozen, along with her late cousin's four little ones and yet, finds spare time and mental ease for her afternoon chats with the neighbours.

There is an art of economizing energy in work. Each activity requires its own special stamina. This is equally true in all spiritual activities called yogas. Stamina develops as a result of continuous methodical practice.

A japa practitioner's attempt is always to maintain his mind in one fixed line of divine thinking. To one who has gained a sufficient poise in this subjective art of single-pointedness achieved through the practice of contemplation, meditation comes naturally. Meditation itself is nothing but a conscious attempt to focus the mind on one channel of thought belonging to the same category. Japa is thus a very healthy and effective aid to meditation, if properly practised and regularly pursued.

Regularity and sincerity are the secrets of success in spirituality. Guard the mind against all excesses and make it immune to selfishness and passion. Watch how imperceptibly the mind ties itself down with things and beings, happenings and circumstances, by its own unintelligent attachments. Even when all these warnings are faithfully obeyed, there is still a subtle danger of the japa activity being muddled with our incorrigible thirst for fruits. The profit motive is the strongest urge in man in all his strenuous activities. Japa polluted by this profit motive (sa-kama) cannot end in spiritual effulgence.

Consider the japa activity as a yajna. Gather the purest and the best of yourself and offer it into the japa as devoted oblation. The potential strength of blessing that lies dormant in japa will thereby be invoked, and to one who is under its grace, meditation is home-coming, after a pleasant and joyous ride through sunny fields and flowery gardens.

The effectiveness of japa, to a large extent, depends upon the spirit of surrender with which the seeker practises it. This idea of surrender should not be merely emotional but must be based on deliberate and conscious understanding. When once we understand the principle behind the surrender we shall discover the bridge that connects the pasture lands of bhakti with the snowy peaks of jnana.

Let us, for example, take a typical mantra and try to discover the attitude of surrender implied in it—*Om Namo Narayanaya*: 'My prostrations unto Narayana'. Prostration is not merely a physical act. It is a conscious attempt at discovering the greater in us and seeking to identify with it. To tune ourselves to the better or the nobler, and thereby gather unto ourselves the very qualities and greatness of the Higher, is true prostration.

In order to prostrate there must be, at least, two factors: the lesser that prostrates and the Higher at whose feet the prostration is offered. Within each one of us there is the matter-conditioned ego and the unconditioned Eternal Self. The seeker is trying to end his false ego at the altar of Himself—the Supremely Divine Self, Sri Narayana. Thus, during the japa the individual practising it will be sincerely striving to surrender totally his personality to Narayana, who is his concept of the Reality.

Thus, a mantra is but a formula that explains to us at once not only what the enduring Truth in life is, but also the technique by which we can reach it. 'Om' is the symbol of the Infinite which is finally attained through the surrender (namah) of all our false identifications with the matter envelopments at the feet of 'the Core of things'—Narayana. When from ourselves our individual-personality-concept is removed we come to experience the *Narayana-tattwa* in ourselves which, being the same everywhere at all times, is Itself the experience of Om, the Brahman.

In fact, it is evident now that japa properly undertaken is not only a preparation for meditative flights but it can in itself serve as a vehicle which can lift us, from the pains and ugliness of our imperfections, to the very Throne of the Infinite, the Perfect.

May you come to realize the bliss of this supreme sadhana—the Japa Yoga.

~

TWENTY-ONE

THE GAYATRI MANTRA[*][†]

The Hindu belief that the Gayatri Mantra was first declared by the Creator Himself, at the very beginning of creation, may be considered an exaggeration, an unavoidable feature in many portions of Vedic literature. But it is a fact that even Western scholars, who are generally accepted as having a better historical sense, consider the Gayatri Mantra as being one of the oldest existing mantras. And, despite the many revolutionary changes that have taken place in our religious beliefs, this mantra continues to have a compelling charm of its own for millions of Hindus. It is not only believed, but it has been actually observed, that when this mantra is repeated with the right understanding of its sacred meaning, the ordinary negative tendencies in a human mind can be erased to a large extent.

The Gayatri is never chanted for purposes of material gain. It is an appeal to the pure consciousness to illumine our hearts—that is to say, it is a prayer to the Self to unveil Itself and to manifest as pure wisdom in our lives.

The Gayatri Mantra is also known as the Savitri Mantra. In ancient Vedic literature this mantra was referred to familiarly as the Savitri Mantra because it is dedicated to the deity called Savitr (the Sun). In some rare old books, it is also referred to as the Savitri-Gayatri. This

---

[*] From Swami Chinmayananda, *Tune in the Mind*, Central Chinmaya Mission Trust, Mumbai, second edition, 1986.

[†] The Gayatri Mantra is first found as the tenth mantra in the sixtieth sutra of the third mandala of the Rigveda.

only means that it is an invocation to the Sun, couched in the Vedic metre called the Gayatri. It is considered to be the most important mantra composed in this metre and, therefore, by tradition it has come to be known as the Gayatri.

The Gayatri metre is generally constituted of three lines of eight syllables each. The three lines of the Gayatri Savitri Mantra are as follows:

Om tat Savitur varenyam
Bhargo devasya dhimahi
Dhiyo yo nah prachodayat.

You will find in the above that the first line has only seven syllables. This is explained generally in two ways: the syllable 'nyam' is constituted of 'ni' plus 'am', and, therefore, they provide the required eight syllables in the line; that the line is to be read along with the Om-kara which would supply the missing syllable. The first is the idea of Sri Shankaracharya. In his commentary on the *Brihadaranyaka Upanishad*, Shankara splits the letter 'nyam' into its two component parts and considers that the rules of the metre are thereby fully obeyed.

The seer of the mantra is the royal sage Vishwamitra to whom all the mantras of the third mandala of the Rigveda are attributed. The Gayatri Mantra is also found in the *Shukla Yajurveda* and the *Krishna Yajurveda*. It is dedicated to Lord Savitr. That Savitr represents the Lord Sun is the accepted version, even though there are some scholars who protest against this. The Sun illumines the world and any prayer for light should certainly be addressed to the source of every light in the material world—the Sun. In the Gita, Lord Krishna says that the light that pervades the sun and the moon are all His light. Thus Savitr, the Lord of Gayatri, is nothing other than the light of consciousness, the Infinite, the Absolute.

The meaning of the mantra is as follows: 'We meditate upon the auspicious divine light of the Lord Sun. May that heavenly light illumine the thought-flow in our intellect.'

The usual prescribed daily worship (sandhya karma) of a Hindu mainly includes repetition of the Gayatri Mantra. The sandhya vandana or daily prayer is a purificatory act. It is a method of reintegrating the mind that runs wild during the day and drowns in total inertia at night.

In the *Manusmriti* we read: 'In the early dawn by doing this japa standing, one ends all sins committed during the night, and by doing this japa in the evening while sitting, one ends the sins committed during the day.' Sin here means, as everywhere else in our sacred books, the agitations created in our mental life by our own negative actions. Such actions leave impressions on the mind which, in turn, give rise to the tendency to repeat such actions.

Over a period of time, the importance of the Gayatri grew to its present status. Eventually, the belief that it cannot be chanted without the sacred thread became widespread. This belief is seldom met with in the ancient texts. When we chant this mantra in our daily worship it is with the *pranava* and the *vyahritis*. The *pranava* before the second line is optional.

Om bhur bhuvas svah
Om tat Savitur varenyam
Bhargo devasya dhimahi
Dhiyo yo nah prachodayat

There are two sandhyas in a day. The term 'sandhya' means the blending point of day and night. In the ancient literature no importance is given to midday worship. In Vedic literature, the Rishis insist only upon the morning and evening prayers. The midday prayer might have filtered into our tradition as a borrowing from Islam.

The best time for morning prayers is between 4.30 a.m. and 5.00 a.m. which is called the brahma muhurta; in the evening the sacred hour is between 6.00 p.m. and 7.00 p.m.

The *Manusmriti* (II:101) gives very clear directions for these prayers: 'After getting up from bed, after answering the calls of nature, purifying yourself completely, disallowing the mind to wander hither and thither, sincerely perform the morning japa standing on your feet and repeat the mantra very very slowly.' Elsewhere we also read: 'In the morning do the japa standing until the sun rises above the horizon. In the evening do your japa sitting until the stars emerge.'

In the ancient days, the daily worship was not as elaborate as it became after the days of the Sutras and Agamas. In the beginning the Veda advises us to sing the Gayatri Mantra both at dawn and at dusk, standing in the water facing the Sun—naturally in the morning the face will be turned eastward, and in the evening, westward. The one who chants the mantra must hold water in his cupped hands and at the end of each mantra-japa offer that water to the Lord. This is called the offering unto the Great Guest (arghya pradana). As this water in the cupped hands is offered, the devotee says: 'This Sun is Brahman' (asavadityo Brahma) and performs the atma pradakshina, turning around in a clockwise direction. This symbolizes the circumambulation of the Lord Sun, equated with the Brahman which is the Self in the worshipper.

The Gayatri is generally chanted a minimum of ten times at each sandhya. However, according to one's faith, convenience and devotion one can chant it any number of times in any sandhya. But never is this mantra chanted after sunset.

In the *Taittiriya Aranyaka** we have a glorious explanation of the

---

* The Aranyakas constitute the Upasana-Kanda of the Vedas—the portion that connects the purely ritualistic section called the Brahmanas with the essentially philosophic portion called the Upanishads.

reason for the daily chanting of the Gayatri and the offering of arghya to the Sun, in the form of a story. The story is a typical example of the Vedic style of mysticism. It has a deep significance in the context of our individual lives.

> On an island called Aruna there dwells a tribe of demons called Mandehas. Their native island is called Man-deha Arunam. These demons arrive every morning in hordes and conquer space, almost reaching the sun, and threatening to destroy Him. The water offered by those who recite the Gayatri becomes as powerful as lightning and strikes the demons who are then forced to retreat to their island. This happens daily.

This story makes as little sense to most people as the pages of a western music score make for me. But when the music score is translated by a musician into melody on musical instruments, the meaningless page becomes a stream of harmony and rhythm. Similarly, this story also needs to be interpreted.

Mind (*man*) and body (*deha*) are the sources of our activities (hence the name of the island, *man-deha*) and they, with their likes and dislikes, their emotions and appetites, evoke in us a host of animal instincts which try to conquer and destroy the spiritual essence—the Brahman, the Sun—in us. The essential brilliance of the human intellect thus gets clouded by the approaching host of such passions and the Gayatri japa has the same effect on them as thunder and lightning upon the demons.

Thousands of years after the Vedas, the authors of the Sutras started recommending more and more items to be incorporated in daily worship. The authors of the Agamas had their own contributions to make to the general form of our daily worship. The Agamas mainly describe the ritualistic regulations and rules for worshipping Vishnu, Siva and Shakti. Each Agama claimed the Gayatri as its own;

and they declared that the Gayatri is presided over by Vishnu, Siva or Shakti, according to the name of the Lord that is recommended by the different Agamas.

The Shaktas put forward the idea that Gayatri is the Infinite goddess and made her a feminine deity. Gayatri Devi soon became the Mother of the Vedas. Even today, it is believed by many Brahmins that if they have chanted the Gayatri, they have chanted the Vedas.

Very many interesting and irrational, though quite effective, beliefs have grown around the Gayatri Mantra and its efficacy. The chanting of the Gayatri Mantra is recommended for anyone frightened of the dark. It is believed to help such persons get over their nervousness and fright. If anyone becomes prostrate with illness as a result of such a fright, then Brahmin priests of true devotion and pure moral life are engaged to conduct a congregational japa by the bedside of the patient.* These beliefs only prove that the very name of the mantra is fully justified. The term Gayatri itself means 'that mantra which protects him who chants it' (*gayatam trayate iti gayatri*).

It is also believed in India that when commencing any important work, if a person detects some bad omen, he must immediately sit down and chant the Gayatri eleven times. If, on resuming his work, he meets with a new set of bad omens he must sit down again and chant the Gayatri sixteen times. This will remove the effects of the bad omen encountered. This is yet another popular belief.

In India a Hindu boy is initiated into the Gayatri Mantra very early in life. This happens during the social ritual called the upanayana, presided over by the head of the family and the family priest. In Vedic literature there is reference to the Gayatri diksha. The term 'diksha' means a discipline which one must undergo in order to

---

* I personally do not believe in these but I am reporting here that those who suffer from such mental weaknesses can find consolation and remedy by repeating the Gayatri Mantra.

become fit for taking part in any Vedic ritual. The word 'upanayana' signifies 'bringing nearer', that is, bringing near a preceptor who initiates the boy by giving him the sacred Gayatri Mantra. It is interesting to note that the age at which boys are to be initiated is clearly indicated. Manu recommends the age of five for a Brahmin, six for a Kshatriya, and eight for a Vaishya. The maximum ages at which initiation may be given are sixteen, twenty-two and twenty-four respectively.

This initiation is glorified in Vedic literature where the Gayatri diksha is equated to a second birth, since this ritual signifies a transformation in the subtle life of a boy:

> The father and mother have given birth to him from mutual desire, so that he is born from the womb; let this be known as his physical birth. But that birth which is given, according to the ordinance, through the Savitri, by the Preceptor who has mastered the Vedas, that is the true birth, the unaging and immortal. (*Manusmriti* II:147–48)

After this initiation the boy is referred to as a dvija (twice-born).

In ancient days women used to chant the Gayatri as freely as men, so says Manu. They also used to learn and teach the Vedas and have their upanayana performed. Thus the Shastra injunctions and our personal observations take us to the conclusion that women too can, rather should, chant the Gayatri Mantra regularly in their morning and evening worship. In fact, there are repeated declarations in the Hindu sacred books that if the effects of the sadhana performed by men are their own, the spiritual benefits acquired by the womenfolk are shared by their husbands, children, their families and the entire society.

The deeper philosophical import of the Gayatri is very clear. The mantra as it stands is obviously an invocation to the Lord Sun to illumine the intellect of the seeker. The sunlight cannot, it is certain, illumine the intellect in us: the white and grey matter of the brain!

In our inner life the Sun represents the light-giver, the illuminator of all experiences, the Atman. This pure consciousness in us, the inner centre of our personality, around which the matter envelopments function with mathematical precision, is similar to the sun, the centre of the universe, around which the entire solar system revolves: each planet and star at its appointed speed, along its appointed path. Hence it is this pure consciousness in us that is being invoked to shine more and more in our intellect.

If the sun were not there, life would be impossible. Similarly, without the Atman the matter envelopments that constitute our personalities would be inert. When this inner sun-of-life is appealed to for a better illumination of the intellect, it reads as an absurd paradox. The infinite light of wisdom, the Supreme Self, is never contaminated in its eternal effulgence. It is ever the same. Its intensity cannot increase or decrease. Therefore, all that the devotee means is:

> May my intellect be steady without agitation. May it be clean without the dirt of passions. May the light of consciousness come to shine forth a brilliant beam of its radiance through my intellect. Thus may my perception of the world be clear, my discrimination subtle, my judgements correct and quick, and my comprehension of situations and beings precise and wise.

TWENTY-TWO

PURIFYING THE MIND[*]

The physical postures one adopts can generate a corresponding attitude of mind. Look in the mirror while keeping your face contorted in a sorrowful expression. Maintain it for two or three minutes: now watch your mind. Is it not feeling despondent, miserable, dejected? Again, look in the mirror and smile happily. After a minute, watch and discover that the mind has caught the cheer and ripples of joy.

Based upon this psychology, the physical movements in ritualism, the devotee's love-play with the Lord's idol have all been prescribed. They are there to help bring into expression the correct attitude of mind (bhavna)—the goal of all spiritual practice (sadhana).

The feeling of freshness after a bath, the special loose dress of silk for prayer, the reserved prayer-corner, the burning of sweet-scented incense, the sandalwood paste on the forehead, the luminous lamps, the decorated altar of the Lord, pleasant music, soothing instruments of accompaniment, the hymns sung, the mantras chanted, the flowers—all these are meant to create a conducive external atmosphere which in turn inspires the required mental bhavna.

A true seeker takes the help of all these in the beginning. He learns to capture the divinely devoted poise of the mind and later plunges into meditation. Many a time the sadhak (spiritual seeker)

---

[*] An extract from Swami Chinmayananda, *We Must . . . (Notes on Self-improvement)*, Central Chinmaya Mission Trust, Mumbai (reprint, 1990).

is rewarded with at least a passing mood of tranquillity, peace and joy. But very often it is whimsical, unpredictable and totally uncertain. When his sadhana is not rewarding, the new initiate becomes weary and frequently leaves it in shuddering disgust.

We generally do not have the patience to inquire why we fail: nor do we have the minimum sense of justice to believe that the scriptures and the repeated assertions of the Rishis cannot all be sheer bluff, a meaningless deception. In a hurry, we are apt to condemn them all and reject them totally, thus exiling ourselves from the exalted ecstasy of successful meditation.

Let us remember that the mental attitude of meditation is not invoked by a mechanical readjustment gained in haste during an evening's 'half an hour'. The meditative mood is to be zealously worked for and earned by each seeker during his entire day's activities. Unless we discriminate and live intelligently almost all the twenty-three and a half hours of the day, we cannot expect even half an hour's meditative mood.

We *must* live honourably and act in a straightforward manner, without tragically compromising our noble convictions and higher ideals. We *must* live in self-respect, refusing to insult ourselves even the least bit. Let us always have a well-guarded personal dignity about ourselves in all our transactions with the world. If our attitude is optimistic, cheerful, heroic, it will flash forth in the very way we stand, sit or walk. But to maintain such a healthy attitude may not always be easy for the beginner. We need not despair. Try, and try again. We can cultivate this ... *We must.*

Just as our state of mind reflects upon our actions, so too can our physical attitude and behaviour, in turn, induce the right mental mood in us. Of the two, strengthening the right physical habits is easier. Thereafter, training the mind becomes simpler and surer. Ultimately the mind is to be tamed and subdued. Conquer it! We *must.*

Therefore, let our physical habits of standing and sitting erect at all times begin to bear their influence upon the mind. Frequently watch and deliberately straighten the backbone. Let us deny ourselves the tendency to lounge and relax in torpid idleness. When our body is erect, our organs perform their physiological functions more efficiently. Let us carry our head erect, shoulders well pushed back, chest always high and let us consciously breathe deeply.

Similarly, glowing, optimistic thoughts, heroic and divine ideals have a powerful and uplifting effect upon the body. Hopeful plans and programmes lend a spring to our strides and attractive buoyancy to our dashing forward into our daily fields of honest labour.

One who thus lives well and full, doing his duties thoroughly, and singing in his heart ever with steady devotion for the Lord, cannot be but an attractive personality—irresistibly magnetic to all others who are miserable, negative and deplorably pessimistic. Such are the people amidst whom a spiritual missionary has to work continuously; but the work is half done when you have charmed them with your sprightliness, when you have given them a new heart with which to live and strive by your joyous optimism and lively cheer.

We *must* learn to discipline ourselves to become such effective servants of the community. And here, not only will we serve more dynamically, but each evening we will experience an effortless gliding into an easy meditative mood at our individual meditation.

If at all we fail in our attempts in meditation, the reason is our own sleepy life, loose living and cheerless attitude during the whole day. Shall we waste a life in the futility of indolence, in the arrogance of hypocrisy, or, shall we peep into our glorious being through the purity of our sincerity and the earnestness of our dedications?

Pure, *we must be,*
Sincere, *we must become,*

Earnestness, *we must befriend*,
Dedicated living, *we must bequeath*,
Joyous living *we must behold*, when we live in
and for the Beloved alone.

VI

VALUES TO LIVE BY

Moral or ethical values are lived so as to stop all unnecessary mental dissipation and thereby to conserve these lavishly squandered mental energies. This inner vitality is the true wealth, Lakshmi. Without this vibrant inner mental stamina you can never achieve anything spectacular either in your outer worldly life or in your inner spiritual world.

—Swami Chinmayananda

~

STANDARDS FOR INSPIRED LIVING[*]

Service (Nishkama Karma)

The Upanishads glorify service as the highest pinnacle of right living. Dedicated and noble work alone can polish an individual to a state of true culture and right discipline. To those who know what service is, work is neither slavery nor drudgery, it is the joy of life. Man is not born to revel in idleness. Nature will whip the idle on to the road of right or wrong activity. Right activity will help him evolve steadily to a state of joy characterized by dynamic outer activity and inner calm and peace.

Vedanta has never permitted escapism, though many uninformed people contend that it does. The earliest Upanishads emphasize that one who cannot live the noble life of renunciation and self-restraint must unavoidably and honestly live a life of intense activity. This implies striving to fulfil one's desires through honest means, teaching oneself to live in cheerful enthusiasm all one's life in the service of man and in the glorification of the Lord.

To one who plunges intensively into life—eager and anxious to daily meet its new challenges, with truth and purity as the standards—actions do not cling. Living an entire lifetime in a spirit of paying homage to the Lord, detached from the anxiety for the fruit of

---

[*] From *The Choice is Yours (Ethics in Vedanta)*, Central Chinmaya Mission Trust, Mumbai (reprint, 1991).

actions and from the ego-sense, is the path lauded both by the Bhagavad Gita and the Upanishads. Such actions are not barriers to spiritual progress: in fact, they are necessary to prepare a student for the highest flights in meditation. To a seeker, dedicated work is a means for the inner purification of his vasanas.

The goal is Self-realization, which is experienced as perfect 'inactivity' and realized through the path of renunciation—the stages of progress from 'animal-man' to 'God-man' are through an intermediary stage called 'man-man'. The animal-man revels in inactivity (tamas), until he evolves to the state of man-man through an intensely active, desire-motivated (rajas) programme of action (sakama karma). Then, through a subtle life of activity that is pursued without motive or desire (nishkama karma), selfish work fulfils itself in selfless work, and selfless work accomplishes its goal of purifying the mind and intellect. Thereafter, the individual gains initiation into the path of meditation.

All activities, whether social, economic, political or domestic, when pursued with an attitude of detachment, can never bind the actor by their results. Results can cling to the doer only when he acts with expectation of and attachment to definite results. The seeker should, therefore, function purely in a spirit of work for work's sake.

Spirit of Sacrifice (Yajna)

'The world is bound by actions other than those performed for the sake of sacrifice. Do thou, therefore, O son of Kunti, perform action for that sake alone, free from all attachments' (Bhagavad Gita, III:9).

Everywhere around us, from the twinkling stars to the flowing rivers, nature serves the world in the yajna spirit of sacrifice. The sun shines, but demands no appreciation from anyone. Rains fall, rivers flow, plants flower, trees bear fruit—all serve the world in order to make it what it is, and yet none demand even a passing recognition from the people and creatures benefited by them. They all perform their duties, as though showing us how to attain fulfilment in their very performance.

The whole world, of cosmic powers and natural phenomena, functions instinctively in the service of others. Even before life appeared on the face of the earth, the elemental forces had prepared the field through their constant activities. In the development and evolution of nature, one easily recognizes different degrees of yajna activities, which maintain the harmonious existence of living beings.

This 'law of seva' is instinctively followed by every sentient and insentient member of the cosmos. Man alone is given the freedom to act as he likes. To the extent he disobeys this universal law of sacrifice, he suffers, because, with his arrogant and egotistic actions, he brings discord to the harmony around him. But when individuals in a community cooperatively strive, without ego or egocentric desires, the cosmic forces that constitute the environment cherish them in return. In short, when man works with the yajna spirit, the outer circumstances miraculously change their pattern to become conducive to the common will of the community that strives for the good of all.

This law of seva was set in motion by nature at the beginning of creation: in short, it is a natural law. One who understands nature's laws and lives in harmony with them will be benefited by nature. The more we seek and probe into the secrets of nature, the more nature reveals her laws, and by obeying them, we increase our harmonious existence with the phenomenal world. The concept of yajna stems from the recognition of the one supreme Divinity that is at once the core of all and yet transcends the universe of names and forms. All are but the one infinite Self—Brahman. This perception of the play of the one Self, both as matter and spirit— both as ourselves and the world around us—is the true vision of the Lord of the Universe. By dedicating ourselves to the service of the nation, the community, the home, and the individuals around us, we are dedicating ourselves to the one infinite Self, who expresses through all. Thus, by seeing Brahman everywhere and His play in all activities, the devoted seeker is never bound by the results of his actions, but he attains the intimate inner experience of the Self divine.

Honesty (Satyam)

Honesty is the spirit governing our inner intellectual world. After we gain experiences in the outer world and assimilate them in our mind, we must digest them with our intellect to convert them into a resolve or conclusion. We must then have the honesty of intellectual conviction to act in accordance with the conclusions we have reached. This quality of the mind is called satyam. However, many of us do not live up to our convictions and, as a result, we suffer. Religion, by advocating the principle 'Be truthful to your wisdom', insists that we constantly and consistently exercise our intellect to guide our actions in perfect harmony with our conscience.

In fact, honesty is not merely expressing our true feelings, in its deeper import, it is the attunement of our intentions with our convictions. If we lack the moral courage to express what we sincerely feel, we cannot live a life of truthfulness. A disparity will be created between thought and word, and the mind will form a habit of doubting and negating its thoughts. This self-doubt depletes our confidence, mental strength, will power and poise.

Unless we are ready to discipline our thoughts according to our reason, chastened by knowledge, we cannot grow to realize the full potential of our true and divine nature. A spiritual seeker must be totally honest, even suicidally honest, for only then does the mind become taintless and free of fear and conflict.

Non-injury (Ahimsa)

Non-injury (ahimsa) in its spiritual import means never having cruel intentions. Non-injury is the attitude that should dominate all our motives. Our intentions should not be polluted by even a trace of cruelty or hatred. Harmlessness consists not so much in never causing physical injury to any being, as in never contemplating harm to any living creature. Physically, non-injury is impossible. To continue living, some kind of physical harm is unavoidable. But even while bringing about unavoidable disturbances around ourselves, if our motives are pure and clean, the harm so brought about is not regarded as injury.

If you protect yourself against a robber in your own home or protest against aggressors, you are not transgressing ahimsa. To kill a serpent or a scorpion in your house is not an act of cruelty. On the contrary, to allow them to flourish in the name of non-violence is weakness, sanctioned only by a misinterpreted culture.

Thus, non injury is a value of life to be applied at the level of our motives. Our motives must be non-injurious and pure. This purity of intention can arise only out of a deep sense of oneness with the Lord's creation and compassion towards all beings, good and bad.

Charity (Dana)

Charity (dana) comes from an inner sense of abundance. The desire to give in charity springs from a sense of oneness in us—oneness between the giver and the recipient. Unless one is able to identify oneself with others, one will not have this noble urge to share all that one has with others who have not as much. Charity is born out of an ability to sublimate one's instincts of acquisition and aggrandizement and to replace them with the spirit of sacrifice.

Giving in charity can create feelings of egotism and vanity unless we give with modesty and humility, ever remembering Him who has given us whatever we have. Many may have the intellectual vision to judge the cause they espouse, the large-heartedness to give in plenty and with appropriate modesty, yet they may not have that element of love which is necessary to feel a deep sympathy with the cause they patronize. To give without sympathy is as futile as building a temple without an idol.

Sympathy generates love in us, and unless this love-element dominates us, compelling us to identify with the cause, we will not spiritually evolve into charitable beings. Charity, honeyed with the spirit of love and the joy of identification, blesses the giver with an inner abundance far outweighing that which was given.

Fortitude (Dhriti)

Fortitude (dhriti) is not merely the ability to live patiently through minor physical or mental inconveniences; it is a subtle boldness that is displayed by a person while facing adversity.

When an individual daringly confronts life, he cannot always expect happy situations, favourable circumstances, and conducive opportunities. When encountering opposition, many a weak individual feels dejected and is tempted to leave the field of work when it is only half done. Many lose their chance of achieving their goal and desert the field of action almost at the moment when victory is imminent.

In order to stick to our convictions, we need a spiritual energy to nurture and nourish our fatigued morale. This inner energy welling up in a well-integrated personality is called fortitude. The strength of faith, conviction in the goal, consistency of purpose, vivid perception of the ideal, and a bold spirit of sacrifice cultivated diligently form the source from which springs the fortitude to remove our exhaustion and despair.

Harmony (Ekabhava)

In nature nothing is disharmonious. The sun and the moon, the seasons, the plants and the animals exist and function in perfect rhythm. It is only in human relationships that one finds bitterness and sorrow. Man alone suffers, not the world of nature. Respect and consideration between individuals must be developed in order to bring about harmony in human relationships.

Without a sense of harmony with others (ekabhava), man suffers from pangs of separateness that condemn him to a life of loneliness. He becomes afraid, afraid of himself, afraid of others. This sense of separateness creates a thousand anxieties and sorrows. These in turn, drive an individual to be selfish, cruel, angry, and even criminal. Love alone is the answer to this general problem of human suffering.

All of humanity asks the same questions: How do we end the sense of separateness and rediscover oneness in love? How can we learn to rise above our sense of limitation and fear? How can we discover our oneness with the world around us? This demand for harmony is in all and has existed in all periods of history, in all cultures, races, and countries.

Having carefully analysed our human weaknesses, the saints and sages advise us to grow in love and gain mastery over our challenges by rising above our limited, egocentric view of life and by exercising a constant awareness of the totality of the world, the entirety of mankind, and the vastness of universal problems. When this total perception is developed, our individual problems pale into insignificance.

When we view our problems from a purely egocentric angle without this vision of totality, the problems assume exaggerated proportions, crushing us down. To live a life of harmony is to recognize ourselves as members of an interdependent humanity, living in a composite universe. It is to merge our life with the resonant cadence of the whole and to bring about a beautiful melody of harmonious existence.

This principle of living in harmony with the external world is not to be construed as a life of idle acceptance or unintelligent surrender to the challenges confronting us. The harmony envisaged by the great religious masters is based on an awareness of the oneness of the dynamic life principle that is the Essence of the universe. This art of practising harmony is to be applied in the din of the marketplace while we sweat with exertion upon the narrow path of adversities. Living in harmony with the conditions around us brings to our heart an inward peace and poise. When we maintain poise, problems and challenges vanish like mist before the rising sun.

Man has to be delivered from his own misconception of himself. When he develops respect for the divinity in him, he develops a sense of holiness, and his reverence towards other human beings increases. Then alone can all economic, political and social disturbances end. Religion or philosophy, whether reached through the church, mosque or temple, cultivates in man this self-reverence. The seeker is taught to perceive a greater Reality, a greater and more divine Presence in one and all.

TWENTY-FOUR

LOVE IN ACTION[*]

To give is any day nobler than to receive, and this is specially true in regard to love. When someone gives us their love it seems like the Lord is smiling upon us, and we are thankful for the love received. But our attitude throughout life should be to give love to all creation. This is the greatest worship we can offer Him.

Some people believe that to the extent that they give love they will be depleted, and therefore withhold their love. They do not understand that nothing else can enrich life as much as giving love. All other glories fade away, but the divinely sweet beauty of love given and tenderness shared remains untarnished under all circumstances. Neither can adversity dim its brilliance nor age destroy its beauty.

Unintelligent people refuse to give love. To all intelligent people of dynamic character, however, the word 'giving' has a different meaning, and every one of these actions provides them with more inspiration. To give is to them an expression of their creativity and mastery of their strength, power, wealth and efficiency. It is the very inspiration in their living, the very breath of their existence. To such people giving love is the noblest expression of their own personality. In the act of giving they experience true joy and complete self-fulfilment.

---

[*]   From *The Path of Love*, The Mananam Series, Chinmaya Mission West, Piercy, California, 1995.

To give love is to expand. Then the lover functions from two centres: from within himself, and from the beloved, a centre outside himself. Thus, the happiness of a true giver of love increases, and his sense of loneliness departs. For, when we give love to all we not only lose our sense of separateness, but we feel good that we are making the world indebted to us, rather than getting ourselves indebted to the world. We are the givers of love, the creditors; the creatures around us are the recipients, the debtors. To receive love is to be forever indebted to the world.

This 'giving of love' must be a natural outpouring, as natural as the song of birds in springtime, or the moonlight comforting the earth, or a mother giving her milk to her child. Our outpouring of love must be a natural, effortless, joyous giving unto the world around us.

The poor cannot give because they have nothing to give. But one who is wealthy and still does not give because of his attachments is also poor. One who has love and does not give it, but demands more love from others can never be rich. He is a 'miser' (kripanah), as the term is used in the Gita and the Upanishads.

When I say 'give', I do not mean wealth or physical strength or power. If we have enough wealth, physical strength or power, we must also give these as an expression of our love, but to give love is to give a part of our own life, to share our joy, knowledge and courage.

This giving is not to be polluted by the vaguest trace of expectation to receive anything in return. Here the giving of love, in itself, is its own reward and happiness. The spontaneity of such happiness enhances the intensity and depth of satisfaction in it.

Such a dynamic expression of love transforms both the giver and the receiver. Give freely and amply of yourself. Imitate the splendour of a solitary flower sweetening the neighbourhood even if it blossoms on a lonely peak!

In such a lavish giving of love the fusion of ourselves with the world can take place, and through this self-unfoldment our sense of separateness ends. Herein lies the wondrous joy of a total freedom from loneliness, fear, anxiety and mental depression.

Remember, even a little giving of oneself is an expression of true love. The mother's love for the child, the child's love for its parents, a person's love for his country or community, and a devotee's love for the Lord are all expressed in self-sacrifice.

If we have not cultivated these capacities we can never be successful in love. We often hear people complain: 'I did so much for him—I fed him, clothed him, protected him—yet, he has no love for me now.' It is indeed one of the most painful of worldly experiences if our friends and relatives do not reciprocate or appreciate our love. But the cause is mainly in ourselves, as we have not given our love freely enough.

The Dynamic Elements of Love

In all forms of love there are some fundamental factors besides the act of giving. These dynamic elements must always be in the heart of the lover. Otherwise, the love manifested is false: it will only be an illusion of love. Such impotent love cannot produce any blessings, neither for the giver nor for the recipient. There are four factors that go into the constitution of love and they form the basis for enduring and productive love: a sincere concern for the beloved; a sense of deep response; an ardent attitude of reverence; and a complete understanding of the beloved.

These four factors are always valid, whether our love is for the world or is turned towards the Lord of the Universe. Sometimes we sincerely believe that we have given love, but we fail to feel the exhilarating joy promised by the great masters. Then we feel extremely disappointed and think that we have been cheated.

But a sufficient quantity of sincere love, when given unreservedly, can never go unrewarded. Where Godlike love is given, joy must follow. We can develop and direct the outward flow of love from ourselves by being mindful of all these above-mentioned basic factors. When they are present, our love is complete, potent, and sincere. Let us now examine each of these.

Sincere Concern

A sincere concern for the well-being of the beloved is the first essential factor of love. A mother who loves her children is always anxious for their happiness. Similarly, if one loves flowers, a pet, or one's country, then one will also be greatly concerned for their well-being.

If, for example, we claim to love our plants but we forget to water them, then it is not true love. We cannot claim to love animals and then mistreat them, or say that we love our parents and then be insensitive to their needs. When love exists, we become immediately and automatically anxious for the happiness of the beloved. In the happiness of the beloved we feel extremely happy, and to a true lover no sacrifice is too great if it is in the best interest of the beloved.

A true lover of one's country will suffer, go to war, or live in poverty if that brings prosperity and glory to his or her country. Where there is true love, the lover is never tired of working for and serving the beloved. A loving teacher never tires of teaching. A loving mother never gets tired of working for her children. A sincere lover of the nation serves the cause of the country day and night. Love and action go hand in hand. One readily strives for that which one loves. And one really loves that for which one labours wholeheartedly. Where there is love, labour becomes a joy.

Therefore, when you love, always be ready to serve the beloved, and work for the beloved's cause. Merely saying 'I love', is not sufficient, we must express our love in action. That is much more noble, compelling and dynamic. Let your hands and legs serve, but do not speak about love. Flood the atmosphere with your heartfelt love. You will then be creating an enchanting magic around you causing everyone to love you.

Deep Response

Secondly, the lover will always have a sense of deep response to the beloved. When one is sincerely concerned for the beloved, the ability to respond readily to his or her needs and feelings will rise in the lover's mind. This 'ability to respond' is the true meaning of the word responsi(a)bility. However, this term is often misunderstood as some burdensome duty being imposed upon us by some power outside ourselves. But as we grow and expand in love we become more sensitive to the silent needs of others. Trying to satisfy their needs becomes a lover's ecstatic passion.

This is most conspicuously seen in a mother. Her love for her children is immeasurable. She is so in tune with them that even when they are far away she knows intuitively when they are not well. This is known as 'telepathy' in psychology. This secret ability to respond with sympathy to the beloved always exists in the heart of a true lover. This is true when there is deep and sincere love, otherwise we only think of our own selfish wishes. Give love, and be sensitive in your heart to the unspoken wishes of the beloved. You will find that this actually happens many times a day. These instances not only surprise you, but they especially thrill the beloved. Each time it happens, there will be an explosion of joy in the hearts of the lover and the beloved.

Leaders become popular, businessmen become more successful, people become great, all because of an instinctive ability to tune into the needs of others. In all such cases they have an intense love for others or their work.

These are two of the four basic factors behind love. One cannot exist without the other. They are both intimately connected with each other. Without 'a sense of deep response' to the beloved, we can never have 'sincere concern' for him/her.

Attitude of Reverence

The divine faculty of effortlessly knowing the feelings and needs of others can never be generated in full measure unless we have the third factor of true love: an ardent attitude of reverence.

We generally meet the world from the surface of our personality and not from its depth, hence, we can contact others only at the superficial level. But, if we delve deeper into our inner nature, we can establish contact with others also at that level. For example, with our eyes we see others, with our hands we physically touch them, but only from our hearts can we touch the hearts of others and evoke their empathy and compassion. With our thoughts we can kindle new thoughts in others and therein unveil new understanding. Thus, to contact the depth in others we must learn to express love from the deeper depths within ourselves.

Reverence is not merely an emotion of love from the heart, or respect due to an intellectual understanding. We can love without respect and we can also respect without loving. We can love chocolate without understanding its ingredients or how it is made. We may understand science and therefore we respect scientists, but that does not necessarily mean that we love every scientist.

The feeling that is generated when a sense of love from the mind and respect from the intellect merge at one and the same altar is called 'reverence'. This can take place only with an integrated mind and intellect.

Our love for others becomes potent when we have a deep sense of reverence for life and all living creatures. Our loving approaches will certainly be rebuked if we have no respect for others. Loving the world without reverence for life and people is like a beautiful curry, well cooked and nicely served but without salt!

Of the factors in reverence, the love aspect is commonly known to us. We tend to misinterpret the word 'respect', however, attaching to it a feeling mingled with fear and awe, thereby distancing ourselves from the object of our reverence. This is not correct, as the root from which the word 'respect' comes is *respicere* meaning 'to look at'. To respect people means to *recognize* them as they are. To show respect is to help them grow and unfold themselves, in themselves, by themselves. Parents should respect their children, and teachers must have respect for their students.

Our relationships often lack true respect because what we call love is an attempt to make use of the beloved for our own purposes. Thus, we try to make them conform to the way we want them to be. This is not love. A true lover sees the beloved with perfect objectivity, and without interfering with the personality of the beloved, blesses him or her to grow and unfold. Thus, pure love has a revitalizing effect upon others. In the presence of such a truly loving person, others grow and expand into a healthier state of being. Without deep reverence for the beloved such a refreshing stream of love cannot flow from the heart of the lover.

Most of us need help to function efficiently as a psychological entity. Rarely, if ever, are we free in our mental life. We need sympathy, applause, acceptance and kindness from others to support our individuality, our ego. In short, we want to be loved by others.

To give love we must become independent in ourselves and be a pillar for others to hold on to. Only one who needs no crutches for his own existence has the power to give love. All others are receivers of love. One who has such an inner strength of personality and a deep reverence for life and people comes to give love, and thereby transforms the world of creatures in his orbit. He becomes an island of peace and contentment in the stormy life of turbulent fears and shattering confusion around him.

Inner Expansion

The ardent attitude of reverence can arise only where there is full understanding. Therefore, the fourth basic factor in love is 'a complete understanding of the beloved'. Without reverence the response will not be satisfactory, and where there is no ability to respond there can be no deep concern for the beloved. Concern for, and response and reverence to the beloved can only be true if they flow from a firm and sure understanding of the loved object or being.

In *Narada Bhakti Sutra*, the means for developing divine love have been described. Sutra 28, the very first sutra in this discussion says, 'Some say understanding alone is the means.' This is true. Without a general knowledge of the object of our love we cannot feel love. With deeper understanding, our love also expands. Superficial knowledge is not sufficient. What is necessary is an understanding that pierces through the outer layers and penetrates into the core of the beloved's personality. Only this kind of understanding assures a steady reverence, quick response, and a real concern for the 'object' of our love.

To pierce into the depth of another, we must lose our selfishness and learn to be one with the beloved—be it a community, nation or the world. As long as we remain overly concerned with our own physical comforts we can never effectively give love. We need to expand into the greater and nobler spiritual dimensions within ourselves. In this inner expansion alone can the sense of separateness with its suffocating sorrows, fears and anxieties end.

The analytical methods of modern physiology and psychology cannot reach these depths. They are not capable of unravelling the mystery of man's personality. Using these methods we understand each other with physical, mental and intellectual information based on perceptions which are largely vague and erroneous. To reach the depths of our being, love alone is the means, the path. It alone has the necessary penetration to reach the required depth to discover the real Essence—the one infinite Self—in ourselves and others.

Until we discover this spiritual centre in ourselves, the God in us, we will be confused and disturbed, an enigma to ourselves and to others. From the Self alone all is known in its entirety, and it is only with reference to It that we can correctly perceive the relative positions of all other factors in our personality. This understanding can come to us only through the words of the great Rishis and by consistently applying and developing our present ability to love others.

Without love we make a hell of this world: with true love this world becomes a heaven. To give love we must have the rich treasure of all these four fundamental factors of love. Ultimately true love helps my understanding of myself and the world around me. The Self in me is the Self everywhere.

~

TWENTY-FIVE

RIGHT AND WRONG ACTIONS[*]

Action by itself is beyond good and bad. It is the attitude and the intention with which we act that really matter. Actions that do not cause regret in us and help us to integrate our personality are considered good actions—punya. Those that leave a sense of guilt or regret in our bosom, that weigh heavily on our conscience and disintegrate our personality are considered sinful actions—papa.

The ancient seers classified these constructive and destructive actions as karmas and vikarmas, respectively. Karmas are all actions that are enjoined in the scriptures, that are noble, and that should be pursued as our dignified duty in life. The constructive activities are of three kinds: nitya karmas, daily duties; naimittika karmas, special duties prescribed for certain occasions; and kamya karmas, purposeful and self-determined work done for attaining a desirable result.

Vikarma refers to those actions that are destructive and therefore forbidden by the Vedic scriptures. These actions, called nisidha karmas, spring from our lower urges and demean our evolutionary status and cultural dignity. They are self-insulting actions, prompted by our ego and its passions.

In addition to karma and vikarma, a third category exists: akarma, or inaction. The scriptures explain that men of realization live in this state, having risen above identification with the body, mind and

---

[*] From *The Choice is Yours (Ethics in Vedanta)*, Central Chinmaya Mission Trust, Mumbai (reprint, 1991).

intellect and thus above the notion of action, whether good or bad. Seekers, in their over-zealousness, often make the error of attempting to adopt inaction as a path. In the Bhagavad Gita, Arjuna entreats Lord Krishna to allow him to pursue the path of inaction. Lord Krishna vehemently rejects inactivity (akarma) and states: 'Perform your bounden duty, for action is superior to inaction. Even the maintenance of the body would not be possible for you by inaction' (III:8).

To sit back physically retired is not the way to reach any goal, much less the state of Perfection. If physical retirement is not accompanied by an equal amount of mental withdrawal from the world of desires, the spiritual future of that seeker is sure to be bleak and dreary, tarnished by mental repressions. The Vedantic scriptures, though describing a goal of 'inaction', insist that we perform actions that are obligatory to our present social status, to our domestic situation, and to the members of our community and the nation. Not to perform diligently all our duties would be inaction. Inactivity brings about the destruction of not only the nation, the society, and the home but of the individual himself, as he becomes victimized by his own idleness and suffers intellectual and psychological deterioration. Even a healthy bodily existence is not possible for one who lives in complete inertia and inactivity.

Thus, a life of dynamic action is always superior to a passive life of slothful inaction. Waste not your time. Never run away from material or personal problems. Sometimes they may attack in hosts, and you may feel incapable of coping with them. Never mind. With faith in yourself and in your ideal, act diligently. A new force, a fresh stream of strength will reach you as though from above, and you will find at the end of the play, won or lost, that you have grown stronger, healthier and mightier. Never fear, never hesitate. Act nobly: act with a will to maintain your ideal. To face problems dynamically and to act diligently are any day more noble than escaping passively from the problems and retreating into a hole of bitterness, self-reproach and self-condemnation.

Not only is an active life of courage and strength good for our inner development, it is essential even for the healthy maintenance of the body. Sunlight, hard work, good exercise all bring a glow of vitality and beauty to the physical body.

Obligatory Actions

Though all these facts may be appreciated, a seeker may still entertain serious doubts as to what kind of work he should undertake. Earlier, we found that all activities in the world can be analysed and classified into four categories. Of these four, actions that are repugnant to the dignity of man and therefore condemned by the scriptures and actions that are utterly selfish are to be totally eschewed by one pursuing a creative life of spiritual living and self-unfoldment.

The remaining two categories, namely the daily duties and the special duties that arise in life together become our obligatory duties, called by the Rishis as niyata karmas. Thus, niyata karma includes both our nitya karmas and our naimittika karmas. The obligatory duties in life include our daily duties, such as entertaining guests, attending marriages, serving in the military and so forth.

People should willingly perform all their obligatory duties. We do not live alone; we are social beings; we live in an interrelated society. Therefore, we have duties not only to ourselves, but we have a widening field of duties towards the world around us. Let us try to fulfil all our obligatory duties as best as we can, with a spirit of detachment, joy and dedication. The more we work with this attitude, the more we are released from our inhibitions, repressions and other emotional entanglements. Mental confusion is swept away, and we enter into a new life of alertness, productive exertion and blissful satisfaction.

True Renunciation

The nature of our duties is determined by the nature of our birth. Each one of us is born with different characteristics and in different environments, and our duties in life differ accordingly. Often we are tempted to run away from our given duties, saying that we are mistakenly placed in the situation. Such a notion may arise in the minds of the students of Vedanta in the initial stages. But environments are not thrust upon us by blind fate. Our inner personality determines and orders our environment. Each one of us is born into a status ordered by our vasanas, and the circumstances around are the exact situations necessary for the exhaustion of those vasanas. Lord Krishna reprimands Arjuna for even considering leaving his field of action thus: 'Verily, the renunciation of obligatory actions is not proper; their abandonment out of delusion is declared to be tamasic' (Bhagavad Gita, XVIII:7).

Abandonment (tyaga) of obligatory duties is considered by Lord Krishna as the lowest and basest of actions. Each individual has obligations towards himself and towards others in society. As long as an individual is a member of society, enjoying a social life and demanding protection and profit from society, he has no right to abandon his obligatory duties.

There are some who give up their duties because of the pain such duties might bring or through fear of bodily suffering. This kind of abandonment falls under the rajasic type, according to Lord Krishna, who explains thus: 'He who abandons action from fear of bodily trouble or because it is painful performs a rajasic abandonment and obtains not the fruit of abandonment (tyaga)' (Bhagavad Gita, XVIII:8).

A man of action and passion will readily fulfil his obligatory duties only as long as they are not painful or too fatiguing. To fulfil all obligations and perform all duties without sacrificing one's own personal comfort is no heroism at all. Such actions have no special reward as far as self-development is concerned. In fact, Lord Krishna says: 'He will attain no fruit whatsoever of his abandonment.'

Performance of one's obligatory duties is itself the most glorious form of tyaga, and can be considered doubly so when it involves sacrifice of one's personal convenience and comfort. Real tyaga always leads one to greater fields of self-expression and joy. A bud loses itself to become a flower, a flower gives up its soft petals and enchanting fragrance to reach the higher status of a fruit. Every selfless action should similarly lift us up to a nobler status in the evolutionary ladder. Our duties are never to be abandoned, but our clinging attachment to actions and their fruits must be relinquished. The Lord thus concludes for Arjuna: 'Therefore, you must always fulfil, without attachment, all your obligatory duties. By performing actions without attachment, one attains to the Highest' (Bhagavad Gita, III:19).

Every one of us, insists the Bhagavad Gita, must, without attachment, fulfil all our obligatory duties throughout our lives. But then, what about our spiritual unfoldment? Lord Krishna assures us that there is no need for anybody to worry about his spiritual unfoldment. When we fulfil our duties, without ego and selfish desires, the existing vasanas get exhausted and the bosom fills with peace and tranquillity. A mind at rest, in its alertness, perceives the Reality that had been shrouded so far by the mind's own agitations. Therefore, Lord Krishna says, 'By performing actions without attachment, one attains to the Highest.'

~

TWENTY-SIX

WE MUST . . .*

Enthusiasm is the very fuel in all great men. With inexhaustible ardour for whatever they undertake to accomplish, they generate an extraordinary drive for action. In spiritual self-improvement and in cultural and spiritual service to the nation, people must discover in themselves the secret of invoking this force of true and flawless enthusiasm.

Pessimists have no enthusiasm at all for anything they do. They always consider life empty, men hopeless, situations tragic and circumstances going diabolically against them. They complain and groan at life. They are angry with everyone around them, against everything that is happening, opposed to every dream, unwilling to act, negligent in duty, and buried in their own imaginary sorrows and defeats. Such people can discover no enthusiasm even to live.

As opposed to these pessimists are the hopeful, cheerful, dynamic and ever-enthusiastic optimists. Optimists are generally of two kinds—the wise and the otherwise. An intelligent optimist believes that the world tends to be good and beautiful and he works diligently to make it so. He has an innately sweet disposition, refined through careful cultivation of looking for only the good in life, and he finds what he seeks! Every successful discovery expands his enthusiasm to search for more, and he thus goes from joy to joy, gaining in

---

* From Swami Chinmayananda, *We Must . . . (Notes on Self-improvement)*, Central Chinmaya Mission Trust, Mumbai (reprint, 1990).

himself and giving to others, achieving for the world and sharing with all. His enthusiasm not only supplies him with a secret pep in his own life, but by its spirited contagion he comes to thrill all around him with his sunny nature and ardent warmth in work.

Even when we work with full optimism and good cheer, most of us detect our zeal languishing now and then, and some of us have a cruel knack of leaving the field at once—strewn with our half-done efforts—and of searching elsewhere for some new springs of enthusiasm. When this is repeated we are apt to find, at the end of our life, a vast desert land of half-hearted acts, partial accomplishments, and unfinished programmes, all littered with miserable failures, and tearful losses—altogether a sheer, dreadful waste.

In such people the flow of enthusiasm is not constant only because they are too impatient. The really great have both the enthusiasm to work and the good sense to wait. Their fervour to work consistently and their patience to await the harvest keeps them all the time intelligently confident and optimistically sure that right results will follow right efforts everywhere in life. Under these attitudes, enthusiasm never sinks in their bosom but sustains them through all their trials and exertions, threats and challenges, and doubts and despair. Patient self-application—with all enthusiasm—in a joyous mood of healthy optimism is the secret 'plan-of-action' of all great men.

Life is a death-long discipline. Constant and alert vigilance over our own thoughts and actions is the stiff price we are compelled to pay for the greater achievements and finer accomplishments in life. Introspection adds polish and verve to our attentive personality to smartly detect the rise of false thoughts, dangerous moods, careless words and inglorious actions. Our alertness gives us the poise to discern whenever we go wrong and the calm courage to correct.

Once we have caught the melody of life and its unerring rhythm, the personality in us becomes fully tuned and ready to initiate great activities. Without such adjustments, and without deliberately cultivating this inner deftness through conscious discipline, any servant of society will bring but more confusion, invite more sinners, and attract more distress into his fields of endeavour.

Regular and ardent prayer, ending with deep and steady meditation alone can unfold enthusiasm, patience, and the inner sharpness to detect and avoid false tones in thought, word, and action. Through prayer and meditation, let us come to feel our oneness with the Infinite Lord. Consciousness of the Presence of the Supreme Power in ourselves need not necessarily spell egoism. Our mental assets must be as real and as readily available for our enjoyment as our money, lands and other material prosperity.

Let us recognize and feel the inexhaustible power in the Self. Let us thereafter apply it entirely, with patience and enthusiasm, to the great and worthy purpose of reviving our culture among our people. Let us not worry about recognition or reward; let us be more anxious about the quality of our work. Let us realize that work is rendered joyous by the very beauty of patient and perfect performance. Let us purify ourselves for great actions, through prayer and meditation, regular and sincere: *we must*.

Systematically, therefore, *we must* train and discipline the mind for right thinking and correct, diligent activity. Right thinking is a habit that can be cultivated. Substitution of positive thoughts, and flooding the mind with creative ideas are methods by which we can flush out the floor of the mind, littered as it is now with the filth of incomplete thoughts and decaying ideas. Having recognized a thought to be negative or wrong, do not waste time in upholstering it to look neat and attractive, but reject it immediately and totally— the power of right thinking expels all false thoughts and induces healthy conceptions.

In fact, this is not a difficult process. It is as easy to entertain noble and elevating ideas as it is to suffocate our minds with wrong

223

thoughts and vicious ideals. It may be that at this moment our minds are full of uncreative thoughts, brought therein by our unconscious wrong thinking. Their easy presence, therefore, may make us feel that to entertain wrong thoughts is simple, and to fight them out of their entrenchment is rather difficult. But to a sincere and heroic seeker, this is not very difficult. In fact, it is easy to entertain positive thinking as it brings in its wake harmony, peace, joy and inner realization.

When the thoughts, unswerving, are rendered straight and when their quality and texture thus change, we come to notice that our actions gather a new glow of perfection, a charm of brilliancy. When the actions are more glorious, our life becomes more productive, carrying with it always the sure insignia of success and achievement. When we look out to the life around us, through a mind filled with the light of clear thinking, we also recognize a larger and meaningful significance to life itself.

In sharing our ideas with others, let us remember that it is our own wealth of inner silence that creates the greater contact, for very often it is found that our silence creates an equally deep silence in the listener, and in that silence his confusion is stilled. To create such a silence in the heart of the listener, the speaker must be great, and the listener also must have the spiritual stuff in him sufficiently well brought out. In silence, that which earlier was not clear to the listener becomes suddenly illuminated and vivid. In that inner silence the still small voice of conscience is rendered more eloquent than at other times.

Let us not forget that the greatest forces in nature are all ever silent. Electricity has no noise. Heat is dumb. Floods creep up silently in the night and sweep away the sleeping villages, against which man is helpless. The silent power of Truth, in irresistible efficiency, is constantly at work—without strife, sound or confusion. As devotees of Truth when we work in society, let us make use of this silent might of the ever-conquering Truth. *We must* learn to be cheerfully silent, gracefully silent, powerfully silent.

If we are conscientious and consistent in our efforts and love, we shall have many, experiences of the efficacy of silence. When all other efforts fail to serve a brother-seeker, then one sits silently next to him the whole evening, without a word passing. Invariably he will cry out at the end of the evening his self conversion, his clearer perception, his changed conviction. This is no magic: this is only because silence always promotes quietness within, and in that quietude all doubts get cleared naturally, automatically.

Finally, the most perfect characteristic in an eminently successful life seems to be integrity—an inflexible, undaunted, firm integrity. And, also, it seems that everyone who has cultivated this trait has drawn from it many an unseen and personal advantage over others who are striving in the same field of achievement.

Once an individual in himself has discovered and fully developed an indomitable integrity, he finds he is master of every challenge, and in all his efforts we observe a self-assurance which is both captivating and rewarding.

Indeed, very few have it, and there is none who is not charmed by it. A man of integrity is accepted, believed, trusted and befriended by all. To attract to oneself such genuine attitudes from others' bosoms is to create and assure a vibrant environment for great undertakings and perhaps, with the others' ready help, a spectacular success. Truly, integrity is a personal asset to man in every field.

The nobility of integrity is not merely in its honour, sincerity and honesty in action, but it is rooted deeper in the quality and beauty of one's own intentions. If the spring of our every thought is pure and if we have the heroism to live unfailingly ever true to the great ideals in ourselves, however impractical and utopian they may be, even in spite of all immediate failures, we still have cultivated integrity.

225

The personality in us, thereafter, unfolds with a glowing poise, and at each apparent failure encountered, with each insurmountable obstacle met, in each moment of social criticism faced and from all empty laughter endured, we come to strengthen our nobility and reinforce our determination to live the honourable life consistent with our ideal and our goal.

Such individuals alone are the evolvers, all others are mere adapters, compromising with circumstances at every turn and adjusting to the changing patterns of challenges. They may struggle on, as hapless slaves to their habits, but never can they come to dominate the outer field and command the world to march on to the appointed goal or end, chosen by their own vision and will. Only a person of integrity has this power over life and its happenings. Naturally, then, integrity is the essential core of every eminently successful life.

No doubt, every one of us has a covetable ideal, a great goal, or a mighty purpose in our mind, and this is noble indeed. But the resolution to live up to it and pursue it continuously wavers at the very sight of the first obstacle. Bhartrihari therefore says that some act till they meet obstacles, others act in spite of obstacles and conquer them, but some act not, fearing the possibility of some obstacle that might arise en route! When the unexpected crosses the path of life, resolution is tested, integrity is put on trial. Often it is tested without any mercy, tried without any charity. Yet, if resolution is rooted in our faith and vision, integrity shall come out successful, and we shall become stronger for the battle.

When a man of integrity thus strides through life's rough path, winning laurels in localized skirmishes with the outer circumstances, a new fire is kindled in him, and with each fulfilled resolution he rises daringly to take up greater resolves upon himself. It becomes a progressive self-disciplining, adding an extra inch to his stature and an added edge to his efficiency.

A straight and dignified man, with his integrity sturdy and serene in both storm and sunshine, is sometimes seen to decay and grow weak and even fall from his high pedestal of strength and glory. In majority of the cases, such falls are due to the unconscious load of negative fears that have stealthily laid their booby-traps in him. If carefully analysed, it will be found that all of them have sprung forth from a lack of clarity in us, a temporary incapacity to overlook some minor disappointment, or a failure to disregard some words or actions of others around. In a weak moment, off guard, any paltry happening can become a stupendous load on our mind. Dragging this dead weight, it is impossible for the man of integrity to maintain his poise and keep his earlier strides.

Therefore *we must* set up a free flow of forgiveness from within us, so that through that rushing flood we can flush out all our negative and suicidal inner disturbances. More than forgiveness, a man who is building himself up for the highest achievement must have the plentiful ability to forget the follies of others around him, the dishonesty of those who are working with him, and the vulgarities of the members of his team. All cannot have true inspiration; even when they are inspired, all may not have real efficiency in them, or constancy of purpose. Forgive them, and if they continue to be bad, forget about them. The poet Robert Browning says:

Good to forgive
Best to forget.

Remember, one of our noblest duties in life is to grow. This is the cry of all evolution. Biological growth was the command in the lower stages of evolution. After having attained manhood, the demand is to grow in our moral stature, in our spiritual worth, in our cultural dignity. This is where study of the scriptures, regular and continuous, and sadhana, constant and sincere, come to serve us. The study of the scriptures clearly points out the goal and the way: sadhana yields to us the energy and vitality to walk the path and explode into the goal.

TWENTY-SEVEN

EFFICIENCY IN ACTION*

What do we mean by action? How best am I to act? What makes me act and what are the personality layers that express themselves in action? If I know the mechanism of action, I may probably be able to understand the technique and the art of adjusting my personality in such a way that my action falls under the highest type of activity, one that brings about achievement for me as well as for my community.

Today we are all students of science, and we are not ready to accept an idea unless we clearly know the complete mechanism of it. This is the spirit of the modern age. Therefore, when the teachers or the scriptures try to explain that we must work, and that the quality of our work depends upon the beauty of our emotions behind it, we are not ready to accept it. We want to know how these are connected. A little knowledge of the instruments of action and how to act in the world outside is necessary. If the mechanism of man as a dynamic creature working in the world is understood, it will be clear how a greater ideal can inspire us to work better.

Mechanism of Action

All living creatures constantly receive external stimuli. The stimuli

---

* From *Vedanta in Action*, Central Chinmaya Mission Trust, Mumbai, fourth edition, 1989.

are called form, touch, smell, taste and sound. These five different types of stimuli reach us through our sense organs. We cannot remain even a single second in the world without receiving stimuli. Through the eyes every form enters; through the ears sounds enter; through the nose smell enters; through the tongue, taste enters; and through the skin, touch enters. Thus, through the sense organs various objects of the world enter into us, inviting us to react to them.

The instrument or mechanism within man that receives and processes the stimuli is called the mind. If our mind is not attentive, but wanders to some other idea, we cannot hear what is said to us. If we are worried or preoccupied, we cannot see, for our mind is engaged with the worry and so cannot receive the stimuli. The mind cannot come to a decision; it only receives the stimuli and then submits it to a higher authority, called the intellect, the judging faculty. The intellect judges how we are to react to situations and what responses we must make. The final decision comes from the intellect.

The intellect cannot judge haphazardly. Everyone's intellect comes to a judgement depending upon his vasanas, or impressions of his past experiences. Past experiences control, direct, regulate and discipline our present reactions to the world, because our intellectual judgements are coloured by their past experiences. For example, if a bottle of whisky is put before a devout Brahmin and a drunkard, the latter would grab the bottle while the former would shun it. The bottle itself is not the source of attraction or repulsion. The quality of vasanas in an individual's intellect determines the attraction to or repulsion from objects. The ideas and ideals that we already have in our intellect condition the intellect's judgement as to how it should tackle the stimuli that have been received by the mind.

Thus, the outer world enters through the sense organs into the mind, the mind receives the stimuli and awaits the intellect's judgement, the intellect judges the stimuli according to the existing vasanas that control it, and when the judgement is passed, the order to act is sent back to the mind. The mind is not only a receiving clerk but also a dispatching clerk. According to the orders passed by the intellect, the mind regulates the proper muscles to act in the world outside. All this happens instantaneously.

The intellect must come to a judgement. But how I judge the situation is different from how you will judge the situation. Our judgements will be different because the ideas and ideals that I am inspired by and those that you are inspired by—the various vasanas under which we work—are different. Furthermore, the reactions of one individual differ from moment to moment. Each individual acts differently at different times, even though the circumstances remain the same. These reactions are determined by the type of ideals with which we work in the world.

Expressing Ideals in Action

Every day we face decisions and temptations. Although we may have high ideals, if our conviction is weak, we compromise easily. Supposing you see a man walking in front of you in a busy street downtown. You see his wallet slip out of his pocket. The man is preoccupied and he is unaware that his wallet has fallen. Supposing you pick up the wallet and realize that it is full of money. Will you think, 'Should I put it in my pocket? No one has seen me. Should I keep it, or should I call the man and return his wallet? What should I do?' You have complete freedom to either keep the wallet or to return it to the man. What determines your response? Your intentions, your ideals, your education all determine your decision. If at that time your negative tendencies are stronger, the wallet will slip quietly into your pocket, and you will try to justify it, saying, 'See, for the past month I have been pleading with God to help me somehow. Honest men are always protected by God. When He wants to give,

He gives it on the sidewalks of downtown!' Thus you justify yourself. However, if you are a cultured man of real education and understanding, of sympathy and concern for others, you will immediately visualize the tragic picture of this man returning home to his wife and children, having lost his wallet. It is a painful scene indeed. It makes you think, 'Let me help him. Ordinarily I cannot afford to give so much money in charity, but here is his own money, and it is certainly charity now if I return it to him. O Lord, you have given me a chance to help someone in need and therefore I will call him and return his wallet to him.' Before the man can thank you, you disappear, and with a growing sense of satisfaction at having done a heroic deed, you go on with your day.

All our actions depend upon the type of ideals in our mind and intellect. The way in which we behave in the world is altered, controlled and regulated by the type of ideals that inspire us. So the question is, how shall we act in the world, how can we improve our actions and gain a greater achievement in life? This cannot be done by working twice as many hours. The idea of the modern commercial world is that if I double my hours, I can double my output. When a machine works six hours, it produces a certain quantity. If it works twelve hours, it can produce double the quantity. But a man's work in society cannot be measured by the hours he works. It is not the quantity of action that matters but the quality. The quality of action is improved only by the ideals that illumine and inspire us. Thus, the nobler the ideals, the greater the shine and beauty of action. The ideals that inspire us at all times to bring out greater efficiency and beauty of action are called noble or moral ideals. Ideals that bring a dispirited and dejected attitude to such an extent that our actions, however efficient they may be, ultimately lead to doom, sorrow and failure, are false or immoral ideals.

The spirit of freedom, the spirit of reverence for one's country, and the spirit of sacrifice for the sake of the common good are all inspiring ideals. Under such ideals, mighty men have done great and ennobling activity in the world, and the fruits of their actions are enjoyed by future generations for decades. Thus, the higher the ideal that inspires an individual, the nobler is the action that he performs in the world.

To jump over the wall of a private house with a concealed dagger, to enter through the window, to move stealthily into the house, to see whether anybody is awake by watching the rhythm of the sleeping persons, and then to go to the safe, collect the valuables, and quietly leave is a skilful achievement indeed. It calls for many qualities of the individual to do it efficiently. But what is the product of all this intelligence and courage? From that day onward the thief finds that he is not happy. Instead, his peace and tranquillity are gone because of the reactions that come to his mind. His best abilities were put forth into a piece of work inspired by negative thoughts. When the goal in one's mind is selfish, even though the work may be successfully accomplished, it is only a sad act of grand theft.

Our scriptures say that work can bring forth real, enduring results, not merely because of the quantity of effort put forth, but because of the quality of inspiration with which the man has undertaken the work. The greater the ideal, the brighter is the action and the product. Mahatma Gandhi was only a barrister-at-law. He would probably have been a successful advocate looking after only his wife and children. But what would have been the total turnover of his work? The same individual, when inspired by the ideal of his country's freedom, became a different person—a mahatma. He brought about a change in the moral vision of the country and of the political leaders and thinkers of the world. The quality of his work was higher and nobler because of the selfless ideals that inspired him.

Imagine that you suddenly hear your house is on fire. You rush home and find that the entire house is in flames. At that moment you see your wife running out of the house with your child in her arms. You then hear spellbound the thrilling story of how the child was rescued. The child was sleeping upstairs in his room. In panic, everybody ran out of the house, and then the mother remembered the child. She asked the fire department to save the child. The chief, in spite of his forty years' experience, said, 'I'm sorry, no human being can go in and come out alive. The whole house is ablaze.' The mother immediately forgot everything, and with superhuman courage ran into the house. She rushed upstairs, took the child, and came out.

After this incident, she would be afraid to go near any fire, but inspired by her great love for her child, she performed a miracle. If this is the potentiality of the human mind, can't she live twenty-four hours of the day as a heroine? She cannot, because she does not have that inspiring goal. An ordinary man may be a coward, but when he is inspired by a great ideal, you find that he miraculously taps a new stream of energy and vitality.

Taking another example, suppose your spouse has fallen seriously ill at home. You cannot take leave of absence from work. Your sister comes to look after your wife during the day, and you take your turn in the night. You serve your wife every night. For months together you do not have a chance to sleep. Yet, out of sheer love for your wife, you do not feel tired. But if your employer says that you must work overtime, you feel like answering, 'Only if you pay me overtime.'

Where did this extra energy come from? Usually by 6 p.m. we are tired, not because of overwork, but because of boredom. On the other hand, when our wife or child is ill, out of love for them we discover new energy which no doctor can explain. If that much energy and efficiency lie concealed in us, what is the secret mechanism by which we can tap them?

Discovering a goal or a vision in life, a great ideal to inspire us, and surrendering oneself to that ideal seem to be the secret behind the new dynamism in our activities. We thereby raise the very standard of activity in us and bring about a greater happiness in the world. Each one will have to discover his or her own goal. There was a time when the ideal was dharma, or religious ideals. Today it is not. Today with the emphasis on technology and raised standards of living, many are inspired to help the poor. This seems to be actively occupying our minds. To serve the underprivileged in the world, to serve one's countrymen, to lift them up, each one of us will have to make his own effort. All efforts cannot be at one point alone; each person can make an impact only from his own position. Thus you can convert your own small office or corner of work into a shrine where you can serve, through your fellow beings, that mighty Lord who is the destiny of the world and who guides it at all times. You alone can discover this new spurt of energy and enthusiasm within yourself. Thereby, your own ideals of work become chastened. You gain an immense amount of reward, not in terms of cash, but in the spirit of joy that arises out of a heart that has done the right action at the right time.

Wrong Responses to the World

Different individuals seem to react to external challenges differently, and these reactions are called actions. One individual acting in the world rises to achievement and success, while another in the same field of work reacts to it so unintelligently that he experiences disastrous sorrows. No doubt, you and I immediately justify our failures, saying that the world is a bad place. We would like to curse somebody for our failure. A bad worker will always blame his performance on his instrument. Similarly, the majority of us are escapists from life, and when we meet with failure we want to attribute it to a cause outside yourselves: 'Nobody was helping me, the world has not given me a fair chance; the environment was not conducive,' and so on. But essentially when we analyse our personality, we find that if we fail, if our actions bring about more and more unhappiness to ourselves and the world, it is not because of the world but because of our own wrong responses to challenges from the world.

Success and failure in the world are our own personal successes and failures. The same situation, the same sun, moon and stars, the same climatic conditions, the same flora and fauna, the same city, may be available to all of us. But I fail in the city and become a tragic figure, while you become a successful person in the same city. How is that possible? It is only because I do not know how to meet my challenges and react properly, while you know how to react to them and are therefore able to make the environment conducive to your development and growth.

We find that the responses of an individual depend upon the type of ideas and ideals he has, and the higher the ideals, the greater his inspiration to act in the world. Every individual must discover this deal for himself. Nobody can give it to another. An artist, a scientist, and a freedom fighter all have their ideals. To the extent that we faithfully live up to the great ideals, dedicating ourselves more and more to them, a pure column of energy seems to spring forth from our hearts and we are able to apply that energy to productive activity.

Many people complain that though they have high ideals, they have no enthusiasm to study, to improve themselves, to live a higher life. Why? 'Because we are exhausted by the time we come home from the office. We live far away from work. Early in the morning we have to commute, and by the time we reach office and return home in the evening, we have no more energy left in us.'

I want to say to such people that they should go to a village in India and observe the farmers. Early in the morning, with a plough on his shoulder and two bullocks, the farmer walks to his plot of land. Where is this plot of land? Not one block, but two and a half miles away. There he ploughs from morning until noon and then he eats what he has brought with him. He has been working in the hot sun. Ploughing is a very strenuous work and he feels exhausted, so he rests until 3 p.m. Again, he ploughs from 3 p.m. to 5:30 p.m. and then along with the bullocks, with the plough on his shoulder, he walks two and a half miles home. The amount of physical energy that he spends on the field are incomparably greater than that of an office manager. When he reaches home, the farmer takes a bath, eats his dinner, and often joins his friends to sing in full-throated joy. He goes on and on with ecstasy and revels the whole night. Where did he get his energy? If a farmer can have so much energy, why do we get fatigued so easily?

When people complain that they feel tired, I am not trying to prove that they are *not* tired. They really are tired. But the farmer is not tired, because being tired of life is not caused by physical exertion. Physical exertion cannot tire you, and if at all there is fatigue, a half-hour of rest will revive the physical body. The fatigue that you and I in the cities feel is only mental exhaustion. The moment the manager wakes up he feels worried about his position, about getting more clients, about getting more pay. In the store he feels anxious because the merchant has more money than he does. Whatever he sees makes him feel troubled. Somebody has a Mercedes, he is anxious that he cannot afford one. By the time he reaches the office, his energy has already started to ebb away. Thus he gets mentally exhausted, even though physically he has not done a bit of work.

In the case of the farmer, he leads a simple life and is happy with his simple comforts. When he ploughs with his bullocks, he feels happy because they are his bullocks. He walks two and a half miles dreaming of his fertile land. He ploughs on and on, and as he ploughs he does get physically exhausted, but mentally he is enthusiastic, and therefore he *does not* feel exhausted. By the time he comes

237

home and takes a bath he has revived or refreshed himself, and there is still a lot of energy in him.

The fatigue that we feel in the modern world is not the fatigue of physical exertion, for with all the modern conveniences, physical exertion is unnecessary. Because of elevators, we need not climb stairs. Because of cars we need not walk. All around us we have comforts to economize our precious energy, and yet we complain that we have no energy at all! Fatigue is caused by mental tension, which is the outcome of having no goal to aspire for. Our goal is only to finish our daily work, somehow or the other, doing as little as possible and getting the maximum pay. This is the extent of our aspirations.

When these negative thoughts come, however much money and security we may have, we will still be dissatisfied. Happiness depends not only on the type of work we do, but also on our mental condition, our mental health. Mental health can be maintained only when there is a greater goal to inspire us, and the higher the goal, the greater will be our inspiration. We discover new resources of energy welling up in ourselves to pour out in tireless activity serving the world. Thus, it is necessary that we have a clear and creative goal in life, so that we may look up to that goal and draw inspiration from it. When we have a goal in life, such as the nation's prosperity, or the country's progress, the goal itself inspires us, and the more it inspires us, the more we find the required energy for tireless activity. As we discover such a goal and surrender ourselves to it, we unleash a new, unknown column of energy within ourselves.

Sometimes we feel momentarily inspired by an ideal, but once the source of that inspiration is gone, we are back again in the old lethargy. Where has that energy gone? The energy was with us, but it has been dissipated into various channels and is no longer available for the 'irrigation' of activity.

Dissipation of Energy

We may build a dam and thereby create a reservoir of water, but if this water is not made use of and taken by canals to the land, then the land cannot be benefited by it. In order to make the land more arable, we need water, and for that purpose we build the dam. But this water contained by the dam cannot create crops, unless a canal system directs the water into the various fields. Similarly, by surrendering ourselves to a great goal, we may find a new enthusiasm and energy, but if that enthusiasm or energy is not properly channelized, it either stagnates or dissipates into unproductive activity.

This leakage of energy takes place, according to the masters of the past, through three dissipating channels. One is regrets about the past. For example, an average student decides that he must get a first class in his exam. He studies very hard for it, but as the examination approaches, he thinks, 'I will be satisfied with a pass—I don't need a first class.' When asked what happened to his determination, he answers, 'I have never received a first class in the past; how can someone like myself ever get a first class?' Thus, the memory of the past has dissipated his confidence and energy. Memories and regrets from the past refer to thoughts such as: 'In the past I have always been inefficient; how can I be efficient now?' Thus, the memories of the past come to disturb us, our new enthusiasm to live a nice life oozes away, and we have no energy for any activity.

A second source of dissipation is anxiety for the future. For example: a boy who has always been a first-class student hopes to get a high rank in his MA examination. The boy enters the examination hall rather pale, and the examiner thinks it is because of overstudy. When the question paper reaches the boy he reads it and faints. An examiner rushes to him. The boy says, 'Please give me some water. I feel dizzy, I need to lie down.' What has happened?

The boy thinks, 'Everything is lost. How can I answer fourteen questions, even though I know all the answers, when there is so little time?' In his nervousness, the boy has forgotten to read the instructions. The instructions say: *Answer any three questions!*

Because of the boy's over-anxiety to get a first class, his efficiency was lost. Many students fail in their exams, not because they haven't studied, but because of such leakages of dynamism, which dissipate their energy and sense of composure. This is why some students fail, even though their teachers expected them to do well. One's success depends upon the mental equanimity with which one acts in the world.

Thus, the dissipation of energy may take place either due to lingering memories of the past or due to anxieties for the future. Even if these two are overcome, the sages of the past say that there is a third cause of dissipation: excitement in the present. You may have noticed some people who sincerely work long hours, yet who give a general impression of being extremely inefficient. No one wants to give work to such a person. He works hard, no doubt, but he cannot come to any decision. In the morning he looks at his desk. The files have already piled up and he is worried about the amount of work. At that time a secretary comes with more files. By the time he takes those files and starts working, he sees a label marked *immediate*. After reading it he remembers the first file, while the secretary has brought in yet another file. He is worried and dejected. He doesn't know where to begin.

On the other hand, if he has composure and self-confidence, he will realize that he should concentrate on one file at a time, come to a decision, and take action so that at least one file is disposed of. If he goes through them one by one, without becoming excited, there will be some efficiency in his work. But if he succumbs to the excitement of the present, it will dissipate his energy and destroy his efficiency.

There are thus three outlets through which our energy is lost: regrets of the past, unintelligent anxieties concerning the future, and feverish excitement in the present. The great seers of ancient India found that once we discover a goal and surrender ourselves to it, we will find a tremendous energy and inspiration welling up in us. After that we should not allow this energy to be either dissipated in the futile memories of past regrets and failures, or in the imagined sorrows of the future, or in the excitements of the present. We must focus our entire energy on the activity. This is the highest creative action in the world. Thereby, an individual who was until now considered most inefficient finds his way to the highest achievement and success.

Training Our Minds

In order to develop this attitude, we need consistent training, because we have already trained our minds in an incorrect way. Not knowing the art of action, we have become master artists in doing things wrongly in life. When each individual does anything wrong, the totality of activity cannot but bring the country to a sorry state.

If, in the socialist pattern, each of us is given a car and we don't know how to drive yet we drive anyway, what would be the condition on the roads? The cars would certainly collide. This seems to be the pattern of the life that we lead. Every one of us is a vehicle. We know how to go forward. The intellect is a very powerful guide when used correctly, but nobody seems to know how to control the mind's energy and direct it properly, or guide it to the right destination.

There is too much chaos in our lives—each person is concerned only with himself. Every one of us is intent on reaching a particular goal, but we reach nowhere, instead we end in disaster en route, because we do not know how to control our minds and pour it into positive activities.

When an individual has discovered new energy within himself, when he has learned the art of stopping the dissipation, and he is able to fix his entire energy on the piece of work at hand, a great joy starts welling up in his mind—the joy of the artisan. This joy can be understood only by experiencing it. For an artisan or a worker, crafting something new—whether a toy or an instrument of precision—brings great fulfilment.

No doubt, to a large extent the mechanization of life in this industrial age has robbed us of the joy that the artisan of the past had. In those days, when they made an article of furniture or a piece of sculpture, they had the joyous satisfaction of creating something. Nowadays because of division of labour and automation, the average worker has been looted of his joy of creativity. Instead, an inert, iron monster called the machine produces everything. Furniture is produced by machinery, clothing is produced by machinery. The worker thus does not have the joy of applying his creativity to his work. Instead, he programmes and maintains machines. To that extent, the joy of creation has gone out of his life.

However, if we turn our vision in a different direction, certainly the joy of having done the right thing in the right way can be ours. For example, even though typing is considered dreary work, if the typist executes his work neatly, without overtyping or making mistakes, he has his dividend of joy from having done his work well. We can discover a joy in the precision and perfection of the work that we turn out. Whether others recognize it or not, we have the satisfaction that we did our work as well as we could.

The artists who have been able to put their head and heart where their hands work have discovered the joy of samadhi, a joy of religious ecstasy, because when the physical, mental, and emotional personalities become integrated, the individual is closer to perfection, closer to the actual experience of joy welling up from within, and in that atmosphere of joy the individual is capable of achieving his best.

Anyone who has a hobby can very easily understand this. A hobby means a physical activity wherein the head and heart act in unison. When the hand is doing something and the head and the heart are involved, the individual says that it is a recreation, a hobby for him. One man says playing cricket from morning to evening is recreation. Yet another man playing tennis or football calls that recreation. If they are asked to exert that much to help their neighbour, they will resist. But in spite of a great amount of energy and perspiration spent in a tennis court, football ground or cricket field, they come away saying that they feel revived.

In summer vacations, some south Indian teenagers go to north India for a holiday. They sightsee the whole day and walk along deserted roads in the midday heat. The local people are afraid of sunstroke. When they look out of their windows, they see these teenagers walking without any protection. They wonder, 'How is it that they are walking in the sun?' They close their windows with the assumption that south India is probably hotter and therefore these boys are walking comfortably. But the teenagers don't know that it is hot. They are living in a realm of their own! They have come to the north to sightsee, and however uncomfortable the heat is, it is fun for them because their purpose is to enjoy the holiday. Thus, walking in the hottest sun, sleeping in railway stations, catching any train and suffering in many ways is an enjoyable adventure, for their head and heart are where their physical bodies are.

After the teenagers have returned home, if the old grandfather were to ask one of them to get something from the corner store, the boy will complain that the sun is too hot! He forgets that when the temperature was at 114°F he was walking five miles on the tarred roads of Agra, enjoying himself all the way. Here the temperature is 80°F and he feels too hot to go out for his grandfather.

You and I feel disappointed and dejected in life not because there is no meaningful work in the world. It is because we have not found an activity that integrates our body, mind and intellect. To work in this way is the art of living that has been described in the Vedas, especially in the Bhagavad Gita.

Thus, to sum up, according to the great teachers, we should discover a goal to draw our inspiration from. Once we have found that goal or ideal, whether it is political, economic or spiritual, a new enthusiasm wells up in us. When there is enthusiasm, sincerity, ardour, and consistency of purpose automatically follow. Next, we should channelize our energy to achieve our goal without dissipating it through unintelligent regrets of the past, futile imagination of the future, or frenzied excitement of the present. If we work in the world with our head, heart and hands fully integrated, the very work gains a stamp of efficiency and beauty. Our reward is indescribable fulfilment and joy.

VII

VEDANTA IN SECULAR LIFE

*The highest prayer in this world is service; the greatest
devotion is loving the people around us; and the noblest
character trait is divine compassion for all living creatures.*

—Swami Chinmayananda

~

TWENTY-EIGHT

THE SECRET OF LARGE PROFITS[*]

Industrial executives cannot understand why, in spite of honest efforts, detailed planning, and great expenditure of energy, our economy is not growing as it should. If it is growing at all, it is a laborious growth. It is a labour pain with constant mental suffering and tension—the kind of tension that brings sleeplessness, high blood pressure, and heart trouble. These are the complaints of modern industrialists. I have this information because they come to me with these complaints. We can only explain that these symptoms are due to tension, stress and strain of the industrial and technological age.

We may look for biological causes for these illnesses, but the root cause is mental. The body is, after all, only a tool, a tool that is wielded by the technician behind it. The one who is wielding the tool is the mind: your inner personality. The tool is necessary, but the tool by itself cannot act. The tool's performance depends upon the knowledge and ability of the technician. It is not our body but the mind and intellect that is acting in us. When the mind is bright and alert, the actions are spectacular, but when the mind is exhausted, dissipated, moody or sorrowful, all actions are painfully laboured.

The situation today seems to be that even though we are sincerely trying to work well, the quality of our performance is dull. There is

---

[*]   Excerpt of a talk delivered on 16 April 1980 to the Annual General Meeting of the Bombay Industries Association, Bombay. From *Vedanta in Action*, Central Chinmaya Mission Trust, Mumbai, fourth edition, 1989.

no brilliancy or vibrancy. There is no definite goal in our personal activity, and thus the mind feels exhausted and worn out. This emotional and intellectual exhaustion decreases our physical capacity and brings about a sudden exhaustion that results in inefficiency and incompetence to face our challenges in life.

This mental and physical debility, though called the problem of modern man, is not new in the history of mankind. In fact, this same problem, along with its solution, was discussed in the Bhagavad Gita. A typical industrialist of today is equivalent to the troubled and incompetent Arjuna when he first faced opposing forces. We may define our difficulties differently—ours may be that the bank is not releasing enough loans, or that the government is exerting pressure, or that the labour is not cooperating. Arjuna may not have had the same problems, but he was also called upon to face a great challenge, the Mahabharata War.

In such situations, you and I are helpless; we are faced with a challenge that we would like to avoid, but that we are forced to meet. Arjuna also, in spite of his efforts, could do nothing to persuade his own cousins not to wage war. An inevitable challenge was placed in front of him, and he was forced to meet it. The challenge appeared to him as futile as trying to break a granite wall with his head! In such a situation, any intelligent man would be tempted to think, 'Why bother about it? Let me retire from this problem.'

The cause of such anxiety is very subtle, and you may not even be aware of it. All worries are due to the psychologically selfish notion that 'I will work only for my family; I will have nothing to do with the world.' Only if you can understand that you industrialists are a rare few, gifted by the Lord with the ability to produce wealth for society or the nation and that you have been doing it successfully, will you have the joy of doing it on a larger and larger scale—not for yourself, but for others.

That attitude is not yet developed. We still have micro-vision.

We still feel, 'Why should I exert myself? Why should I sweat for others? I will work only for myself.' And when this mood overtakes us, we may think, 'Why not run a simple, quiet shop?' or, 'Why not a small restaurant?' or, 'Why not just sell something on the roadside? Even if I sell popcorn, I can live comfortably! Why have I entered industry and got crushed by the very machinery I created?' This doubt rises in us because of a lack of values and understanding and, above all, a lack of vision. Please think.

The Bhagavad Gita's Solution

In the Bhagavad Gita Arjuna confronted this same situation and he similarly thought he should run away from the problem. He felt that the situation was futile and should be abandoned. Krishna had to hold Arjuna back by the shoulders and admonish him, saying, 'Do not run away, you must learn to face the situation. You must come out and confront your challenges.'

But in order to face such challenges, a lot of courage is required. This courage comes only when the mind is strong and poised, for only then can it rediscover its own efficiency, ability, and beauty of performance—all of which ensure profit and success in life.

How does this equipoise come about? It comes when the individual's mind is ignited by a larger vision, when he comes to understand his importance in life, his nobility, and the great contribution that he is expected to make during his lifetime. Even though the situation outside seemed impossible before, he now develops the courage to face it. He realizes that he has been selected to do that particular job. He recognizes his own importance.

With the teaching of the Bhagavad Gita, this mental vitality returned to Arjuna. He was brought to see the shallowness of his micro-vision, his self-centred view of life. His vision expanded to macro-vision, with the understanding that he was not a solitary individual, fighting against the world of multiplicity, but was one with the whole universe, one with the Lord who is the cosmic Person. The whole universe arises in Him, exists in Him, and disappears in Him, just as the waves rise, play, and disappear into the ocean. The ocean in dynamic play is the waves. The waves are, in essence, not anything other than the beautiful, serene depths of the ocean. The oneness of the larger reality of life and the incidental play around was perceived by Arjuna.

Once you understand that the entire world is one harmonious tapestry, and that all individuals are interrelated, with each one of us having certain responsibilities and duties to society, then you will no longer ask, 'Why should I feel responsible for my neighbour?' You will naturally feel extremely interested and responsible for your neighbour, because your neighbour is not someone different from you.

You may object, saying, 'My neighbour cannot be me. I am limited in my body. What do I have to do with him? He is a different person. His name, his job, his attitudes are all different from mine. How can I feel one with him?'

I will answer this point. Just think for a moment. Have you ever paused and looked at your own hands and legs? Is the hand like the leg? Are not the shapes different? Are not the functions different? Are not their names different? The hand is not called by the name 'leg', and the leg is not called by the name 'hand'; yet are they not both yours? The toes, the nose, the eyes, the ears, the hands, and the fingers are all different. Your entire body has many different parts and functions, but they are all a part of you. I do not say that you are the possessor and these are the possessed. But are they not all you? If I cut off your ears or toes, is that not doing harm to you?

Please think. You know that even though your limbs are of different shapes and functions, they all are you because you live in them. Their joys are your joys, their sorrows are your sorrows. If you understand this idea, then you will see the whole universe as one mighty expression of the divine Spark of Existence. Life is then seen as One, expressed through diverse forms. If this much is understood, a macro-vision automatically comes.

I am not talking to you of esoteric philosophy. This is a very practical and necessary philosophy if you want to live effectively in the modern world. In fact, this is not mere philosophy. Developing a macro-vision is the practical need of the day. The times are rapidly changing. Frontiers are no longer frontiers, oceans are no longer safe boundaries. If an atomic war happens, it will not be between two superpowers alone; all countries will suffer at the same time. It all depends on which way the breeze is blowing. An atom bomb may burst in Moscow, but if the breeze happens to be southward, the rest of Asia will suffer for no fault of theirs. Is it not true that little incidents in insignificant countries are causing the mighty powers to tremble? The days of isolated warfare are gone. An incident happening in one part of the world has repercussions all over the world. Today, all nations have become woven into one fabric.

This large macro-vision does not come automatically to an individual. It has to be cultivated. The entire discourse of the Bhagavad Gita had to be given to Arjuna before he was able to throw off his moodiness and overcome his mental confusion. Once his mind became calm and serene, Arjuna was able to rediscover his efficiency and potency.

It is very important to note that Krishna did not alter the situation. He did not order the situation to change. Every one of the Pandavas and Kauravas was standing on the battlefront ready to advance. Krishna did not bring new forces or new allies for Arjuna. He merely talked to Arjuna, thereby lifting him out of his mental confusion.

When Arjuna was mentally upset, he wanted to run away from the situation. He became pessimistic. But once the mind became quiet and calm, though the situation remained the same, Arjuna found a new courage and confidence within himself. He rediscovered his efficiency and declared to Krishna, 'Certainly I will face this problem.' Where is the problem? The problem was no longer a problem: it was only a game, a sport. With that self-confidence, Arjuna advanced, and he found that victory came to him.

This attitude of mental poise is unavoidable if you really want to become an industrial visionary, a developer of a macro-economy. Even today in the universities we do not speak of ordinary economics, but macro-economics. The micro-age is gone. But this adjustment in our minds, in our viewpoint, in our vision, has not yet been made.

Applying the Bhagavad Gita's Principles to Today's World

This macro-vision is not new in history. We find it taught even in the ancient Vedic scriptures. In fact, it was this macro-view that enabled the Indian civilization to survive natural declines and again rise to glory. It is because of this vision that, in spite of many calamitous political and economic situations affecting India, Indian culture and civilization have remained as precious as ever. Many are the cultures elsewhere that have arisen, sparkled for a moment, and died away completely. Where is the Greek culture today? Where is the Roman culture, the Egyptian culture, the Macedonian culture? All of them arose, blazed for some time, and slowly died out. Only in libraries do we have books reporting their existence.

Indian culture has survived because of the macro-view of Hindu philosophy. However, today after centuries of foreign rule, India has been culturally broken down, and the great sagacity of its culture has been virtually lost. The Brahmin class failed the Indian people, for they thought it was not necessary to study or practise the tenets of this great culture. The other members of society also did not know anything. We cannot hold anyone to blame now. It is a phenomenon that is inevitable in the world of space and time where nothing exists permanently. India's cultural beauty and eminence have thus today receded to their lowest ebb.

The Hindu scriptures contain a great body of knowledge that enables civilizations to adapt to changing times. Those scriptures are not ignorant of the need for economics and politics. In fact, they have precious insights into both. Many industrial and technical men have benefited by reading them. Great thinkers in the West are studying the scriptures of the East and bringing out fresh insights, new political and industrial visions, and new attitudes in life based upon the Upanishads, the Bhagavad Gita, or the Dhammapada of the Buddhists. These books are becoming more and more attractive to Western scholars. Western man is pursuing this study to learn how to tune and readjust the mind and reduce stress and strain of the modern technological age.

In India today, most people, even industrialists, still practise religion, though on a superficial level. If you go to any industrial complex in India, be it small or large, you will find in many places a picture of the Lord with an incense stick lit beside it. Those industrialists seem to be deeply devoted. But if you listen to the prayers offered, you will hear: 'Oh Lord, I am giving you incense, yet you don't give me anything.' Then the devotee sits down right in front of the Lord, at his desk, and starts cutting everybody's throat! If profits are not good, he loses his faith. It is all because such people have misunderstood what faith in God is.

Admittedly, some faith is there. Externally it is there, but the tuning up of the mind and the spirit of surrender are absent. You need not make God your proprietor—that may be too much. All right, make Him a one-penny partner in your company, just a penny partner with no voting power. Let Him also sit in at your Board meetings. The Lord is so clever that if you make Him a one-penny partner, within six months you will find that He becomes the managing director of the company!

Try it. Surrender your worries to Him. You will find that your mental weakness, exhaustion and fatigue get reduced and your mind becomes calm and serene. When the mind is thus calm and serene, your efficiency increases; your performance, your attitude towards others, your vision of life as such, the way you meet challenges change into a new tempo and beauty. With these inner qualities, your activities gather a momentum that cannot but attract success in the modern material world.

TWENTY-NINE

~

RIGHT ATTITUDES FOR SUCCESS[*]

You and I are alive. Therefore, we cannot but be active. As long as we live, we have to act, for life pulsating through the body becomes activity in the outer world. Since actions flow out of every living person until he or she dies, it is important to understand how they can be organized, altered, or disciplined in order to bring about happiness in the community and a sense of fulfilment and satisfaction to the individual. This is called the 'art of action'.

Action is inevitable, because it is the signature of life. Life expresses itself in action, as death does in inaction. But actions may vary from man to man. A farmer working in the fields perspires and sweats with exertion. A poet in the midst of his greatest creation doesn't seem to be working at all from the farmer's point of view. From the standpoint of a poet, a scientist is wasting public money. From the scientist's standpoint, an ordinary thinker is wasting his time. From all their points of view, Buddha sitting under a tree in meditation is an idler, an unnecessary leech upon society. Each one may point to the other and say that he is an idler, but each one knows how vigorously he himself is working.

A great painter was once sitting near a wayside pool, throwing stones into the water and watching the play of light and shade upon the ripples. An ordinary man, walking along the road, carrying milk

---

[*] From *Vedanta in Action*, Central Chinmaya Mission Trust, Mumbai, fourth edition, 1989.

to the nearby town to sell, jealously looked at the man and thought, 'This fool is sitting idly from morning to evening, eating food that is brought to him. How unfair! I have already put in eight hours of work and I cannot make both ends meet. What an injustice!'

The simple villager did not know that the person against whom he had complained was none other than Michelangelo, the great painter, who wanted to observe the play of light and shade on the waves so that he could capture their alluring beauty on canvas. He was vigorously studying, but others thought he was idling away his time. It is that man, the so-called idler, who produced immortal paintings and sculptures while the milkman who was supposed to have worked and toiled so honestly for society died leaving no trace, nothing for posterity to remember him by.

Everyone must work, but what matters is how to work and in what way one should work. Being in the sun for the whole day alone is not work. That is only one method of work. The question at hand is what type of work can we do and how can the maximum be brought out of us.

Working for Personal Gain

The great sages of ancient India observed that the type and the quality of work that people perform can be classified into three categories. The first of them, they said, is the lowest type, and since I do not have a better word, let us call it *labour*. When I say labour, I am not using the term in a derogatory manner.

The man who works in society only for the sake of wages, for profit, is called a labourer. A great political leader of a country may be a labourer if he is putting forth his intelligence, mind and body for his society with the idea that he will accumulate power, money and prestige for his personal gain. If you ask such a person why he wants wages, he has no motive greater than to furnish his house beautifully for the sake of his wife and children, for his own pleasure. The man who is self-centred works only for the profit that comes to him. With the profit he does not think of starting a hospital or serving society. If that is the limited ambition with which a man is pouring out his energy into the world, that person falls under the classification of a *labourer*.

In the same profession in which a labourer is working, there can be another individual who is not a labourer. Next to Mahatma Gandhi, who was inspired by the most selfless of ideals in the political field, one can see a labourer in the same political arena. It is not the field of work that matters. It is not the position that gives one dignity and glory in society, but, rather, it is how one acts. If a person works with the idea that he will gain something from society with which he will benefit himself—if this is his self-centred, limited point of view, even though he may be a scientist, a great thinker, a writer, or intellectually the greatest genius in the country, he is only a labourer from the philosophical point of view.

Working for an Ideal

In contrast to the labourer, the second variety is called a *worker*. What is the difference between a labourer and a worker? If one asks a worker why he is working, he will say that he wants to bring about a change in society. His eyes are not on personal profit, but on success for society. Success in what? Every worker has a picture of an ideal heaven, of a perfect society. He will struggle hard in the world because he is inspired by a great enthusiasm and vision of life, and he strives to bring that vision into actuality. He wants nothing else from life. He is ready to starve, he is ready to suffer, but what he wants in the world is only success for his ideal. The political workers, the spiritual missionaries, or the great cultural thinkers struggle to realize their ideals in the world. To the extent that their ideal is achieved, they are happy and feel that they have succeeded. Thus, a labourer wants wages so that he and his wife and children may be more comfortable. A worker, on the other hand, is inspired by an ideal for a greater cause than himself.

Working with Joy

The third variety is very rare. Labourers are many in the world, and workers are few in number. But the third variety, called *men of achievement*, is very few indeed. It is these people who give a fillip to the general cultural beauty of society and uplift the entire generation to a higher standard of life, a higher dignity of morality, a greater virtue in living. Such mighty men are called saints and seers, prophets. They are embodiments of great virtues and values. They live an ideal life, inspiring others even after their death. The fragrance of their thought and the might and glory of their ideals gather a new momentum as the years pass by. Christ died two thousand years ago, and yet we find that his glory becomes more and more compelling as time passes.

One may ask the man of achievement, 'What is it that you want in the world; why are you working? O Buddha, why did you work; O Christ, why did you work; O Mohammed, why did you move from place to place, preaching against many odds?' Men of achievement work in the world not for profit, nor for success, but from a feeling that they are doing the right thing, irrespective of whether or not they will be recognized in their lifetime. All that a man of achievement wants is the secret joy in himself, the sense of fulfilment that he did the best he could. He does not care whether others recognize him or not.

The men of fulfilment do not work for a more comfortable life, nor do they work in the world outside for bringing a heaven upon earth, but by practice and precept they try to lead mankind to live an ideal life. More often than not, such men have been persecuted by society, for they are too idealistic for their age. Against all such obstacles, a man of fulfilment lives on, inspiring others by his joyous way of life and thus bringing about a new movement of moral change in the country. In time, the morality, the culture, and the civilization of the society always receive a fresh impetus because of their work. Christ, Vivekananda, Shankara: all of them gave a push and a fillip to the ideal—a life that they themselves lived and experienced, not merely conceived and talked about.

Thus, men of achievement are not mere labourers or workers, they are seekers of self-fulfilment. By living the idealistic life in society, in spite of the fact that the people around them were not living nor willing to live the ideal, they thrilled and inspired their generation, instilling in them an awe and a reverence for the perfect life. Such ideal individuals alone have uplifted the world and brought about a greater consciousness of the higher joys in life.

Integrity

Today we hear from many professionals and businessmen that they cannot afford to be honest in business. How sad! It needs real heroism to create beauty or progress in the country. It is not for the coward, or for those who compromise with their ideals. If we are not ready to make sacrifices, no society can come forward. We cannot expect a miracle to happen, an angel to come down and suddenly, with a magic touch, make the entire country glow.

It is by individual sacrifice alone that progress is possible. Everywhere, in all fields—political, economic, and cultural—progress has taken place in the world only because of such sacrifice. If just a few people, after realizing the goal of life and the art of living were to enter into the business world and live an ideal moral life, finding fulfilment in the work itself, not caring for the petty earnings, they would inspire others also to live in this way. Until we are ready to make a sacrifice, we cannot do anything to improve society. It all rests upon our individual shoulders to improve the world. The neighbour is not going to help improve relations between husband and wife and children. Each one has to understand and live the right life in the home, and only then will the home be beautified. In our own lives, whether at home or in society or in the institutions where we work, we must have that integrity so that we are able to work with a sense of fulfilment rather than for a fleeting hour of success or for a little extra money in the wallet.

Responsible Living

Many of us from each stratum of society have a tendency to complain that we can't make ends meet. Why is this so? The more we earn, the more difficulty we encounter in making both ends meet. It is all because our stomachs have a knack, it seems, of growing larger than our belts. We have to learn to keep our stomachs in check, or else nothing will be sufficient to fatten the body or the stomach. If the stomach continuously grows larger, then something must be done. Today, modern man, whether he is wealthy or not, seems to think that the stomach has grown so large that he sees nothing beyond it—the head also is a stomach and so is the heart! Nothing lies beyond the stomach, because the appetite to live the sensuous life has become insatiable. How will such a person ever be able to work?

We have so many desires to satisfy that even our two hands, two legs, and twenty-four hours a day are insufficient. There is, therefore, disgruntlement at all times and discontentment in the heart. A man who is discontent cannot act beautifully in the world outside; he cannot have a great vision.

However, if we observe a man of success in any profession, we find that he has no time to waste in the cafés, no time even to go near the movie theatres. Most people, if they have a little time at their disposal, go aimlessly around the shopping malls, just marking time. Why? Because they have nothing to crave for, to demand, to achieve for themselves. All that they want is to live at the physical level. Such people should be counted as animals, because animals also live solely at the physical level. If people remain at that level, they will live a mere animalistic life, and a higher happiness, prosperity and peace can never be theirs.

Prosperity, culture and progress are possible because we have a mind and intellect. If we do not tap this resource, national progress will be impeded, the general progress of the world will be hindered and you and I shall despair continuously. We will quarrel endlessly amongst ourselves, criticize every government that is elected, and die in sorrow and tears, never gaining the joy of having truly lived.

In order to live and bring out the best in ourselves, we must have a goal in life, a mission, an inspiring ideal. Keeping our focus on that ideal, we must work in the world. Thereby, our work becomes chastened. The work itself becomes its own reward and a great joy wells up in the mind, not in terms of what we get on the first of the month, but what we give to society as best we can, from the situation we are in.

All of us have only twenty-four hours a day, whether one is a mighty personality making history in the world, or is struggling to earn his livelihood. Yet we find that the individuals who make history—often within a short span of ten or twenty years—accomplish remarkable deeds and leave behind lasting contributions for successive generations. Often it is a wonder to many as to how one single individual can do so much work within a short time, contribute so much to the world, while others working harder, leave nothing behind.

When we act, the glory of action is not dependent on the environment, nor on the work, but on the motive behind the work.

Work gathers a new momentum, a new ardour, only when the intentions behind it are noble. Take sculpture as an example. Of the countless sculptors, some sculpt political leaders or wealthy socialites, others create fountains for parks. Now observe the beautiful sculptures in temples and churches. The sculptor here did not just sculpt a shape, but he imparted to it the great love and reverence for the theme that he was depicting. Such art pieces become immortal. They are more than stone. They speak. The artist seems to have poured his heart and soul into the pieces of stone, and the stone then reflects the immortal message of the heart of the sculptor. So too in any field.

~

THIRTY

OUR CHILDREN[*]

Today's children are different. They are more intelligent and perceptive. They have developed many distinct traits to cope with the fast pace of life of the present age. Often they know more and perceive more than their own parents.

With the rapid growth and spread of modern science and technology, there is a totally altered environment in which our children have to live. They are thus moulded by the new atmosphere, and nature has faithfully enhanced their abilities to meet the world around them. Thus today's children are different in their emotional nature and intellectual grasp.

They have learnt to live in an alien atmosphere of minimum love and concern from even their own parents. They see everywhere around them utter selfishness and free-for-all competition: each one for himself. The child never sees anyone living in a spirit of self-control or sacrifice. Nothing is sacred to the parents—all are madly running around seeking escapism in paltry pleasures and pastimes. The children have to cope with this unfortunate and confusing sense of insecurity within, and a harsh world of neglect and lovelessness without.

No one can doubt the fact that our understanding of our children

---

[*] An extract from an article published in *Tapovan Prasad*, Vol. XXIII, No. 6, June 1985. (Based on a paper sent by Swami Chinmayananda to the First National Conference of Principals, Headmasters and Correspondents of Chinmaya Vidyalayas, held at Bangalore in May 1985.)

is almost nil. We have never tried, and we are also not competent to see the world and our behaviour from the child's standpoint. The educational system of the last century thrust upon our children is slowly crushing them into ugly twisted caricatures! The system is not geared to meet the needs and demands of children in a world that we have perverted for them.

The problem has achieved mammoth proportions and the task ahead appears to be very strenuous. It needs the immediate and urgent attention of all sane and intelligent people. We are definitely growing into a nation of heartless brutes, extremely uneducated and uncivilized. To curb the rot and put the nation back on track, we may sometimes have to be extremely brutal and unrelentingly severe. After yet another decade of neglect, the tragedy will perhaps deepen to become a problem without a solution.

No doubt there is around the world a slow decay in living life's enduring values. But everywhere we perceive behind the confusion and sorrow some redeeming features: a love for the country, a belief in a social or economic order, a sense of revolt against the existing system. But the rot in India has no such ideology—here every vulgarity in politics and commerce, in religion or social systems, in professions and industry, is based upon and springs from a callous and outrageous selfishness.

We must at least save our children who are to be the citizens of tomorrow. The path seems to be obscure to many. Opinions are so varied and self-contradictory from place to place, that many feel the roaring onrush of a stupendous calamity for man and his hard-won culture and sensitivity. Yet, we must strive to evolve a method to satisfactorily meet the urgent needs of children in their homes and in their communities.

The child is not a miniature adult. Therefore we should not try to cram into him our adult ideas in his early years. He has his own way of seeing and enjoying things and responding to day-to-day happenings. Let him live his life and grow up to appreciate his poetic world of ideals, rather than drive him to learn the more practical rules of life.

It is Rousseau who insisted upon the importance of a healthy environment at home for a child and who stressed the importance of the influence of the mother upon the growing child. He pleaded for the child's rights. His writings called for a redefinition of parental responsibilities. They made such an important impact on the existing values and beliefs that the French Parliament condemned the book and ordered every printed copy to be confiscated and burnt!

Rousseau's ideas were a reaction to the break-up of family life in the Europe of his times. It was a plea to women, as mothers, not to neglect their responsibilities towards their offspring. No 'nannies' can replace a mother. He stated 'where there is no mother, there is no child'. He insisted upon liberty, freedom of movement and free-play of all the five senses of the child. Do not rush the child into premature speech, he wrote. When he has something to say he will discover the words to express it. Leave him alone.

To Rousseau, the object of education is not vocational: it is to produce a man out of the child. 'A well-educated man is he who is best equipped to bear the fortunes and misfortunes of life,' declared Rousseau very eloquently, as though echoing the ideas of the Rishis, which we find in our ancient treatises on education.

Leo Tolstoy had his own theories on education and these were much influenced by Rousseau's ideas. He opened a school for the simple peasant children where there was no punishment meted out for being late or absent: 'If the school is run properly, children will run to their class well or ill,' was his argument. The main thrust of early education in his school was on reading out stories and fables, from the Bible and from literature. When the children got interested they taught themselves to read with minimum help!

Homer Lane is yet another daring educationist who conducted

experiments in the countryside outside London. He viewed children who committed crimes from a distinctive angle. Instead of pitying them as 'poor little sinners', he admired their vigorous dynamism and considered them as stout-hearted little ruffians. For him they all had admirable qualities but these were misapplied. He sought to channelize their over-enthusiasm and give a purposeful direction to their sense of heroism. For him that was true education as it helped retrieve children from their wrong ways, enabling them to become successful men.

Lane believed in the efficacy of work to discipline the minds of children—not just work thrust upon them but work that they voluntarily took up and enjoyed doing. Rudolf Steiner, Maria Montessori and Rabindranath Tagore are others who gave much thought to systems of educating growing children.

We all start our career at birth arriving into a strange world with no evident knowledge of it. Thereafter starts our struggle to experiment and discover our abilities to see, hear, smell, taste and touch. After that we learn how to move, coordinate, and function with our main instruments of action. When the child has crawled out of his infancy and reached the stage when he can move about, watch and observe, he is fit for self-education. The child's endless sense of wonder at things, his steady sense of inquisitiveness, his silent but very thoughtful attention to everything said and done around him in his world, his experiments with love, affection, anger, jealousy, covetousness, instinct of acquisition, grabbing, fighting, kindness—the entire gamut of emotional life—is the next stage. During this time education starts and this highly impressive period is the most crucial time in building up the child's entire future.

At this juncture, his main study is from example and he imitates all the elders that he watches around him: parents, servants, maids, neighbours, their children and visitors. From everyone children pick up certain traits, habits, words, ideas, dress sense, even their accent and inflections of speech. The child is never tired of observing and learning from everyone and from every situation.

Hence it is important to provide the child, at this nursery level, with a happy and cheerful atmosphere; and with the ideals of affection, tenderness, concern for other living beings, appreciation of the good and the noble, recognition of beauty in things and charm in people. Children are slow to grasp the subtle, therefore, we have to openly exaggerate the noble virtues: be a bit shamelessly demonstrative. Touch the children. Tell them that you love them, that they are beautiful, intelligent, good and noble. Repeat that again and again! Demonstrate your readiness to sacrifice for others. Let children see that you are very anxious to be helpful to others. This can very quickly impress them and sink into their personality. Thus noble character is easily formed.

The teacher is a twenty-four hours, 365-days-a-year professional. Children are very observant, especially of their teachers for whom they have love and respect. No action of the teacher is insignificant to the children. They watch and watch, and learn to imitate and reflect upon their teacher's actions and words.

When the child is five, he becomes fit for regular schooling. Everywhere the entrance to primary classes starts at five. Now his limbs are steady. A healthy child has enormous energy to burn up and needs frequent refreshment to replenish the energy drained away in playing, fighting, running around and also in studying, singing, howling and screaming.

Now we must start taming his behaviour to enable him to conform to a happy social life with others, while he is encouraged to grow in his knowledge and abilities. Art and craft classes provide the best environment in which to polish behaviour. The wild ones are to be especially treated with love and kind persuasion. In extreme cases punishment must be given in the presence of all other children, as an example. Yet, never show any rancour towards the punished child. Keep on loving him and express your endless concern for his safety and comfort.

From five to ten the child stretches his emotional and intellectual abilities into ever-widening fields and this is the right time to emphasize the higher and noble values of life. This is done through stories, and children pick up their own ideals to admire and revere. The Puranic stories, toned down to their level of understanding, stories of great saints and sages, mighty heroes of science and politics and social workers who had moulded the character of people, are all very easily absorbed by them. Animal stories from the *Panchatantra* hammer into them the concepts of good and their distinctive features. They will see how in the confrontation of good and evil, the good alone wins in the end. Recitations, mass chantings, and group songs are very effective at this stage.

Between the ages of ten and fourteen, they need a little more material to handle as their minds have unfolded to a greater extent. Now the child appreciates ideas that it can wrestle with and enjoys the flashes of wonder at understanding life and its ways. At this stage they can enjoy and enrich their minds with books like *Gita for Children*.

For individuals in the age group of fifteen to eighteen years, help them to sink their ideas into their own minds. Encourage them to express their opinions on things they have studied. They must be helped to overcome their shyness. Encourage them through compliments and generous presents for what they have tried to express. Never, at this stage, should we criticize the mistakes they make. Leave them alone to grow up—do not hasten them.

When they are between eighteen and twenty years, they have reached a fuller stage of mental and physical development. Now they are ready to have a deeper understanding and this is the time to introduce them to the early steps in sadhana (spiritual practice). This will enable them, when they are by themselves, to discover that with diligence and practice, they can control the mad onrush of their own wild and crazy mind. A little japa and daily sessions of a few moments of inner quietude of the mind will be very helpful to them. We can slowly lift them to a conviction in themselves that 'man needs self-control if he is to control his own mind'. Without such a tuned-in mind, excellence in life's activities cannot be assured.

When the youngster reaches perhaps twenty or twenty-five, he is ready to be initiated into the highest. Without any hesitation teach him or her the Upanishads (Isa, Kena and Kathopanishads) and the Bhagavad Gita (Chapters II, III, VI, IX, XII and XIII). The rest he can study by himself. Leave him alone to grow up at his own pace.

This kind of a graded system, if followed faithfully, will enable us to complete the education of our growing generation more effectively, both in their inner values of life and also in the outer objective sciences. The secular education will make them proficient to meet the challenges in their professions, and the values of life inculcated will mould them to be better persons in society.

Can we conceive and plan out in every detail a system of education for our children based upon the above ideas? This will be the job of our educationists. Will they take up this national challenge and face it wisely with determination and courage?

~

THIRTY-ONE

YOUTH ALONE CAN*

From time immemorial the march of history has brought about great changes, of progress or decline, of ups and downs. These reflect the quality of human endeavour in any particular period of history. The fundamental truth is that the present situation is a product of the past. The past is modified in the present and becomes the future. The modifications may be a degradation or an improvement. Thus, there are examples of a glorious past which on account of the poor contribution of the living generation turned into an inglorious future. There are also examples of a sad past modified into a glorious future by brilliant efforts of the living generation. After the last war, eastern Europe came under the oppressive rule of Russia and suffered from the 1940s to the 1980s. But this year, they reacted all of a sudden and, by united efforts, overnight they freed themselves from oppression. Germany was divided into two by the Allies after the last war and separated by a wall. Now the wall has crumbled and the will of the people has asserted itself. Rebuilding a united Germany has started. By breaking down the wall and selling it they made more money than had been spent to build the wall!

The present suffering is no doubt the product of the past but that does not mean that we have no escape from the past and that

---

* Swami Chinmayananda's address to the youth on 13 October 1990 at Dr H. Narasimhaiah Auditorium, Bangalore. From *Youth Renaissance*, souvenir brought out by the sevaks of Chinmaya Mission, New Delhi, 1994.

we have to continue to suffer. No, it is possible to act in the present so as to bring about a glorious future. To continue the past and the status-quo (present), the old bandicoots are sufficient. The old leaders will continue what the earlier generation had been doing. Do you think that the present government is a change from the earlier one? Was the earlier one a change from the one preceding it? No. There is no point in accusing them as they are all used to continuing the status-quo or even making it worse. Then who is to bring the change? It is the Youth. That is why I have chosen the subject for today: 'Youth alone can'. Roll up your sleeves and strive to rebuild the country.

The present can change the past by intelligent, well-planned, continuous effort. While thus working, many sacrifices may have to be made. When is it that the community or society has not had to pay in sweat and blood in order to rebuild a better place for the next generation? The amount of sacrifice to be made depends upon the conditions prevailing. Consistent and intelligent effort is called for. But if the youth has no ability to think, to plan, to bring about the necessary changes, and has no consistency of effort, the future cannot be built. It will be sadder than the present.

Therefore, if the youth is to contribute rightly to reshape the present into a more harmonious and happy future, they must have knowledge, and not merely information. The information that you gather from your studies must inspire you to dedicate yourselves for the reconstruction of the present. Then only will life be fulfilled. Animals and birds also make and have little ones, look after them, teach them to look after themselves as they grow. If man also lives only at that level and is engrossed in earning and enjoying himself, he is not in any way different from an animal. But man has the intellect to know what is right, to act rightly to the best of his ability, to gain the joy of fulfilment, and to lead a rewarding life. We always glorify such people—a Mahatma Gandhi and other great

271

men in different fields of activity. They are all people who contributed significantly for the welfare and progress of the community. They gave more than they got from the world.

See the difference between Ravana and Rama: both were great, but while Ravana was intent on grabbing, acquiring and subduing others, Rama was constantly thinking of the welfare of the people, serving and sacrificing for them. The glory of man is the ability to sacrifice for the sake and benefit of others. We want such young men of perfection, beauty and excellence in every field of work, as it is a highly competitive world that we will enter in the twenty-first century. A nation cannot be built by third-rate people. Objections are immediately raised. We must help the poor and the backward. The mistakes of the past must no doubt be corrected. But we must not make more mistakes. A mistake cannot be corrected by more mistakes, but only by a logical and intelligent solution. This requires knowledge and wisdom. Mere information will not do. Information must be digested, assimilated and transformed into knowledge. Youth possessing such knowledge will be the true leaders.

It needs a lot of vision, insight, heroism and courage, to live up to what you believe in, the ideal that you have kept before you. That ideal should be chosen uninfluenced by your likes and dislikes, and by keeping your mind open to ideas from others, taking time to examine and criticize your own predilections, and keeping out selfishness. Once you have decided on your goal, hold on to it and put forth consistent efforts. When you work for a great ideal, obstructions are bound to come, for this is the law of life. Nature provides these obstacles to bring out the best and noblest in the individual striving to reach his goal, bringing greater glory to him. This is how one grows.

Mother Ganges comes down from the peaks of the Himalayas and after flowing through an extensive area of the country reaches the Bay of Bengal. Do you think that her journey to the Bay is a smooth one without any obstructions? She encounters many obstructions during the journey. In places where there are no obstacles you are not conscious that there is a river as she is silent. When she encounters any small stones there is a soft musical sound. When bigger rocks are met, there is a bigger sound and some bubbles and froth are seen. She gathers her white sari and goes around the rocks. Where the stone is small she jumps over it with laugher. If she encounters a mountain, she rubs her shoulders at the feet of the mountain and moves along its sides till she comes to the end of the mountain, then goes round and continues her journey till she reaches the Bay. Similarly, you must have a goal and the determination to reach it, despite the obstacles that you are bound to encounter. With each obstacle that you overcome, the greater is your glory, the greater is the sense of fulfilment. It is a rewarding experience worth all the efforts, thought and planning involved in it. Do not sit back and think that the present leaders can take us forward to a glorious future. No, they can only carry on. This is no doubt necessary. But the revolutionary changes that we seek can be achieved only by enthusiastic, well-disciplined thinkers. The changes that Gorbachev brought about in Russia have been made possible only by the courageous efforts of many dissidents who suffered untold hardships inflicted by the government. They persisted in propagating their views which in the fullness of time, Gorbachev accepted.

So though the present is a product of the past, don't sit down and say it is our fate. Every moment man has freedom to start a new way of life. For this, two things are unavoidable. First, the right thing must be chosen as our goal and for this, a capacity to think properly is necessary. Thereafter, instead of theorizing, you must have the heroism, the large-heartedness, the muscle necessary to live up to your ideals. Look at Prahlada. The eight-year-old boy stood firm against the might of the greatest tyrant—his father Hiranyakashipu. The meaning of the word 'Hiranyakashipu' is 'one who is wrapped in jewels', meaning an utter materialist thinking only of money, wealth and power. He banned God in his kingdom and proclaimed himself as the God who only was to be worshipped. But Prahlada had full faith in God and the courage to suffer all the persecution of his father, until the Lord came in the form of Narasimha to destroy Hiranyakashipu. So Prahlada by his efforts brought about the destruction of exclusively materialistic policy and installed a higher culture.

So, whenever you want to bring about desirable changes, do not be swayed by propaganda. Think for yourself whether this system of pure materialism and secularism will take us to our cherished goals. With knowledge, start thinking and planning and if you have the heroism to strive, put forth your efforts to reach a greater goal. When Communism had ruled, the communists believed that the highest happiness belonged to them. But after twenty-five years of suffering and privation, things became worse and as they came to know of the relative prosperity in capitalistic countries, they began to long for a change. When the Iraqi army invaded Kuwait and saw the prosperity there as compared with the under-development in their homeland, their eyes were opened. They looted everything in Kuwait and took it to Iraq. Once the army realized the relatively poor conditions in Iraq, they refused to suffer any longer and made demands for improvement in their condition. Everywhere in the world, wherever revolutionary changes have been brought about, it is the youth who have spearheaded the movement for change.

So, friends, it is only the youth that can rewrite the present history into a more pleasant and beautiful future. We may commit mistakes sometimes but then we must provide something for the future youth to do! So let the future youth correct us; as we are correcting the past, let them also have a past to correct. Thus, like a relay race, each generation tries its level best to reach out to the next generation to carry on the change.

So, now we have to turn over a new leaf. We must learn to give up narrow selfishness and have a noble goal. It is not that an entire generation will do this, but if the leaders and the educated class, with a newly inspired enthusiasm, come to live a nobler life, others will get inspired and follow. *Yad yad aacarati sreshtah, tad tad eva itaro janah.* As the Gita puts it, consistency of purpose and a spirit of dedication and, if necessary, sacrifice, should characterize the new spirit.

~

THIRTY-TWO

THE LEADER[*]

In every organization—political, industrial or commercial, secular or sacred—the real fire is supplied and maintained by its leader. He is the captain, the one in the top cabin who steers the ship and has, due to his position, a better vision than those who sweat and labour in the belly of the ship, in its machine room.

The leader must have vision, and yet a visionary can never be a leader. The leader must see ahead and at a safe speed steer clear of all obstacles and put the sails up in the most advantageous winds and take the ship under his command to the required harbour.

A true leader should give his serious attention continuously to fostering a spirit of teamwork. Selfishness in team members breaks the spirit of collectivity and there soon arise personal groups, based on caste or creed or 'native place' whose narrow interests bring continuous conflicts into the organization.

When we look around, with scientific detachment, we clearly see three main types of organization:

1) An institution based entirely upon the power, strength or wealth of the executives. They dictate to everyone and often such institutions grow and quickly expand. These are autocratic institutions. The person at the top soon gets a crazy sense of self-importance, and his arrogant attitudes and dictatorial efforts are felt by the others below

---

[*] From a collection of writings/speeches by Swami Chinmayananda published in *Youth Renaissance*, souvenir brought out by the sevaks of Chinmaya Mission, New Delhi, 1994.

as insufferable tyranny. The institution crumbles!

2) The second type of organization is what is very popular with people of our times—often heard of but rarely seen—the democratic institutions. Here the organization is created to fulfil certain demands and desires of its members, and so long as the members are satisfied they limp on making a lot of noise but really accomplishing nothing great, except, of course, satisfying the demands of the members. The moment a fair section of the members are dissatisfied, the organization crumbles. It gets destroyed by its own few dissatisfied members: enemies within plan and destroy it.

3) All long-surviving institutions are organized upon the basis of mutual love and respect for the leader, a sense of reverence for the very programme for which the institution works. Here the organization is based upon harmony. This sense of harmony and cohesiveness can arise only when all members are truly inspired with the goal set up by the institution and work dedicatedly to achieve it. Such organizations alone can stand firm against all strains from without, because within them they have a team of strong members holding together and functioning as many hands but as one head-and-heart.

The members, office-bearers and executives of such an organization work in a single spirit of joyous excitement, from which unity of purpose, tireless enthusiasm, cheerful pursuit and such other virtues arise. This is referred to in the Gita as Karma-Yoga—functioning in the yajna spirit. It is ego and its selfish desires in our hearts that compel us to break the homogeneous harmony and the joyful rhythm in the day-to-day working of the institution. Unless the members are dedicated to the idea for which the institution strives, the best in them cannot stream forth to enrich the total achievement of the institution.

What we have so far discussed gives us a clue to understanding the causes behind the continuous progress of a flourishing institution, which undertakes stupendous tasks and spreads great blessings all around for its members and for the community as a whole.

A mere volume of rules or some spectacular performance by an individual (or individuals) in an organization cannot by themselves help the organization to serve the community for a long time. And when that organization serves and manages only for profit, the institution never survives for any length of time. Like weeds they spread and flourish and are gone with the seasonal rains. There must be a unison of objectives and ideas. Each must know what they are collectively striving to achieve and in that great scheme of achievement, which exactly is the part each is responsible for.

If an individual's objective or idea is not in unison with the organization, he will be very unhappy and if he is not booted out unceremoniously he may wreck the melody of work within the institution. If the objectives and ideas of the members are harmonious with the aims and objects of the institution, the place becomes a temple of joy-in-work and the result can be seen as blessings upon all.

In many institutions discord starts mainly due to lack of proper and effective communication. It is indeed a delicate art. Secretive manipulations spread fears and discontent, but too open a system of communication is also dangerous for the growth of an organization.

The *Panchatantra* beautifully expresses this art of communication. It says:

Some things a man must say to his wife.
Some to his friends; some to his sons.
All these are trusted people, but,
he should never tell everything to everyone!

We must, therefore, use our discrimination at all times in communicating information. Never put your foot in your mouth!

FORTHCOMING TITLES

The Penguin Swami Vivekananda Reader
Edited by Makarand Paranjape

In his brief lifespan, Swami Vivekananda left an indelible imprint on the minds of all. On 11 September 1893, he made his dramatic debut on the world stage as a last-minute, uninvited participant to the Parliament of Religions at Chicago. To a standing ovation, he proclaimed his message of tolerance and universal acceptance in the 'name of millions and millions of Hindu people of all classes and sects'. Speaking against sectarianism and bigotry, this young speaker in flaming robes struck a chord in the hearts and minds of his listeners. Until his death on 4 July 1902, Vivekananda taught, lectured, wrote, published, and travelled tirelessly. His dynamic personality, the shining and noble example he set, and his love for and service to his country, continue to motivate millions to this day.

The Penguin Swami Vivekananda Reader is an unmatched compilation of his selected works aimed at a general audience. The carefully chosen works, including speeches, essays, letters, poems and conversations, show that Vivekananda's words do not merely inspire, but propel action. With a detailed life sketch and a scholarly introduction, this edition is compulsory reading for all those interested in the making of modern India.

PENGUIN
Non-fiction/Spirituality

Sri Sathya Sai Baba: A Life
Bill Aitken

Born to a poor family in the village of Puttaparthi in southern Andhra Pradesh, Sathyanarayan Raju was a bright, talented and confident boy whose charitable nature and religiosity belied his tender age. Deeply suspicious of his spiritual precociousness, his father made him go through a traumatic exorcism. But the boy already had a devoted band of followers and, when he was thirteen, announced that he was the Shirdi Sai Baba reborn. Today, Sri Sathya Sai Baba has an estimated thirty million followers worldwide.

Acclaimed travel writer and self-described 'spiritual nomad' Bill Aitken tells us why so many—royalty, wealthy industrialists, influential politicians, as well as the poor—flock to Puttaparthi. Sai Baba's message, he reveals, can be summed up in one word: love. It is as simple as it is profound, not unlike how his devotees see the Sai himself—the embodiment of deep spirituality wedded to simplicity, elegance and grace.

Yet, the Sai phenomenon is less about producing vibhuti from thin air and more about modern-day miracles. Miracles like free schools and universities, super-speciality hospitals which provide free treatment to all and revolutionary projects like the one which has brought drinking water to a million villagers in drought prone Rayalseema.

Aitken is a rarity—a genuine spiritual seeker with a keen eye for cant and superstition. His study is neither a hagiographic exercise in myth-making nor a dry, objective account of the Sai's life. The result of many years of inquiry and research, this biography bears testimony to the enduring relevance of the sacred in our times.

VIKING
Non-fiction/Biography
India Rs 450